WARDEN'S HUNT CLUB

Huntin' Poachers - No Limits

Anthony J. Petreikis

ISBN 978-1-09833-918-0 eBook 978-1-09833-919-7

CONTENTS

THIS BOOK IS DEDICATED to my wife, Laura, and my three children, Garrett, Kaylee and Nathan. Whether I had good days or bad, they were always there to make them better! I love you all.

ACKNOWLEDGEMENT

There are so many people who deserve to be acknowledged that I could never "name" them all. For me, family is more important than anything. Specifically, I need to start with my wife, Laura. She was the best partner that a game warden could ever have while at home or in the field. As you read the cases inside, you will come to realize that many of our memories together were made at work. We had good days and bad ones, but always worked well together. Whether at work or at home, when you know what your partner is thinking, it's easy to work toward a common goal!

My kids (Garrett, Nathan and Kaylee) never complained about the demands of my job. I probably missed as many events in their lives as I attended. For over 20 years, I worked more holidays, birthdays and weekends than I didn't. Although I'm sure that they got frustrated, they never really complained or caused me any more guilt than came naturally. For that, and just being there, I will eternally be thankful.

My parents (Jim and Sandy) made me who I am. When you become an adult, you come to realize where you got your traits from. I got most of my artistic side from my mom and a lot of my personal drive from my dad.

Moving up the line, my parents also came by their traits naturally. Although I never had a chance to know my grandfathers, I did get to know my grandmothers (Sophie Petreikis and June Rokus). Grandma Sophie was possibly the most driven person that I ever met. Grandma June was a great talker and passed down her artistic trait.

The last two people I will mention by name are my brothers (Jim and Chris). When we were young, we fought like cats. As adults, there's nobody that I would rather share a fishing boat with! I always look forward to our time together.

The Kids

Although not too many people write a divided acknowledgement, I think it's necessary under the circumstances. There are some cases in this book that involve horrible situations. At first, I questioned mentioning those cases at all. The more that I thought about them, I realized that if I didn't talk about them, you wouldn't "really" know what being a game warden is all about.

After I started writing the book, I was talking with Sandy Long. Sandy just happens to be my favorite paralegal. Working in the Mercer County States Attorney's Office, Sandy was always smiling and happy to see me. Sandy was one of very few people that I actually shared my book writing aspirations with. While talking with Sandy, I told her that I intended to write about cases where children had passed away. I told her that in some way, I might be able to give a gift to their families. A child who never had an opportunity to make a name for themselves would forever be written into a book. In my "old age", I have also come to realize that working those cases was personal for me. I don't want the same thing to happen to anybody else—officers and parents alike. Maybe, just one parent, will read about those tragedies and avoid a disaster.

Sandy told me that I was right. She told me that she had lost a child. As she continued, my eyes started welling up. She said that as a parent, when you lose a child, your biggest fear is that they will forever be forgotten to time. Sandy lost her daughter Becky

Sue Long (22) in a horrible car accident. I don't know Becky's story and didn't work the case, but if she was anything like her mom, the world has missed out on getting to know a special person. For that talk, I must thank Sandy and Becky. They helped give me the courage to move forward with the writing of those stories.

PREFACE

I was probably only a few years into being a game warden when I had thoughts about writing a book. As my career progressed and I told people stories of my exploits, many of them asked me to write a book. Having the fire started, I intentionally never read another game warden's book. If I got around to writing my own, I didn't want to influence my writing style. I wanted my book to be my own "creation".

In my 24th year of service, I decided to start putting a book together. I had two years of work left and had hoped to publish the book on month that I retired (that didn't happen). I wanted to give it as a gift to my family, friends, "the Kids", my coworkers, future officers and the people of the State of Illinois (who had funded my career). I also recognized how big of a part of my life being a game warden had become. I knew that it would be hard to retire and just not be "one" anymore. I figured that it would personally help me if I had compiled that part of my life into something that I could "give back".

With a goal in hand, I made a "loose" outline of what I wanted to cover in my book. Although I had stories that I really wanted to tell, I had others that just seemed to fall into place. I even had one that came to me at the "eleventh hour". I was already writing the book when Maci's case touched my life in a big way. I wrote that chapter within a month of the accident happening.

None of the cases that I wrote about are just a copy of a field report. That said, old case reports are a nice reference to have. The facts are as I remembered them and many of my reports helped to refresh my old memories. It always seemed easier to remember my personal feelings than it was to remember the minor case details. It was neat to go back and read many of those reports again. I remembered many things that I had forgotten over 20 years. The most enjoyable parts of the book to write were the areas where I could "freelance". It was when I was simply talking about a thought or an opinion. There weren't any mistakes to make there. You can't make a mistake when you are simply talking about your own thoughts or feelings.

Since I mentioned thoughts and feelings, all of them discussed in this book are mine. They do not reflect the opinion of my wife, the State of Illinois, the Illinois Department of Natural Resources or anybody else for that matter. Occasionally, I mention what I believed people were thinking, but police officers are constantly trying to determine intent. We make our decisions based on all the facts of a case—including what the intent of the violator was.

For the readers who are not game wardens, I hope that my book opens your eyes to what we do as game wardens and experience as people. If you're a young game warden, I hope that my book gives you some working ideas and personal drive to work hard and smart. If you're an old game warden, I hope that you've had similar experiences and enjoy some of my thoughts about how things happened and why. If you're a violator, hopefully I didn't give you any "tricks of the trade". If you are someone that I arrested, I hope that I included your story in this book. Not because I have any angst for you (and hopefully you not for me), but because I think that, in some way, it would be neat for you.

You made it into "The Book". You can brag if you want to and you will have an opportunity to see what I went through to catch you. If you're a poacher that I didn't catch, but came close, it would be neat for me to hear your story too!

All of that said, the likelihood that I wrote your story in my book is not very good. In my career, I wrote in excess of 1,000 primary case reports. Some of those reports just documented minor incidents, but the overwhelming majority of them involved some sort of enforcement action. Aside from my primary case reports, I also wrote hundreds of supplementary reports. Those are reports where I was not the "primary" report writer, but simply wrote a report to supplement another officer's report. Often, I was right next to the other officer, but it was their turn to write the report.

Since this book only covers about 50 case reports, if you made it in here, there was something in your case that I wanted to tell. It could have just been something quirky, but it was important to me. After writing for over a year and reaching the 110,000-word mark, I realized that I could never completely tell 25 years' worth of stories. I would have to write an encyclopedia to do it.

In the cases that I wrote about, I tried to give credit where it was due. I would expect the same from anybody else. You will see that Laura was with me for some of the cases. She was always a great partner to have with. I didn't write about "her cases" (even if they were great ones) because I wanted her to be able to write her own book. Many of the cases where we worked together, but she wrote the primary report, were definitely worth writing about!

In order to make sure that I didn't "embarrass" anybody who didn't want to be mentioned, I didn't use any offenders' real names. If I did use a person's real name, I will have written both their first and last name in the book. Most of the time, if I thought they were important enough to mention by name, I also talked about them a little. Everybody else will just be called by a single name. It's not their real name or a derivative of it. In "The Blue

Thing", all the officers are just named a rank. It was not necessarily their rank, but I wanted you to understand what was really happening during those cases.

I hope you enjoy the book and my writing style. If I ever meet you after you had read my book, please let me know what chapter you liked the most!

SAYINGS AND PHILOSOPHIES

As conservation police officers (CPOs), we get a large amount of windshield time. To keep from the occasional boredom, I would try to solve problems, come up with inventions, define ideas and explain why things happen as they do. Over the course of years, I believe that I have come up with some interesting sayings to share. They are lines that I have written while on the road. I cannot say whether somebody else has thought of these before me. I can say that I have not read them before. They are thoughts that I have generally had as a result of something else going on in my life.

"The character of a man is determined by the intent of his actions, not the result of them."

Most people will never look past the face value of this saying. It is, however, a very deep thought! I had been working as a CPO for about 14 years. At that point in my career, I had worked under three different direct supervisors. It would be easy to say that they were all good or bad, but that would not be fair or reality. I believe that all three of those supervisors were good people. I don't believe that any of them had bad intentions for what they did. They all had traits that I would try to emulate as a supervisor later in my career. They each also had traits that I would try not to

1

emulate. This saying is not about those supervisors. It is about my fourth supervisor. I will just call him Amos.

I would not consider myself an employee that wanted to cause any problems—literally at all. I spent every year trying to stay off the "problem radar". That said, I am an opinionated person who had worked very hard up to that point in my career. The reason I emphasized the hard work is just that officers who work hard tend to have a lot of work experience. When you are both opinionated and experienced, you may not want to listen to some Amos who does not know what he is talking about. This is especially true when one feels like their supervisor displays bad intentions within their actions (and you consider yourself a person of integrity).

Well, that is where I landed with Amos. To make matters worse, Amos seemed to be a very spiteful and hateful person. I can honestly say that Amos is one of the worst human beings that I have ever met—and yes, he was a police officer. Amos seemed to target Laura and I every opportunity that he had. Eventually, it got to the point that Laura threatened to quit. That caught our Captain by surprise, and we were sent to work for a different supervisor until Amos transferred south. Laura's threat hit the Captain especially hard since she had been his intern 15 years earlier. If I had threatened to quit, the Captain may have handed me a pen—who knows?

After the Captain retired, I had an opportunity to clear some air—and yes, I was very honest. The Captain said to me that he was sorry about how it had all gone down. He said that he did not realize Amos was such an Amos. I advised the Captain that I had a hard time forgiving him for what he had allowed. I went on to explain that the worst part was the "hate". I am not a hateful person by nature - very much the contrary. The Captain had allowed Amos to do things to my wife and I (and other officers) that was totally unacceptable. I explained to him that the hate I felt inside for Amos was terrible for me. I had literally not felt that level of hate for another human being ever in my life. It was a burden that I had to fight with for years. Hate is a burden that I do not wish upon any GOOD human being.

The Captain eventually said that there was nothing that he could have done. I told him that the solution was easy. I advised the Captain that he was "THE CAPTAIN". Literally, all he had to do was take away Amos' ability to discipline people. Amos seemed to thrive on holding people accountable for anything—unless they were his friends. This appeared obvious when I was in the field and became even more evident when I was the supervisor of our District. My later promotion gave me a direct view of what I was held accountable for and what others were not. The Captain did not have an answer for my solution. Although I truly believe the Captain is a very good person, I question his ability to step outside of being a "company man" in order to do the "right thing". He seemed to just stay in his comfort zone. Since Amos is also really good at "crop dusting", maybe the Captain just couldn't see past the fog?

Okay, so back to the saying. Intent is the most important thing when it comes to human nature. I would look at situations that Amos had put Laura and I in and say that he had intentionally done something bad. That is what created the "hate". When something has been done wrong to you and the offender made a mistake, you can generally find a way to forgive them (depending on the result of the mistake). When that same thing is done to you with bad intentions, maybe the offender does not deserve forgiveness. Yes, that is a rough statement. Then again, what if they apologize and claim they are truly looking for your forgiveness? Should you attempt to understand the intent of their apology? Do they really mean it? How about if the offender repetitively does things to intentionally hurt you and never asks for forgiveness? At that point, you are dealing with a BAD human being—whether

3

he wears a uniform or not. That is where we eventually got to with Amos.

One of my final supervisory dealings with Amos was my annual personnel evaluation. Needless to say, Amos did not give me a "glowing report". Being that I was an experienced, opinionated officer, I was not going to hold back. I marked the "I do not concur" box and advised that I wanted to write a rebuttal. Well, the first rebuttal of my career landed me in Springfield. As a general rule of thumb, there is not a good reason to be in Springfield (as a field officer). Between the time that I was evaluated and the time that I arrived in Springfield, I had written this saying. From what I heard, Amos was allowed to blow smoke while Laura and I gave our side of the story (yes, she had a rebuttal as well). During my conversation with the "brass", I let it all fly. I explained the history of my relationship with Amos and my previous years' work. During that year, I had doubled nearly every officer's field report total in my District. I also told this saying to the brass and explained my thoughts behind it. Although I do not believe my evaluation ended up where it should have been, it was much improved over where Amos had it.

I can say that my saying and the understanding of it has made me a better person. I frequently have thought about this saying long after working for Amos. I've thought about how Hitler had killed millions of Jewish people (and others) during WW II and what his intent was for doing so. I also thought about the fact that Truman likely killed hundreds of thousands of people by dropping two bombs and what his intent was. The result is the same in that innocent people were killed. Yes, I know the numbers are different. The fact of the matter is that both Hitler and Truman ordered the killing of innocent people. Their intentions were different and thus their character is as well.

A thought about Hitler and Truman didn't make me a better person, but I wanted you think about this saying at the highest level. For me, I started (and continue) to look at myself and the things I do a lot closer. I have caught myself many times about to do or say little things that may not be the "right thing" to do or say. It has given me a better grasp of my own moral compass. In fact, I think my kids have started to figure out my weakness. My daughter tended to be clumsy when it came to her food. She used to spill quite frequently. I got to the point that I would not allow drinks in the car. At a moment of weakness, I allowed the kids to have dinner on the road. Yes, my daughter spilled her drink. I was very angry and letting her hear about it when she said, "But Dad, I didn't mean to do it." I stopped and thought about what she had said. I was able to bite my tongue until it was cleaned up. Yes, she uses that excuse quite frequently now. A large part of growing up is the ability to anticipate when bad things that are about to happen. A sign of maturity is changing course so that they don't. I am sure that she will learn this concept soon. I cannot say that I do not raise my voice, but I do try to turn those situations into teaching situations. Okay, maybe sarcastic teaching situations.

Maybe I should thank Amos at some level for making me a better person by being a bad one.

"One can perpetuate success by the realization of what made them successful..."

This is a saying that I wrote later in my career on one of those boring drives. I was just thinking about luck and how people try to define it. Early in my career, I would work very hard (physically) to make good cases. After making those cases, people would often tell me that I had done well. I was one of those people that would respond with, "It's better to be lucky than good." I look at it now and think that it was my way of trying to be humble and not brag about the case. I also realize now that it is a "self-diminishing" statement.

As I worked throughout my career, I found that it got less physically demanding to make those good cases. The reason that it got easier is that I started to define the things that made me successful. All officers do this at the subconscious level daily. On every stop, officers should be looking for the things that they recognize as a "lead" or "hint" to some illegal activity. If the officer verbalizes what the hint is, the violator may consider it stereotyping. It is, however, not a bias to stereotype in that way. It is good police work to recognize that someone with dancing bears in the back window of their VW may have drugs in the car. If you are driving through a parking lot, and you see a dancing bear sticker on a parked VW, you may want to look in the windows. Now, that does not mean that you should not look in the windows of the other vehicles—you should. Because an officer has a heightened awareness from a stereotype, it does not mean that they have a bias. Bias indicates an understood preference, which you do not necessarily have with a stereotype. Most officers don't care if the violator has dancing bears or hunting stickers. They just want to catch a "bad guy".

As a supervisor, I told my officers this saying in my first District Meeting. I never really heard what they thought of it. As far as I know, they thought I was crazy. Crazy that I bothered to think about it that much, crazy not to realize that they had already thought of it...or that it was just a crazy approach to supervising. Prior to that meeting, I never had a philosophical conversation about enforcing the law with the officers in my District. In fact, I will say that most officers have likely had very few philosophical conversations about law enforcement. It makes you wonder if they think about it—since they don't talk about it. I am not sure, but I wanted my officers to start thinking about it if they weren't already. With that saying, I tried to challenge them to stop and think about their good cases—after they have made them. Don't just move on to the next case. I challenged them to think about how they got there. I challenged them to think about the variables of the situation and the WHY. If you can figure out why people do what they do, you are on the verge of perpetuating success. There are two directions you can move from knowing the why. You can move toward the most likely "who" and identify potential violators. You can also identify what the result of the action is. If you are cognizant of both and recognize when you see the potential violator or the potential result while working, you have taken the next step in perpetuating your success. Now all you must do is interview of the suspect. He will likely think you already know the details of his exploits because you have been able to fill in the gaps with WHY.

An example I used for this saying involves people baiting deer in Illinois. It kind of amazes me how infatuated people have become with deer antlers. I suppose that people have always been that way. I think everybody wants to kill a big buck. Even the people who claim to be "meat hunters" would generally like to have a head on the wall that is deserving of their family name. Yes, I know that you cannot eat the antlers. You also cannot mount the meat. Don't let them fool you; most meat hunters keep their antlers too. Some meat hunters likely claim that status because they cannot repeatedly kill a big buck. For some hunters, the desire to kill a monster gets the better of them and they succumb to baiting.

I found, over the course of several years, that competition was the key to finding baited deer stands. If people are competing for the attention of the deer (especially if there is a giant buck in their area), they will be more likely to bait for deer. From there, I began to look at maps of the areas where I had found bait over the years. I had spent hundreds of hours walking timber in order to make those bait cases without realizing the connection of why to where. When you looked at the map, it was obvious. The people hunting smaller tracts of land (40 or less acres) near similar properties were competing to kill the same deer. If you walked through those tracts, you were very likely to locate baited deer stands.

I also identified a second hunter competition. This competition was based on the deer's time and location. That is the amount of time that the deer spends somewhere. Will it spend time on "my" property or the neighboring one? I found that people who hunted property bordering a sanctuary were also more likely to bait for deer. I attributed this to the fact that those sanctuaries garnered most of the deer's time. The deer would not need to leave the nature preserve, the corporate property or even a large piece of private land where the owner is an anti-hunter. As I progressed in my career, I could find a baited deer stand much faster than I could early in my career. I would look for baited stands based on the map in conjunction with what I saw on the land (timber, brush, grass, etc.). Yes, this would be the same as working "smarter not harder". But "smarter not harder" does not necessarily give you direction of how to be "smarter". My saying hopefully does.

"Without goals, one is simply living - not achieving."

As a person, I have always been goal-oriented. If I decided I was going to do something, I generally figured out how to get it done. I'm not someone who asks for help, but rather one who wants to do it himself. It doesn't matter if it is simply carrying a cast iron bathtub out of a house or inventing something to solve a problem. I always enjoyed the challenge of the task. Equal to the challenge, I enjoyed the satisfaction of achieving my goal.

As a CPO, I worked much the same way. I constantly set goals. As I got further along in my career, I did it more often and tried to set my goals at levels that I truly thought I could not achieve. I found that I pushed myself even harder to reach those goals. I did not always reach my goal, but found myself looking for new ways to reach them. I suppose you would call it "thinking outside of the box". All the methods "outside of the box" worked for me at some level. The only drawback that I occasionally ran into was an inefficient method. In those cases, it simply took too much time to reach the desired result. Over the years, the goals that

I set and the challenge of developing new methods to achieve them helped to keep the job interesting. While I was in the field, I figured that everyone was setting goals. Like every agency, we had our underachievers. I figured that they either didn't set their goals very high or had let the administration get to them. If they had let the administration get to them, they likely decide that they weren't doing "anything" for this agency (but suck a paycheck). Most of those people likely didn't want to do anything from the start and just looked for an excuse to justify their inaction. All they needed was one other person to be miserable with them—and they had their support group.

When I became a supervisor, I wanted to get everyone to set their own goals. If they got to pick their goal, how could they not want to achieve it? Their goal didn't have to be hard to achieve, it just had to be something that was distinctly achievable. So, I gave my officers a blank book and asked them to write their goal (or goals) down. If I never followed up on it, many officers would likely never write in the book. Maybe they would write in it once and never look at it again. Some officers would even say that it was a stupid idea. As a goal setter, I figured that the people who refused to try it just needed an excuse not to fail. If you never set a goal, you can't fail to achieve it. Because I didn't want to exploit anybody's "failure", I told my officers that it was their goal to achieve and I would not inquire directly what their goal was. The only thing that I ever asked was whether they had set a goal and if they had achieved it. Some did and some didn't. The ones who did would often share more and were proud of working toward their goals and what they had accomplished. The others usually had little to say about it.

In the first year of being a supervisor, I had to take a series of supervisory classes. At first, I thought, "I don't need a class to teach me how to supervise." I didn't want someone to tell me how I needed to think—no brainwashing here. I wanted to be the supervisor that "I" wanted to be. The reality is that each class gives you ideas to incorporate into how you supervise. One class answered a question that I didn't even have. That was simply that not every person is "goal-oriented". You can try to get them to set goals, but some people truly don't care about them. As a goal setter, that is hard to accept. In trying to bring all my officers into the realm of "goal-setting", I wrote this saying. I wanted them all to experience the challenge of trying to achieve a goal—and the satisfaction of doing it. With most of my officers having many years still to work, I also wanted them to experience the fun that I had in challenging myself to do something I had not done before. A new goal can make you look at an old job in a new way. It helped me to keep my job fresh and fun for over 25 years.

"The fear of failure can create divided attention and make the likelihood of failure even greater."

This was something that I wrote as both a supervisor and a kids' wrestling coach. In the Game Warden world, you never know what is going to happen. You could be conducting a boat safety check and within seconds be wrestling with the operator. Any stop can go bad in the blink of an eye. Especially if the person you are dealing with is under the influence of alcohol or drugs. Like nearly any fight, a hand-to-hand "police involved fight" will generally end up in a wrestling match. If you win, you get to take them to jail and don't get any team points. If you lose, you could lose much more than being humiliated. Realistically, the police officer is betting a Ferrari against the Bad Guy's Yugo. If the officer loses against a true Bad Guy, he may get killed. If the Bad Guy loses, he goes to jail. The Bad Guy can quit at any time and just accept going to jail. Yes, the officer can try to disengage, but he cannot just give up when he does not know what the end result will be. Losing is not an option.

During any police "wrestling match", you should not be thinking about what is going to happen if you lose. Likewise, you should not be thinking about what is going to happen if you win. You must be focused on the task at hand. In your mind, you are always be wrestling a state champion. You should also always anticipate that the match will go into triple overtime. In other words, it is going to be hard; you are going to get hurt and it is going to take a lot longer than you had hoped for. During the match, you should minutely be focused on completing the tasks necessary to win. Not winning, but what you are doing to get there. As an officer, you must stay on top. You must get one of the bad guys' hands behind his back. You must get a handcuff on his wrist. And so on...

Then reality kicks in... While you are wrestling with this guy as a police officer, his radio is blaring, yours is sounding off in your ear, the motor is running, his wife is yelling at you, the dog is barking and all of this is happening between the seats of the boat. And that is really not that "bad" of a scenario. What if he has three friends with him instead? As a police officer, you need to focus well enough to win without putting yourself at risk from another threat. You must be aware that the wife has a knife, the dog has teeth and if you fall overboard, you are in the water (with 25 pounds of uniform weight). Depending on the environment, a police officer cannot focus as minutely as a wrestler can. Neither a police officer nor a wrestler has time to think about the result instead of the task. Hopefully, for both, there will be plenty of time to think about the outcome when the match is over!

METHODOLOGY TO WARDENING

As you read this book, you have most likely catch onto some of the "tricks of the trade". You will also see that I didn't work with other officers very often. Laura would obviously be the exception to the rule. Early in my career, I realized that I didn't work the same way when I was working with another officer. I felt like I didn't push myself as hard as I normally would to catch "bad guys". I also felt like I would miss things that I didn't miss when I was working alone. I don't know if it was because I was trying to accommodate the other officer or if I was relying on them. Either way, I didn't feel like I was as good of a game warden when I was working with somebody else. I'm sure that some officers thought I was asocial, but that really is not the case. I enjoy talking with people, but I also take work very seriously. Maybe too seriously. Since I always took pride in my work, I found that I preferred pushing myself at work over being social.

Over the years, I saw many officers that frequently worked together. Some worked together so often that I wondered if they could do the job on their own. When I became a Sergeant, light was finally shed onto the key difference between me and those officers. As a Sergeant, I had to take what they call a DISC Survey. The DISC survey breaks down a person's personality into four different categories. I'm not an expert on DISC Surveys and cannot completely describe what you learn from them. I can tell you that they are worth taking and some of what I learned from mine. After getting the results from my survey, I had a class that broke down the results and told me how to apply what I had learned.

I was told that I am a very high "D" and a high "C". The high "D" is one of the least common traits. It indicates that I am a multi-tasker that is very goal-oriented, amongst other things. The high "C" means that I like numbers. When you put them together, you get someone who pays attention to numbers that sets goals for themselves. Since your personality is not infinite, you cannot be great at every personality trait. If one or two of your traits are high, the other traits will generally suffer. The traits that suffered for me were social and service. That's most likely why I'm not on social media and do not find myself mingling within the little "huddle groups" at the back of a classroom. It is also likely why I didn't look for people to work with all the time.

The most common personality trait? Yes, that would be social. I believe that is why social media sites are so popular and bars and churches never go out of business. That is also likely the reason why some officers feel a need to work with someone else all the time. It is not because they cannot do the job on their own, but rather that they would prefer to do it with someone else.

As a supervisor, the class teaches you how your personality interacts with your officer's personalities. It helps you to plan for the struggles that you may be facing with some of your officers. As a high "D", it helped me to understand that some of my officers will actually work better as a tandem unit. The high "D" in me still says that two solo patrols can cover twice as much ground as that single tandem unit. In the end, I believe that every officer can benefit from knowing their own personality traits. If nothing else, it may help them better understand themselves and why they work the way they do. At a grander level, the officer will be better at communicating with other officers and the public. I truly wish that I had a better understanding of my personal traits earlier in my career.

Communication with other officers and the public is one of the most important parts of law enforcement. I am sure that police academies vary, but new officers will always be trained in communicating with their supervisors and radio telecommunicators. They will also be thoroughly trained in interview and interrogation skills. Depending on how good of a communicator an officer wants to be, there is a never-ending list of additional training that they can seek out.

At about the 10-year mark, I realized what I consider to be the most important phrase (I will call it the **Key Phrase**) in our profession. Nobody ever mentioned it to me, but I am sure many officers naturally use it. I often wondered if those officers recognize that they use it and why. If they don't, maybe my explanation will help in their use of it. For the officers not using it, hopefully they will start. It will not only help deescalate incidents and investigations, but it will also help to eliminate officer complaints. It is a phrase that helps to bridge the communication gap between an officer and the violator.

I first used this phrase when I was dealing with some belligerent violators. It calmed the entire situation down and everybody left as happy as they could be (under the circumstances). Thinking about the phrase later, I was able to understand why it works. I was also able to further develop how, when and why to use it. The phrase is simply, **"I'm not saying that you're a bad guy, but you made a mistake today."** Depending on the situation, I will follow it up with something like, "You actually seem like a really nice person." I may even spend some time justifying my position on who they are as a "good" human being.

Law enforcement is not meant to be a personal attack on the person who has been stopped or apprehended. The officer is simply doing a job that has to be done and serves many pur-poses. Although many people fully understand that, some do not look at it that way. They take it personally that an officer has stopped "them". How many times have I heard, "My gosh, nobody else ever gets stopped for this." I've heard it thousands of times in one form or another. Once they believe they are getting a citation, some of those people go into full defense mode. From there, the situation can escalate rather quickly if it is not diffused.

By using the Key Phrase, rational people will generally be calmed down. They will be brought back to the reality that you are just doing your job. As an officer, I just wanted compliance from the offender and to make it home at night. If the offender thanked me for being nice, that was even better. They may not be happy about the citation, but hopefully they realized that I was just doing my job. I never meant for it to be personal.

Even if you do not believe that the person is a nice guy (as you have told them), use the Key Phrase. In their mind, they may believe that they have pulled one over on you. They may think that they have the upper hand in the situation. Who cares what the offender thinks in that regard? They have complied and you have completed your job without escalating the incident. You have succeeded in your job goal. On top of that, when the situa-tion is over, it will be unlikely for them to complain about you. You have told them that you like them. It's harder to complain about someone who likes you.

Within the same realm of compliance, I also occasionally found a need to articulate fairness. As I stated above, one of the most common complaints from the public is how they are treated in comparison to another person. That complaint is easily dif-fused if you can tell a person that you have treated everybody else the same and do not believe it would be fair to the others if you treated them differently. This alone is part of the reason that early in my career I set standards for what people would be cited for. As I continued throughout my career, there is not any group of people who could ever state they were treated unfairly. Good, bad or ugly, they were treated the exact same as everyone else. Being able to honestly tell a violator that fact helped to diffuse arrest anger many times.

ARA

Throughout my career, I have had to teach at all levels of school. I have also taught many groups outside of school. One of those groups was the Police Explorers. Police Explorers are teenagers that have shown an interest in being police officers. These kids are hopefully starting to build a resume and not trying to learn how to skirt the law. When I went to teach my first class, I wanted to teach them what it meant to be a police officer and what it took to be a good police officer. Anybody can respond to a "common" call and handle it competently (if they have been trained to do it). Special calls may take a special officer. As game wardens, you must be proactive in order to be good at the profession. While en route to teach the class, I thought about what it took to be a good proactive police officer and came up with "ARA". ARA would comprise the three stages necessary to be good at "proactive" police patrols. ARA stands for **Awareness, Recognition and Action.** I believe that you need to be effective in all three stages to be effective at proactive police work. To illustrate ARA, I'm going to use a story from when I was working (as a Sergeant) with one of my CPOs. It is not a special story, but has several facets to help with the illustration.

On this day, I was working with CPO Audrey Hoftender. Audrey is a good CPO. More importantly, she is a good person. Audrey was fun to work with and always acted like she was learning from you—even if she already knew what you were telling her. Audrey was assigned to work JoDaviess County at the time. JoDaviess County is possibly the best "game warden county" in the state of Illinois. It is highly timbered and has a huge deer and turkey population. It is also on the Mississippi River and has borders with both Wisconsin and Iowa (in the northwest corner of our state). All those factors lead to opportunities for a game warden.

Audrey was driving us to a local taxidermist so we could do an inspection on his facility. It was late in the afternoon as we drove behind a couple of industrial buildings in Galena. Audrey was multitasking as she drove, and I was enjoying having someone else drive for me. Looking behind the industrial buildings, I saw a car parked with the driver's door open. There was a subject (Driver) sitting in the driver's seat and another subject sitting on a piece of steel just outside the door. I told Audrey that they looked suspicious as we drove past. Audrey said she caught a glimpse but hadn't seen two subjects. In her defense, she was responding to something on the computer (one-handed driving is not uncommon for a game warden). Audrey asked if I wanted to stop and talk with the subjects. I said, "Yeah, let's go back and do a 'welfare check' on them."

As we pulled up, the guys weren't nervous, but they were guarded. You could tell something wasn't right. Audrey was down wind as we talked to the guys. Suddenly, she caught a whiff of cannabis. The whiff led to the two subjects being cited for their indiscretions. As Audrey filled out their paperwork, I saw a dandelion growing next to the building ahead of us. It was early April and had been very cold that spring. I had not seen another bloomed dandelion anywhere up to that point. This one was big and proudly bloomed out. I instantly wondered if the foundation of the building could be that warm. Walking over to the dandelion, there was warm water coming out of a drain tube from the wall of the factory. The water had black soot in it and was draining into a storm sewer. I made Audrey aware of the flower, water and soot for later investigation.

Returning to ours suspects, I made small talk with them as Audrey continued with the paperwork. During our conversation, I asked Driver how much he had paid for his bag of weed. It was not a "normal" bag of weed. It actually had four "balls" of weed in the bag. Driver asked, "Do you really want to know?" I nodded and was thinking, Yeah, or I wouldn't have asked ya. Driver told me that he had the ability to get his hands on some gold. Driver said that the dealer is willing to take gold in payment. He told me that the dealer took one gram of gold for a quarter ounce of weed. Of course, I gave that information to Audrey too.

This case occurred in the last couple years of my career. I like it as an example of awareness because there were several awareness issues brought up during one stop. It is not uncommon to have several issues, but they are usually not this diverse. Seeing the car, seeing the dandelion and smelling the weed are all examples of awareness.

"Awareness" is the most basic stage. As a police officer you need to be aware of what is always going on around you. In fact, I would say that everybody should try to be aware of their surroundings. Most people wanting to be a police officer naturally have awareness. Some can be taught it and everybody who "wants" to be a good police officer will get better at it over the course of their career. Even officers that "just want to collect a paycheck" (JCAP Officers) get better at awareness. They most likely fail further down the line of ARA and claim a failure in awareness. This is because there is little accountability for a failure at the awareness stage. It is almost impossible to tell someone that they should have seen something when they claim that they didn't. In comparison, failure to act in a later stage can open an officer up to discipline, litigation or both. It's less painful and easier to just say that you didn't see it.

"Recognition" is helped with training and even more so with experience. I often said that I was a much better officer at the 20-year mark than I was after 10 years. That was in large part due to experience. As Audrey and I drove past the car, I recognized that the two subjects at the vehicle were suspicious for that location. During the check, Audrey recognized the odor of cannabis. I recognized that the dandelion growing was not normal for that time of year. I also recognized that I didn't normally see cannabis packaged in the manner that I saw it that day. In these instances, recognition is married to awareness, but it is different. Some people would have seen the vehicle and never thought anything more of it. Some people would have smelled the cannabis, but not recognized what it was. I was never a drug user. It took me about a year (after I was hired) to get good at identifying the odor of cannabis. Some people would have seen the dandelion and just thought that it was nice to see an early one. They would never have given another thought to why it was early. And some people would have just been happy to catch someone using drugs. They would have dealt with the arrest and not asked another question. How many times have you heard someone say that they saw something but didn't think much of it? A good proactive police officer slows down during a stop (if they can) and pays attention to the details. Sometimes, they may have to look at things more than once to have them register in recognition. There are times when I feel like something is just not right, but I can't put my finger on what it is. I just strike up a conversation with the person while I try to figure out what is going on. The "cream" will rise to the top—it works.

"Action" is the pinnacle of the stages. After seeing the car and recognizing that something wasn't right, I asked Audrey to go back. Could we have continued on to the taxidermy inspection? Sure, we could have. Sometimes you are responding to a call or there is something that you literally must do. Make a note of what was going on and work it later. If you didn't spook the "prospects", they will likely be back. They probably think you are just a JCAP.

Another nice thing about this case is that there are several levels of action within it. The first was making the stop. We then moved on to asking where the cannabis was located. The next two levels take a lot more work. A sample of the water coming out of the drain tube needs to be taken. It needs to be submitted for testing. If there are pollutants in the water, it will need to be addressed. The final level is the trade of gold for cannabis. As you think about that one, you should be thinking about how to catch the dealer. Who would take gold in on trade for cannabis? Will the dealer be a pawn or artisan jewelry shop? Will the "Driver" show up on any of the local pawn shop records? Is there someone else that repetitively brings "scrap" gold into the local pawn shop? Gold that they got from the "Driver" will likely always be cut or broken. Sometimes, game wardens are not equipped to handle these types of cases. If so, bring in the EPA to help with the water and share the drug info with local authorities. Take some sort of action, you never know where it will lead. You may surprise yourself in how "good" you really can be.

At the recognition stage, the JCAP officer may have just driven by. He may be intentionally driving with "blinders on" all the time. While driving, the JCAP may not look at things to see what is "actually there". If JCAP is action-ineffective, he sees and recognizes the car as suspicious but never stops. In the mid-levels of action-ineffective, the JCAP stops, finds something and figures out a way to keep from doing any paperwork. JCAPs are a liability for their department and their community. JCAP may have just let a DUI drive down the street. If the DUI kills someone, the department will possibly be sued. Much worse is that an entire family's life has just been changed forever. If the accident never happens, there are still two possible bad results. If JCAP just drove by, the "bad guys" may become more brazen or expand what they are doing. If JCAP stopped and harassed the suspects but did not make an arrest, he likely just moved the problem somewhere else. If that's the case, it's just a matter of time before JCAP moves the problem again or a proactive officer must do JCAP's job. You must remember that for as long as JCAP is working, he is filling a position that could have been filled by a good proactive officer.

Becoming the "Old Bull"

During ARA, I mentioned slowing down. That was really hard for me to do in the first couple of years. I was always trying to find the next "big thing". I figured that if I checked more people, I had more opportunities to find a violation. I believe that in my early years I was also too focused on finding certain types of violations. Quite often I would succeed in finding what I was looking for, but I'm sure I missed many violations while getting to the one I wanted. Around the third year, I started to slow down during my checks. Checks are not necessarily enforcement stops. I could be checking a fishing license, doing a welfare check or just stopping to talk with someone. I believe that officers need to spend more time at each check rather that hurrying to the next one. By slowing down, I had an opportunity to see more, hear more and get more out of the check. Obviously, the length of the check had to be within reason and not an illegal detention. It was a personal challenge of mine to find the violation. If I missed the violation, I figured the violator would be bragging about it to his buddies. I didn't want to be branded the "gullible" game warden. I would rather be disliked for being too thorough.

Let's break down a check so that you get an idea of what I'm talking about. This is more representative of where I ended up than where I started. Binoculars and watching people before they know you are there is of paramount importance. I would watch people until I felt like I knew who I was about to check. While watching them, they would litter, hide fish, do drugs and poach animals.

On parked vehicles, I would look at the license plates to see if I would be checking an Illinois resident. I needed to know if they were eligible for their resident licenses. I would also look through a parked vehicle's windows. If I had not seen the people yet, I would have an idea if I was looking for more than one person. During daylight, I would shine a strong flashlight through the window into the dark areas of the interior. I would frequently develop probable cause for a search just by seeing contraband sitting in plain view.

If I had pulled into a parking lot within visual range of my next check, I would try to keep my eyes on the subjects as I parked and exited my squad (especially if they saw me pull in). If they appeared suspicious in any way, I was pulling my binoculars out. I would exit my squad and keep my eyes on the subjects as I approached them. When I was within good unaided visual range, I would frequently take a "tactical" look at something. What I mean by a "tactical look" is that I would turn my head to the side or angle it toward the ground. I acted like I was looking away or down. I would not actually look away. I was just giving the person "the opportunity that they had been waiting for". Frequently, the person would hide or move something while they thought they could. I would continue my approach as though I had not seen anything. I may even go through my check that way. Waiting until the very end and then addressing what I had seen.

I would also use "tactical talking" as a distraction technique. Sometimes as I approached people, I would see them doing something suspicious. If I did and was already within verbal range, I would intentionally try to ask them about something. Usually what I would ask them about wasn't even relevant. If I had seen some guys smoking dope, I might ask them if they had caught any fish. I knew that they had not been fishing. Prior to answering the question, they would almost always hesitate. It was kind of like a Yogi Berra question. It was something that a person would have think about beyond face value. They would think that they were not fishing. They might think that I was a stupid "fish cop". They may wonder why I asked them if they were fishing when they clearly didn't have any fishing equipment. They may even start to think about how long it had been since they went fishing. Maybe they were just relieved that the cop didn't see what they were doing. Really, all I was doing was trying was buy some time. Time to close the gap from me to them without them destroying the evidence or running.

As I approached people, I would be looking at what I could see hidden inside their pockets. I would be looking for the "odd" bulges. Many times, I could literally see the outline of a cannabis pipe or hitter box in someone's pocket. It was fun to tell someone to hand me the pipe in their pocket when I had never checked it. When I asked people for their identification, I would be looking closely as they opened their wallet or purse. When they pulled out their ID, I would be looking at everything that I could see. Sometimes, I would see rolling papers, plastic baggies or other IDs. Many people would hand me their Illinois ID card and have an out-of-state driver's license right behind it. Some of those people would have a resident Illinois hunting or fishing license. Were they eligible for them? Plastic baggies sticking out of any pocket, wallet or purse needed to be asked about. How much legal stuff do you really carry in your pocket in a plastic baggie?

I would be looking at everything sitting on a table. Cup holders in a bag chair are one of the best storage spots for drugs and paraphernalia. If someone was sitting in a bag chair, I made sure to see what was in the cup holder. If they had an open tackle box, I would be looking to see what they had sitting in plain view. If they were hunting, I was looking for bloody hands and parts of any animal. Just finding one clue could lead me to the violation I was looking for.

Beyond the Check
Each check also offers an opportunity to gain intelligence. It may be on the subject that you are talking with, his friends or just general intelligence. A game warden needs to be curious. Ask

questions. If the person was fishing, I wanted to know if they had fished anywhere else that day. Had they caught anything at the other place? Was there anyone else over there? Had those people caught anything? If they were hunting, had they heard any gun shots around them? Some people really wanted to tell the game warden about a neighbor's illegal activities. They just didn't want to make the call. Ask them and give them the opportunity to tell you. I got to the point at the end of my career that I could get a violation from most of my hunting checks. The question was: how hard would I have to push myself and would I breach what was a reasonable amount of time (for the check)? With enough time, I felt like I could open the door. Once I had it open, the case usually grew to something bigger than what I had initially uncovered. If the people were "really nice", I would actually feel guilty because it seemed so easy.

While looking at everything and gaining verbal intelligence, I would also be reading the person's verbal and physical clues. Some people would indirectly tell me where something illegal was located. They would ask to go get something, but wanted to do it by themselves. Usually, it was their wallet in their vehicle. I would ask them to wait for me. As they had to wait for me, they would get anxious. When I was ready, we would go and get their wallet and whatever else they were hiding. In other areas of the book, I mentioned people literally pointing out illegal things. I would always look for those nervous habits. People also have trouble when they tell stories and act it out at the same time. They would tell me one thing, but would show me that they had done something else. You must pay close attention to pick up on those inconsistencies. Each situation offers different opportunities to catch a "bad guy". As I said before, the key is taking your time and getting **everything** you can out of each stop. Even if you just leave with information for a future case, you are better off than you were. Remember to write it down in your "things to work on book".

Many poachers are simply opportunists. They kill something extra because the opportunity presented itself. Those poachers may not have taken any precautions to avoid being caught. Although they will take after-the-fact precautions, they still are more prone to being apprehended. For others, they enjoy the thrill of the poach. Those guys take precautions and premeditate what they are doing. They have run the scenarios through their heads. They already know what they are telling the game warden when they get stopped. They are the ones that get a name like "Johnny Poacher".

By working locations, not people, you give yourself an opportunity to catch both Opportunists and Johnny Poachers. When I say that, I am not saying to discard intelligence. I am also not stating that I would take a pass on a known violation or violator. I often listened to officers stating that they needed to catch "Johnny Poacher". If you can figure out where Johnny hunts and are confident in your information, catch Johnny. If you spend all your time trying to catch Johnny, many other poachers are getting away with their deeds. It is similar to what I had done as a young officer. If there is too much time and focus spent on one person, the larger picture is lost.

As I worked and cleared my locations, I simply added more locations to my list. If you keep doing that, you will eventually catch your Johnnies. The key question becomes, "How do you identify likely poaching locations?" Common sense tells us that we catch a poacher where there are things to poach. The location will be dictated by the species being poached. Proper habitat for the species is the single most important factor. Find the habitat, find the species and find the poachers. I would let the poachers help me in my endeavors. Do you want to know where the best hunting spot is? Ask a poacher. They know where the animals are. Heck, they will likely enjoy educating the game warden and bragging about the area. They have definitely thought about what it would be like to hunt there. They have also thought about the risks of trying to do it. For some poachers, it's not worth it. For others it is.

Another common theme that I found for Johnny Poachers was remote locations. I never knew a poacher that wanted to be caught. They will look for locations where they cannot be seen. They will also be conscious of seeing you before you see them. They will want to be able to run or destroy evidence before you get to them. If they were a poaching fisherman, more often than not I had to walk further to get to them. With road hunters, look for roads that have no houses or houses that are way back off the road. They want to eliminate complaint calls.

Another thing to look at was an exit route. I don't know if Johnny Poachers think about it, but I caught a lot more of them in locations where there was an escape route than I did on a dead end. Animals always want an escape route. It is likely a built-in defense mechanism for humans too. Johnny Poachers definitely have stress and likely get anxious about what they are about to do. Since it is a premeditated act for Johnny Poachers, they are reducing stress by having an escape route.

So that brings us to time. This is the million-dollar question. Obviously, opportunists are hunting during or close to legal hunting hours. Maybe they see a deer before or after hours and just cannot resist. Maybe they see one on their way to or from their hunting spot. Johnny, on the other hand, does not want to be predictable. Although Johnny likes the "cover of darkness", he can literally be caught at any time of day. If someone was willing to give me information, I wanted to know the time more than anything. By working my locations, I just had to pick the right day of the week. I may not catch Johnny this week or next, but I would catch him.

One of the most important things that I told my officers when I became a sergeant was, "Get to the deer and get the violations." I'm sure that they already knew it, but maybe they had not "defined" it. I consider there to be three different types of deer. There are physical deer. Yes, those would be the ones that you can literally touch. It makes no difference if the deer are lying on the ground, in the bed of a truck, in someone's garage, hanging in a meat locker or sitting at a taxidermist. There is a "paper deer". Those would be the deer that exist on paper. They may be in an IDNR harvest report, a newspaper or in a taxidermist ledger book. Even though they do not physically exist in front of you, they did at one time. There is record of the deer that will be hard to refute. The last deer is a verbal deer. Even though they do not exist in front of you (and possibly have never existed), they do exist in someone's mind or words. All the different types of deer allow an officer an opportunity to catch a poacher. Very simply, an animal was killed and could have been poached.

The physical deer is the easy one. If you get to it while the hunter is still in the field, you need to get every detail you can from him. Those details need to be cross-referenced with every-one else in the hunting party (try to do it tactically). As an officer, I was looking for any inconsistencies. Those inconsistencies could be in the hunting parties' statements or between their statements and the physical evidence. It's an easy red flag if the deer has another hunter's tag on it. Figure out how, when and where they got the deer.

I love paper deer. You have nearly an unlimited amount of time to review them and look for inconsistencies. I came up with a standard method of reviewing paper deer. I would use it on nearly every paper deer that I found. In the last 15 years of my career, I realized that I could literally work on paper deer investigations all year long. Once they are recorded on paper, you just need to fig-ure out how to get to them. Think outside the box. Come up with paper deer that nobody has thought about reviewing.

Verbal deer are the ones that I tended to give leniency on. It's not that the hunters deserved a "break". They had broken the law just like the paper and physical guys. Many times, these were the deer that I had elicited from people while I was having a casual conversation with them. Hunters like to talk about hunting and brag about what they have killed. By just asking a few questions, I could get a bunch of information. I wouldn't be taking notes, but I would remember their name and cross-reference whatever information they had given me with my computer. I think I gave more breaks on verbal deer because I felt guilty. The hunters thought they were just having a conversation with me. They really had not intended on incriminating themselves. I was just able to make them feel comfortable enough to tell me more than they should have. I kind of felt like I had stacked the deck.

One of the last things that I am going to mention in this chapter is "Bridging". I coined this term around my 15th year of service. About that time in my career, I was looking for ways to keep the job challenging and fun. Bridging helped me to do that. It is simply bridging a case from one poacher to another. I would ask more questions of poachers that would lead me to information about other hunters. Often, I would get information about other hunters that were not in their group. They would just be people that the hunter knew about. I would follow up on the information that I had obtained and try to make a case on the next hunter. Sometimes, I could make two or three successful bridges from one hunter. The best I ever got was six bridges that connected seven different hunters. It started with one deer poacher and led to six more.

Finally, what is a "shit magnet"? A shit magnet is just an officer that is constantly getting into good arrests. Because it happens so often, people start calling the officer a "shit magnet". Like many other officers, on and off throughout my career I carried that title. The reality of the situation is that a shit magnet is just a curious proactive officer that puts themselves in the right location on the right day at the right time on a regular basis. I feel as though the use of my methodologies, sayings and philosophies made it so I could put myself where I needed to be when I needed to be there.

In no way am I claiming to be the "Ultimate Game Warden". I have watched plenty of other officers claim that title. I will say that I was a good game warden who worked hard and seriously thought about what he was doing–and why. For the general public, maybe this chapter gave you a little look into an officer's mindset and methodology. For old game wardens, you already knew all of this. For the young game wardens, I hope that you take a little of what I have said here and build upon it. I hope you become much better than I ever was. You will not stop getting better unless you already know everything.

RUNNERS

Runners create an inherently dangerous situation. If you're chasing someone, you are trying to catch them. If you succeed, you have caught someone who does not want to be caught. If they do not suddenly have a change of heart (which some do), you may be getting into a fight. On television shows and in the news, suspects run from officers every day. With me, it was not that common of an occurrence. As I got better at reading people, I always tried to set myself up to avoid having to chase someone. I felt like I could generally tell if they were considering running. If they were considering running, I could say they were "on the fence". I just had to figure out how to get them to stay on my side of it. Sometimes, I had to diminish their violations so that they did not feel like they needed to run. Other times, I had to continuously give them orders to get their mind off running. While verbally trying to convince them not to run, I would try to eliminate their escape route. The chase was over before it began if they had nowhere to go. Sometimes, it can be hard to close the escape route, maintain a safe position, preserve evidence and verbally control the situation all at the same time. This is especially true when you are operating as a solo unit. Complicating that further, back-up units may be a long time in getting to you. With all of the situations that I put myself in, I feel like I did a fairly good job.

Very early in our careers, Laura and I located most of the restricted fishing areas in Will County. What I mean by restricted is that nobody could fish at that location. One of those areas was the Lake Renwick Heron Rookery. This area is part of the Will County Forest Preserve system. Because of the nesting birds, nobody could enter the area for fishing or otherwise. The rookery is in the middle of an urban area and is pretty much encompassed by roads.

As Laura and I were on patrol one morning, we happened to be driving past the rookery and spotted two guys fishing on one of the lakes. The lakes on this side of the rookery were long narrow strip pits. Each one was separated by a little dike that was covered with waist high grass. Driving past the guys, we parked our squad down the road and snuck back through the tall grass. By the time we reached the end of the lake, one of the guys (I will call him Old) had worked his way around to the opposite side of the lake. He was about 50 yards around the bank from where we were. The other guy (I will call him Fat) had worked his way down one of the dikes and was also about 50 yards away. Laura and I talked about it and she was going to catch Old while I caught Fat.

We agreed that we would each work our way toward our guys. There were three breaks in the dike where I would have to cross a strip of water in order to get to get to Fat. Staying on the opposite side of the dike from Old, I worked my way toward Fat. When I got to the first break, I could see that there was gravel on the bottom of the three-foot break. I was able to hop across the break without being seen or heard. As I approached the second break, the grass started to get really short. I stopped and looked at the break. This break was about six feet wide and appeared to have a similar gravel bottom. There was no way to stay in cover and I was going to have to step in the water to cross the break.

At least the water was only about six inches deep. I stood up just high enough to see Fat. He was about 30 yards from me. At that point, I was convincing myself that I had it in the "bag". I was definitely in better shape than Fat and he was only 30 yards from me. I figured I would stand up, identify us and hop across to Fat, who would be waving his hands in the air.

I stood up and identified us to Old and Fat. As I began to direct them to stay where they were, Laura stood up too. Old and Fat took off running like two gazelles. I thought, no biggie, I will be on Fat in no time. Jumping to the middle of the break, my foot sank about 15 inches into a gray slurry mud. For a second, I thought that I may be stuck there. Listening to the suck as I pulled my foot out, I started running up the dike toward Fat. Fat had opened the gap up between us to about 40 yards. Reaching the third break, it was just as bad as the second break. By the time I emerged from the third break, Fat was 50 yards ahead of me. Fat was closing in on the railroad tracks at the end of the dike. When Fat reached the tracks, he scaled the hill and disappeared into the brush. By that time, I was only 30 yards behind him. Reaching the base of the tracks, I went up the hill on Fat's trail. At the top, I looked down the tracks and couldn't see Fat anywhere. I couldn't hear Fat moving in the brush. Fat had literally disappeared. Normally, we would all like Fat to disappear......just not this Fat! I looked around the area and could not find a trace of Fat. I figured it was not a big deal since Laura would surely have grabbed onto Old.

Starting back down the dike, I could see Laura but not Old. I figured that Laura had him sitting in the grass somewhere. As I got closer, I gave Laura a hand gesture asking where Old was at. She shot me one back, asking the same about Fat. I hated to admit that I didn't catch him. When I finally made it back, I asked her what happened. She said that she had chased Old into the timber, but couldn't find him. He had disappeared. I told her my story and said that I thought for sure she would have caught an

80-year-old guy. Laughing, Laura said that she couldn't believe I didn't catch a guy that was 100 pounds overweight. Our first chase had not ended up as I expected. Would I do anything different? Yeah, I would have chased Old instead of Fat. Not saying I would have caught him, but I didn't catch Fat.

It's a Swamp Thing

Moving ahead to 2000, things started to heat up. It was mid-June, and I was working at Des Plaines Conservation Area (DPCA). Being a direct shot down I-55 from Joliet and Chicago, DPCA was almost always busy. It was early afternoon on a warm sunny day when I had worked my way to the Kelly Road parking lot. It is likely one of my favorite spots that I have ever worked. The lot was on a dead-end road on the west edge of DPCA. Because of the remote feeling, people breaking the law were comfortable going to that lot.

I always tried to park my squad just outside the entrance of the lot. I would exit my squad and walk in. If I did that, the people in the lot couldn't see my squad before I could see them. I caught the fishermen before they ditched their poles and the druggies before they ditched their weed. As I walked into the lot, I saw there were several people fishing in and around the area. The parking lot is bordered on the north and south sides by Kankakee River backwaters. The backwaters extended about a mile both north and east of the lot. On the north side of the lot there was a large cement water intake housing. The housing took water in from the north backwater and moved it to the south side of the lot. The entrance road came in on the west side of the parking lot. Northeast of the lot was about a square mile of timber and fields. If you could not swim, the only entrance or exit to the lot was either on the road or through the timber.

Looking at the cement housing, I saw there was a female subject (we will call her Jill) fishing on top of it with her three-year-old daughter. Walking over to Jill, I identified myself to her.

Asking Jill if she had a fishing license, she told me that her boy-friend (later identified as Jack) had it. Jill told me that Jack was fishing with his mother (we will call her Mom) about 100 yards to the east. Walking to the east, I located Jack and was able to check his fishing license. Confirming with Jack that he was with Jill, I asked him if he had Jill's fishing license. He said that he did not. After questioning Jack about it, I told him that I would go back and talk with Jill. Of course, Jack decided to accompany me. On our way back, we stopped and talked with Mom and checked her fishing license.

When I got back to Jill, she claimed that she thought Jack had bought her fishing license for her. Jack and Jill told me that they lived together, so I asked Jack if I could hold onto his fishing license to help write Jill's written warning (using the address). Jack agreed and suddenly got really nervous. He broke out a cigarette and asked if he was free to go. It is one of the only times that I have been directly asked that. I told Jack that he could leave if he wanted to. Jack then asked if he could go over by his mom. I again agreed, but thought that I just told you that you could leave. Jack never directly asked me for his fishing license back. Jack quickly walked over to Mom while I walked back to my squad. Driving back to the lot, I parked right in the middle of it. When I parked in the lot, Jack was pacing back and forth and smoking hard. I tried running a background on both Jack and Jill through ISP, but was having trouble getting a response. Changing Jack's name a little, ISP told me that he had four warrants for his arrest. All of them were for driving offenses. Telling Jack that he had a warrant for his arrest, he said, "This is bullshit." Jack proceeded to tell me that he did not have a warrant for his arrest. Trying to reason with him, Jack reiterated that it was "bullshit" and started to walk away from me. As soon as I took a step toward Jack, he took off running. I immediately gave chase. Jack zig-zagged between the cars in the lot like he was on a rail. Every time he cut the next corner, I tried to follow but lost traction in the gravel. It was frustrating because

I would close the gap in the short straight-of-way and lose what I had gained in the next corner.

Finally, Jack took off toward the timber. My squad door was open, and the engine was still running, but I was going to catch Jack. When Jack hit the timber edge, he continued into the woods on a deer trail. I was about 20 yards behind Jack and gaining on him. Jack still had his cigarette in his hand and would occasionally look back over his left shoulder. I felt like I was running hard, while Jack was making it look easy. That didn't matter because I knew I had enough left to finish the deal. I was so focused on catching Jack that I was not looking at the trail. Suddenly, my left shin caught a six-inch log that was suspended across the trail (about a foot off the ground). I immediately did a header and found myself lying on the ground. By the time I regained my feet, Jack was about 40 yards ahead of me. I really wanted to keep chasing him, but had been knocked to my senses. My portable radio did not work that far from my squad and it was still running.

Hoping that my squad was still in the parking lot, I started to run back that way. Our radios back then would only work if we were within about 100 yards of our truck. I had not had contact with ISP radio in a while and was likely not returning their calls. When I reached my squad, I advised ISP of the chase and requested a K9 unit. Not only were they sending the Grundy County K9, but the ISP airplane was relatively close too. I coordinated with several officers and posted an officer on every edge of the mile woods.

Jill had found an ID by the time I returned, so I was able to complete a background check on her. ISP advised that Jill was wanted on a warrant for a driving offense. I handcuffed Jill and had her come over by my squad. Jill asked me if her daughter could go with Mom (the daughter's biological grandmother). I advised Jill that I would have to do a background check on Mom. Sure enough, Mom was wanted on a warrant too. Her warrant wasn't valid in Will County, so I was able to let the little girl go into her custody.

About 30 minutes into this ordeal, I had Will County Sheriff's Police and three other CPOs on scene helping to secure the perimeter of the mile woods. The ISP airplane was circling overhead and the Grundy County K9 unit had arrived at my location. I really didn't think the airplane would be able to see Jack under the treetops. For some reason we couldn't cut the K9 loose and things were starting to look kind of bleak. I figured Jack would just hunker down somewhere until we were gone. I was wrong. Jack was not smart enough to take his red shirt off and decided to make a break for it across an open swampy marsh. The marsh led directly to the campground where CPO Mike Bronson had parked. Mike was field training a recruit that day. The pilot was able to direct Mike and the recruit to the edge of the swamp. When Jack exited the muck, Mike and the recruit were waiting for him. They were able to hook Jack up without further incident.

Because Mike was short on interior room, one of the Will County Sheriff's Deputies brought a stinky wet Jack back to the Kelly Road parking lot. CPO John VanZant had arrived and eventually helped me transport Jack and Jill to the Will County Jail. Jack was charged with Resisting Arrest. In cases like that, the State's Attorney's office generally wants a report prior to the initial appearance. It was always hard to get a report done that fast. When I went in to drop the report off, the assistant state's attorney was excited that I had arrested Jack. I was told that Jack had tried to burn Jill's house down (with her in it) the previous week. Jack had two new Aggravated Arson warrants that were waiting to be entered into LEADS. I think Jack still is my personal record—six warrants on one guy. Suddenly, it made sense why Jack would commit another crime trying to avoid arrest. Very seldom will somebody run because they have a traffic warrant. Even more amazing was that Jill was fishing with Jack. Who wants to fish with a guy that just tried to burn her you up in a house!? As for Jack, he eventually pled guilty to Resisting Arrest and was fined $350. Not surprisingly, I believe Jill did not cooperate in the prosecution on the other charges.

Since I mentioned CPOs Mike Bronson and John VanZant, I should tell you a little more about them. They were both part of my original District. For new recruits (like Laura and I), being original District members is special. Those members are the people that you knew when you were young on the job. They helped you through your mistakes and likely helped to make you who you were as a warden. Mike was one of the older members when we joined the District. He was more of an old school game warden that seemed to always be smiling. John was in the class that was hired just before ours. When we moved into the north end of Will County, John headed to the south side. John was about as "laidback" of a game warden as you will ever find. Nothing ever seemed to bother John much. He was someone that generally calmed things down if shit was hitting the fan. I enjoyed working with both Mike and John when our schedules permitted.

The Breast Stroke

Not even a month after Jack and Jill, I was again working at Des Plaines Conservation Area. Shortly after nightfall, I would always venture through the Kankakee River boat launch. On this early July evening, most of the traffic had exited the Kankakee River. As I drove toward the launch, I observed a boat out on the river and a vehicle pulling an empty trailer through the parking lot. I pulled my squad down onto the PWC launch and parked. The PWC launch was on the opposite side of the dock from the boat launch. After dark, PWCs could not legally be operated so that launch was empty.

After exiting my squad, the car with the trailer turned the corner and headed toward the launch. The car's headlights lit up the side of my squad. It made me uncomfortable since I always tried to be "stealth". Trying to diminish my bad choice in parking locations, I figured that the guy (we will call him Stroke—as in breaststroke) in the boat would see me before I could check him anyway. Looking out at the boat, I saw Stroke staring at my squad. He obviously realized who I was. Stroke reached behind him, grabbed a life jacket and quickly put it on. I walked out onto the dock so I could conduct a safety inspection on Stroke's boat when he came in. When the car finished backing the trailer into the water, Stroke pulled his boat up near the launch and turned his motor off. Stroke yelled at me, "What's up?" I told him that I was going to conduct a safety inspection on his boat when he got it trailered. Stroke acknowledged that he understood and started his boat back up. Stroke proceeded to drive about 100 yards out across the river. Obviously, something was not going right. The guy in the car (Trailer Guy) was not in on it since he was standing by the trailer with the bow strap in his hands. When Stroke got all the way across the river, he yelled, "I'll meet ya at Big Basin" and took off flying downstream. Trailer Guy reeled the strap back in and prepared to leave.

Yeah, I was a little irritated at that point. I hopped in my squad and started for Big Basin. Big Basin was a bar on the Des Plaines River that had private boat docks and a boat launch. Several miles downstream from the DPCA boat launch, the Kankakee and Des Plaines Rivers come together to form the Illinois River. Stroke was going to have to drive his boat down to the Illinois and then several miles up the Des Plaines River to get to Big Basin. He would have to pass numerous hazards between the two locations. As I was driving, I figured that Stroke would either get in an accident or just never show up. Of course, I also figured that I needed to beat Stroke to Big Basin—if he was going to show up.

Arriving at Big Basin, I parked in the lot. Stroke had not arrived yet. Trailer Guy pulled in shortly after me. I walked over to Trailer Guy and asked him if Stroke was drunk. Trailer Guy said that he didn't know anything. I walked down onto the dock with my flashlight.

I couldn't believe it, but after about 10 minutes I saw Stroke coming up the Des Plaines River. As Stroke pulled into the harbor, I shined my light on him and again identified myself. I told Stroke to pull his boat over to the docks for inspection. He complied. As Stroke was trying to tie off, he told me that he knew I would be there. Stroke had all the normal signs of being drunk. Besides the normal signs, Stroke was being a stroke. Every time I asked him for something, he acted like I was inconveniencing him. When I got done with the inspection, I asked Stroke how many beers he had to drink. Stroke asked me, "Did I say that I had any?" We repeated that exchange two more times. I asked Stroke to exit the boat and walk with me up to the pavement. He agreed. On the blacktop, I asked Stroke one more time how much he had to drink. He said, "I've had my legal limit."

I asked Stroke to do some field sobriety tests for me. He agreed. We went through the HGN, One Leg Stand and Walk and Turn Tests. Stroke did miserably on all of them. I asked Stroke if he knew the English Alphabet. After saying, "Not very well," Stroke blurted out his best rendition. Messing that up too, Stroke asked me, "Am I in trouble?" I advised him that he was. After confirming it with him again, Stroke turned and started to walk away. I told Stroke to hold up. He immediately took off running to the east across the parking lot. He was not real fast, so I initially just kept pace with Stroke while I was yelling at him to stop. As I looked ahead, I saw that we were approaching a rock embankment that separated the lot from the river. I was right behind Stroke on his left side. The embankment was both to the right and straight ahead. I knew that when Stroke got to the embankment he would have to turn to his left. I was going to tackle him like a linebacker. Readying myself for the sack, Stroke threw me a curve ball. He continued straight off the rocks diving headfirst into the water.

Stroke was still wearing his life jacket. He had his head down under the surface of the water and was using something of a breaststroke above his head to help propel himself forward as he was kicking. After about 20 seconds' worth of "swimming", Stroke lifted his head out of the water to see how far he had made it. Looking back at us, he swam in a loop and stood up in the water. It was only a couple of feet deep. Stroke went over and hid under a dock before finally giving up.

I arrested Stroke for operating a watercraft under the influence of alcohol (OUI). Of course, he had to tell me that it was just "suspicion" of the violation. When I stuck him in my squad, Stroke immediately put his wet feet up on my dashboard. As he pushed on my dash, I told Stroke that I would arrest him for criminal damage to State property if broke it. He took his feet down. When we arrived at Channahon P.D., Stroke refused to provide a breath sample and was released later that evening. Stroke eventually pled guilty to OUI and was fined $500.

In the Shadows

Jumping ahead to 2005, I was working my first full year in the Quad Cities. Although I was comfortable in my patrol area, I definitely did not know it inside out. One thing that I had figured out was that Hennepin Canal State Park was a treasure trove of activity. If things were slow, I could almost always count on finding something there.

It was 11:30 p.m. on a chilly mid-May night when I saw a car parked in one of the Hennepin Canal parking lots. The headlights were on, but I could not see any people in the car. This lot is the first one west of the Route 67 bridge on Big Island Road. About 40 yards away, the bridge spans the canal and one branch of the Rock River. The bridge consists of very large overhead steel beams. The steel beams come down and disappear into the surface of the bridge. On my patrols in this area, I would generally drive past the parking lots and try to see what was going on in and around them before I would pull in and "work" them.

Driving north on Route 67, I continued past the intersection with Big Island Road. I decided to continue up to the fishing areas north of there and then come back to see if the car was still in the lot. When I got done checking those areas, I drove back toward the parking lot. As I approached the intersection of Route 67 and Big Island Road again, I could see there were two vehicles parked in the lot next to each other. Turning the corner onto Big Island Road, I could see three guys (Runny, Lumpy and Joe) standing outside at the rear of the vehicles.

Pulling into the lot near the vehicles, there was a big Pro Series speaker box sitting on the ground between them. Parking my squad, I exited the vehicle and identified myself to the subjects. I immediately noticed that Lumpy had a huge bulge in his right front pants pocket. It looked like Lumpy had 2/3 of a grapefruit shoved down into his pocket. I asked the subjects what they were up to. Lumpy told me that he was just buying some speakers. I walked past the subjects and in between the two cars. Shining my flashlight into the vehicles, I saw that a female was sitting in the driver's seat of the black Chevy.

Turning back toward the subjects, I asked Lumpy what he had in his pocket. Lumpy turned his right side away from me, put his hands in his pockets and said that he had a bunch of stuff in them. All three of the subjects suddenly got really nervous. Lumpy pulled a phone out of his left front pants pocket and showed it to me. I asked Lumpy if he had a gun or weapon in his right pocket. Lumpy said, "I'm not going to lie, it's pot." Lumpy pulled a giant bag of cannabis (165 grams) out of his pocket. Yes, I know it is amazing, but sometimes it is just that easy. I told Lumpy to hand me the bag. He complied. It was obviously going to be a felony, so I put Lumpy in handcuffs, searched him and put him in my squad.

As I walked around to the driver's side of my squad, I saw Runny reach into the black Chevy and pull some more radio components out of the back seat. As he was setting them next to the speaker box, I was putting the giant bag of pot on my dashboard. With Lumpy in cuffs, I would have thought that everybody knew the speaker deal was off. In reality, Runny wasn't trying to complete the deal. What Runny was doing is a common tactic for someone who has something illegal. Those people will generally do one of two things. They will either try to separate themselves from the illegal items or they will point them out to you. They don't literally say, "I have something illegal" and point at it. You need to watch their hands and body language. They may tap on it, push on it or repetitively rub it. They will also try to hide it when you are not watching. I always found it fun to act like "Columbo". I would act like I didn't see or recognize what they were doing and then spring it on them. Runny was trying to separate himself from the speakers and radio components. You will not see a much better example of that. In other situations, you need to be aware of someone who "wants" to leave their jacket or something else behind and walk away from it.

I walked back over by Runny and Joe. I asked them if they had any cannabis. They advised they did not. After checking them and their vehicles for contraband, Runny and Joe started complaining about being cold. I walked over by the speaker box and radio equipment. I lifted one side of the speaker box up and could hear what sounded like broken glass sliding around inside. At that point I figured that Runny had broken the window out of a car, stolen the speaker and was now trying to sell it. I asked Runny where he got the speakers. He said that all the stuff was his girlfriend's brother's. Runny said that he was just trying to sell it for him. Runny started complaining about being cold and asked if he could sit in the car. I agreed and returned to my squad with the serial numbers from the speakers and radio equipment. At my squad, I ran checks on Runny, Joe and the radio stuff. I was told that Runny was wanted on a warrant.

Walking back to the black Chevy, I tapped on Runny's door. When he opened the door, I told him that he had a warrant for his arrest. I stepped back about two steps. Although I had searched the vehicle, it was still possible there could be a hidden weapon inside. I advised Runny to step out of the vehicle. He swung his legs out, stood up, said "fuck you" and took off running toward the bridge. I had stepped too far toward the back bumper! I chased Runny for about five steps and thought about the bag of cannabis sitting on my dash.

I ran back to my squad, hit the rollers and took off toward the bridge. Yes, Lumpy was strapped into the front passenger seat. When I hit the corner, I could see Runny sprinting down the bike path on the other side of the road. I knew I could cut him off if I drove down to the next entrance (about a block away). I hit the gas and headed toward the next entrance (down Route 67). In order to get up onto the bike path, I had to pass a pizza place. When I cut the corner, one of the delivery guys was heading out to his car with a bag full of pizzas. He was nice enough to swing them out of the way as we headed up onto the bike path. By the time I made it up there, Runny had turned around and was running back toward the bridge. Runny ran up the bridge embankment and onto the bridge. I couldn't follow Runny in my squad, so I had to drive a small loop to get up onto the bridge. When I finally got up on the bridge, I couldn't find Runny. Milan and Rock Island Police units came and helped in the search. We never did find him. As I thought about it later, I figured that Runny had hid behind one of the big steel bridge beams. I think that after I drove past him, Runny took off running back the other way.

Lumpy was dropped off at the Rock Island County Jail that night. He never really said anything about the chase. I would think that it was pretty interesting for him. I can't imagine that too many people get that kind of a "ride" in a squad. Lumpy eventually plead guilty and was fined $3,751. Runny's speakers and radio equipment were seized as evidence. I never found out where they were stolen from. A lot of people who have stuff like that stolen never enter the numbers into LEADS. Since the speakers were never entered into LEADS, I eventually tried to return them to Runny. For some reason, he never came to picked them up. In fact, I never saw Runny again. I found out later that Runny had been a local problem child for several years.

The Landing of Lincoln

On a late afternoon in February of 2006, I was heading toward my house from Kewanee, Illinois. The fastest way to get home is to cut through Cambridge on Route 81. As I was nearing Cambridge, I could see a set of squad car lights up ahead. The squad was on the opposite shoulder of the road with an old Lincoln in front of it. As I got closer, I saw the Lincoln pull up onto Route 81 and start heading in my direction. I then saw the squad continue behind it. I figured that the squad had completed a traffic stop and was going to turn its lights off. The squad followed behind the Lincoln as they both sped past me. There were two guys and a girl in the Lincoln (we will call them Bonnie, Clyde and Jack). I turned on my Henry County radio and was able to hear that they were in a pursuit.

It's my understanding that our squad trucks only go about 95 miles per hour, so I knew I was not going to be part of the pursuit. I did a U-turn and figured that although I would not be in the pursuit, I could be a close back-up unit. As I got up to speed, I lost sight of both units. They were about a mile ahead of me. I listened as the Henry County unit kept calling in the speed changes and conditions of the pursuit. At one point, they advised that the pursuit was in excess of 105 miles per hour. As the units approached a set of curves, the Henry County unit discontinued the pursuit. I slowed down and figured that I would turn around and head back toward the house.

As soon as I turned around in a driveway, Henry County advised that the Lincoln had crashed next to a creek. Turning back around, I knew that I was only about two miles from the creek. The three occupants had reportedly exited the Lincoln and were fleeing the scene. Almost immediately, there were officers reporting that they were involved in a foot pursuit of Bonnie, Clyde and Jack.

When I arrived on scene, there was smoke and flames shooting out from under the hood of the Lincoln. The Lincoln had driven off the south side of the road and crashed into a tree. Parking my squad, I couldn't see anybody around the squads or the Lincoln. I ran over and looked inside the open driver's door of the Lincoln. There wasn't anybody inside. Looking across the road to the north, I saw a police officer running to the north. He was in the brushy grass that had grown up on both sides of the creek. As you got further from the road, the brush and grass got thicker and had more trees mixed in. On both sides of the brushy grass, there were harvested farm fields that extended for a few hundred yards to both the east and west.

Initially, I did not want to leave the Lincoln, but then another Henry County squad pulled up. When the officer got out, he told me that the Lincoln had been stolen. I told him that I was going to drive my squad along the east side of the creek through the field. It was one of those days that I was really happy to have a four-wheel drive truck. Driving up a tall ditch, I started north across a cut corn field. About the time I got to the top of the hill, I saw Bonnie, Clyde and Jack running through the field northeast of me. They looked at me and took off to the northwest. When they reached the hedge row, they cut through it and continued down the hill. There were a lot of big trees in the hedge row, but I saw a path that had been cut through it to the north of me.

Driving up to the cut, I motored through the hedge row. When I got to the other side, Bonnie, Clyde and Jack had made their way to the next hedge row northwest of me. There was a fence in that one. I watched as all three of the subjects jumped the fence and continued back down the hill toward the creek. There were not any cuts in the second hedge row, so I was going to have to continue on foot. Parking my squad at the fence, I got out and yelled at Bonnie, Clyde and Jack to stop. They didn't even look back at me. I advised ISP of the foot pursuit, hopped the fence and took off after them. I was making up a lot of ground as they reached the creek. In this area, there was not any brush along the creek. The creek had been straightened and consisted of a ten-foot-wide and six-foot-deep ditch. The trio had to work to get through it. As I reached the east side of the ditch, Clyde was pulling Bonnie up on the west side. I thought about jumping across and grabbing Bonnie, but figured that we would both get hurt. As they were starting across the next field, I jumped down into the ditch and climbed out the other side.

After another 200 yards, I was on Bonnie's heels and they were all looking over their shoulders. Bonnie doubled over and said that she couldn't go any further. Clyde and Jack were trying to rally Bonnie into running again. She refused. I called ISP and told them I had the trio stopped and wanted a back-up unit. I drew my gun and had it at the "low ready" (pointed at the ground). Clyde and Jack had the baggy gang banger look going on. I could see bulges in Clyde's pants pockets. I yelled at all of them to get on their knees. All three of them looked at me. Clyde and Jack yelled, "Fuck you, pig!" I stepped closer to Bonnie and grabbed her left arm. I told her to get on her knees and jerked her forward to the ground. Bonnie complied. Clyde and Jack backed up and started to heckle me. They were telling me to leave Bonnie alone. As Clyde and Jack continued to yell at me, they started wildly waving their arms around and touching their pants near their front pockets. They started the "Fuck you, pig!" chants again.

Clyde suddenly yelled, "If you're going to fucking shoot me, shoot me pig!" Then he yelled, "I love you, Bonnie... Now shoot me, you fucking pig!"

Clyde put his hands in his front pants pockets. I yelled at Clyde to get his hands out of his pockets. He was obviously grabbing something inside of his pockets. Clyde suddenly jerked his hands out of his pockets and said, "I'm getting a cigarette, you fucking pig!" Clyde had a lighter in one hand and a pack of cigarettes in the other. As he worked a cigarette up in his pack, I saw a Kewanee Police officer break out of the brush about 100 yards south of us. When the Kewanee officer reached us, he went toward Clyde. I holstered my gun and grabbed Jack's right arm. I whipped Jack to the ground and cuffed him. When I stood up, the Kewanee officer was pepper-spraying Clyde. The pepper spray didn't seem to affect Clyde, but I was down wind and was catching the mist. As my eyes started burning, the Kewanee officer tackled Clyde. I helped the Kewanee officer get Clyde handcuffed. As we put the cuffs on Clyde, Jack and Bonnie had regained their composure and were yelling at us "fucking pigs" again.

About the time the Calvary arrived, we had the situation calmed down. Bonnie, Clyde and Jack understood that they were getting a free ride. We searched them and did not find any weapons. We also did not find any identification. They all ended up being juveniles. What a nightmare! Did Clyde really want to commit suicide by cop? I found out later that the stolen Lincoln was one of their grandparents' cars. I wished that I had a lot more information going into that whole ordeal. It was not a good situation, but it could have been a very bad one.

Ivy

In May of that same year, I was working along the Hennepin Canal near Rock Island. Shortly after noon, I located a few vehicles parked by the Route 92 bridge on Canal Road. Generally, when vehicles were parked there, the occupants would be fishing in either the Rock River or the Hennepin Canal. Seeing the vehicles well in advance, I parked about 50 yards prior to reaching them and walked the rest of the way in. Sometimes, I would opt to drive past the vehicles and walk back to them. Either way, I didn't want the people to know that my truck had stopped by their vehicles.

Reaching the vehicles, I looked in the windows. I could tell that I would be checking fishermen. Crossing the entrance gate, I walked toward the bank of the river. In the 30 yards between the vehicles and the riverbank, I would be walking past the Hennepin Canal. As I passed the canal, I checked, but couldn't see any fishermen. Continuing up onto the towpath, I saw two fishermen (Biggun and Grill) on the bank of the Rock River. The nice thing about the towpath is that it lies between the canal and the river and is elevated about 10 feet higher than both. I always liked the fact that I could stand on the towpath and see the fishermen on either bank.

Biggun and Grill had poles in the water and were talking amongst themselves. Biggun's name is fitting. He stood about 6'2" tall and weighed about 260 pounds. I knew Grill from checking him several times before. He was shorter and lighter than Biggun, but was in much better shape. I called him Grill because he literally has a full golden "grill". Every tooth in his mouth was gold. Biggun was standing with a pole in his hands and Grill was sitting on a bucket to his left.

Like always, before I walked down to check them, I stopped to look at Biggun and Grill with my binoculars. It might seem like over-kill when they're only 15 yards away, but it really helps. When I focused on Grill, I could see that he had something in his lap. My initial thought was that he was trying to tie on a fishing lure, but his line was already in the water. Looking more closely, I could see that Grill was trying to roll a blunt. After he loaded it up, Grill wound it meticulously tight and licked the paper to seal the edge.

As soon as he got done rolling it, Grill looked over his right shoulder and directly at me (I must have been burning a hole in his back).

I lowered my binoculars and walked down the side of the towpath. It's steep when you first start going down and levels off along the bank of the river. Keeping my eyes focused on Grill, I saw him palm the blunt into his left hand and curl it down toward his knee. Since Biggun and Grill were both looking at me, I acted like I was just coming to check their fishing licenses. I identified myself and began asking about the fishing.

Reaching Grill, he was staring out into the river. He acted like he was watching his fishing line. Stepping over to Grill's left side, I told him to hand me the blunt. Grill said that he didn't have one. Asking him to hand it to me again, he refused and began to stand up. Grabbing Grill's left arm, I told him that I had seen him roll it and asked him to sit back down. Grill said that he wasn't sitting down. When he got all of the way up, Grill ripped his arm away from me and started running toward Biggun. I immediately gave chase. Keeping up with Grill, he turned and started running up the towpath embankment. I can remember questioning whether I would be able to keep up with Grill if he made it to the top. Grill was about five feet in front of me, but had started scaling the hill. This put his waist was at about my eye level. Focusing on his pants, I can remember thinking about Grill's puffy cargo pockets. I knew that if I could get a hold of them, I would have a chance to stop the chase. Just as Grill reached the rim of the towpath, I dove and grabbed onto his cargo pockets. Jerking Grill toward me, he fell back, and we rolled down the embankment.

Ending up in a pile of brush and briars, Grill kept trying to get away. I held on and started yelling for him to get his hands behind his back. He refused and just kept trying to stand up. As Grill reached his feet, I pushed him over into a tangle of vines and climbed onto his back. The vines were in such a thick tangle, that it was like laying on a series of webbing. "Webbing" that was keeping us suspended above the ground. Every time I started to get one of Grill's hands behind his back, he would wiggle his body back and forth. When he did, the vines would give way and we would drop a few inches toward the ground. When we dropped, I would lose leverage on Grill's wrist and he would suck it back up under his chest. To make matters worse, Grill started yelling at Biggun to come help him. At first, Biggun stood there with his fishing pole and told me to let Grill go. When he started to walk toward us, I pulled out my pepper spray and told Biggun that if he didn't sit down, I would be spraying both of them. Grill started complaining about his asthma and told me that I was hurting him. Hell, I was breathing worse than he was! Biggun told me to stop hurting Grill as he sat in his chair. I told Biggun to have Grill to put his hands behind his back and it would all be over. Biggun sided with me! He told Grill, "Just put your hands behind your back." Grill didn't listen to Biggun. Pulling my handcuffs out, I pushed down on Grill's back and the remaining vines under us broke loose. When we were on solid ground, I was able to get the first handcuff on Grill's left wrist and pull his hand behind his back. Getting the other wrist back, I had Grill handcuffed. The whole thing only took a few minutes, but I felt like every muscle in my body had been strained to its limit!

I can remember thinking, "All of this over a freaking blunt!" I helped Grill to his knees and searched his pockets. I located a baggie of weed, but couldn't find the blunt. Grill cynically said, "You got my weed." Calling ISP, I requested a back-up unit. They said one would be en route. I searched the area where we had wrestled and around Grill's bucket, but never found the damn blunt. I did find a box of cigarillos with one missing. I'm sure it was the one that Grill had used to make his blunt. There was also a pile of tobacco in front of Grill's bucket. He had obviously split the cigarillo and dumped the tobacco there before I saw him rolling the blunt.

Escorting Grill, I had Biggun walk with us up to my squad. Biggun sat on the ground as Grill stood in front of my squad. Searching Grill, when I went to check his right sock, he pulled his foot away from me. The second time, I grabbed Grill's ankle and could feel a bulge in the top of his sock. Reaching in the sock, I pulled out a big baggie with four smaller baggies. The smaller baggies all had little white rocks inside. There was the "ah-ha" moment. Now it all made sense!

About that time, my back-up unit (a Rock Island County Sheriff's Deputy) arrived. I helped Grill into my squad and started my truck. I asked the Deputy to watch Grill as I went and checked again for the "lost blunt". He agreed. I went back and searched everything, but couldn't find it. Grill later told me that he still had it in his hand when we started wrestling. It must have gotten mixed in with the rest of the debris on the ground.

When I returned to my squad, I field-tested the white rocks and confirmed that they were cocaine. Of course, the cannabis in the baggie tested positive for THC. Biggun agreed to take care of the fishing equipment for Grill.

Heading to the Rock Island County Jail, Grill and I had a bit of a heart-to-heart on the way. We talked about life and all the times that I had checked him before. He was always legal, and we would joke around together. I told Grill that I was surprised that he (of all people) would cause me so much trouble. Grill was very apologetic for what had happened. Grill told me that he just used the "crack" to lace his own blunts. He said that if he was rolling for other people, he wouldn't put crack in them. Grill went on to tell me that his mom had asked him to quit using drugs. He told me that she also said that he wouldn't quit until he got caught.

Reaching the jail, I helped Grill out of my squad. I could see that he had blood on his hands and scratches on his forearms. Looking at myself, I saw that I was all scratched up and had blood under my fingernails. The meat had been pulled away from the bottoms of the nails. When I saw my nails, they instantly started hurting! I asked Grill if he had any communicable diseases. He said that he didn't.

Walking into the jail, I had to sign Grill into their book. Just before custody of Grill was turned over to the Sheriff's Deputy, he stepped over and gave me a big "man-hug". I was a little surprised, but thought that just maybe I had helped him turn a page in his life. After exchanging pleasantries, I left the jail. I never did see Grill out fishing again. I don't know if he gave up drugs, fishing or both. Hopefully, his mom was right, and he just started fishing somewhere else.

As I headed toward the office, Capt. Hunter told me that I needed to report the "job-related" injuries and get a blood test done. I went to the local hospital and had a blood draw. I had to go about six months later and do it again. Capt. Hunter talked Grill into having his blood tested too. Both of us came back clear every time. I didn't realize the worst part of the whole case until the day after the arrest. All the vines that Grill and I had been wrestling on were poison ivy. Every one of those little cuts on my arms was infused with "ivy juice" and had started to bubble up. It took about a month to get the poison ivy to go away!

A couple of months later, Grill pled guilty to the possession of a controlled substance and was fined $3,052. He also got 24 months of court supervision. Grill was 26 years old at the time of the arrest and I was 36. I'm just really glad that Biggun stayed out of it!

Boating Hazard Style

The last runner I will write about is going to be Luke. Laura and I had been out patrolling in the "Normandy" on the Mississippi River. What we called the "Normandy" was a commercial flat bottom boat that is super wide and heavy. Although it was very stable, you got soaked every time you used it. Part of every wave came over the side and landed in the boat. Having finished our patrol, we were sitting at the 55th Street launch in Moline. We had put the Normandy on the trailer and were getting everything locked down when I saw Luke coming down stream in a small Boston Whaler. Luke had his motor wide open and was skirting our bank. As Luke approached the launch, I walked toward the dock. I knew that Luke was going to blow through the boat launch no-wake zone. In Illinois, you must stay a minimum of 150' out from a public boat launch. The intent is to make it safe for people to load and unload their watercraft.

After Luke passed the launch, he slowed down and started "plowing" water. He circled out toward mid-river and continued turning until he was driving back up stream. As Luke approached the launch again, I yelled at him and waved for him to come in. Luke casually turned his radio down, turned his boat toward mid-river, looked over his shoulder at me and hammered down on the throttle. All while I continued to yell and wave at him to come in. Luke headed back up stream.

I told Laura that we needed to launch the boat again. Laura backed me into the river, while Luke had circled around and was coming back. When I floated off the trailer, Luke was passing me. I yelled and waved at him again. He just kept it pegged. I got the Normandy started, hit the strobes and took off after Luke. Luke looked at me, looked back forward and hunkered down like he was going for it. When I got up to speed, Luke was about 80 yards ahead of me. We were traveling pretty close to the same speed. I was not catching him, and he was not pulling away from me. Every time Luke curved a little, I could cut the curve and make up a little distance. I was able to tell ISP about the pursuit, but there was too much wind and motor noise for us to hear each other.

This section of river can be very dangerous. It has a lateral wall. The wall is partially above water and partially submerged. It divides the river almost in half for a few mile stretch (above Lock and Dam 15). There are several breaks in the wall where you can go from one side of it to the other. If the water is really high, you can cross over the wall in some areas. There are also a few small islands and Arsenal Island, which is connected to the Lock and Dam.

As we approached the I-74 bridge, I had closed the gap between us to about 40 yards. Luke headed down the chute (channel) on the northeast side of Arsenal Island. Following him down the chute, Luke flew past an anchored fishing boat. At the end of this chute, there is a small old cement lock. The water flowing through the cement lock is very turbid. Without hesitation, Luke entered and passed through the lock. I slowed down just before I entered the lock, but followed Luke through it. Exiting the other side of the lock, Luke had opened a 75-yard gap between us. Following him up stream, Luke went back through another cut in the lateral wall. I lost sight of Luke through the trees and shrubs on the exposed part of the wall. When I got to an opening, I crossed through the wall but could not see Luke up or down stream. I could see a set of wakes going up stream toward the I-74 bridge.

Following the wakes, I reached the head of Arsenal Island. There were two people in a red boat that pointed me toward downtown Moline. I followed around the head of Arsenal Island until I could see the docks in front of TGI Friday's. It is a large set of docks that is set up to accommodate numerous watercraft. From the outer tip of the docks to the bank is about 50 yards. There was no Luke in sight, but there was a large cabin cruiser tying off at the outer most dock. I slowed to an idle as the guy tying off the cabin cruiser looked at me. I gave him the two-handed "what" gesture. The guy pointed to the dock on the other side of his boat.

Luke suddenly appeared on the dock and started running toward TGI Friday's. The dock system there only attaches to the bank in one location. Luke needed to run about 20 yards on the first stretch of dock and 30 on the second stretch before he could cross onto the bank. I hammered the Normandy down and shot in between the docks behind the cabin cruiser. As I approached the 30-yard stretch of dock, I pulled the throttle into neutral and spun the Normandy sideways. As she glided up to the dock, I jumped onto it right in front of Luke. Luke stopped and said, "Screw this!" He jumped into the water toward the bank of the river. I was able to finally tell ISP where we were located and what was going on. I asked them to send me a back-up unit. The water was up to Luke's chest. He started wading toward the bank. I ran down the dock to the bank. When I reached the bank, Luke turned around and started wading back to the dock. The Normandy was still running. The last thing I needed was for Luke to take off in my boat. I ran back onto the dock, while Luke turned and started wading back toward the bank. After doing this about three times, two bouncers from TGI Friday's asked if they could help. I agreed. I stayed on the dock and asked them to grab Luke if he came to the bank. They agreed. Luke walked out to the dock and hid under it. I told Luke several times that he could not get away and needed to give himself up.

Luke stayed under the dock for about a minute. The whole time that I had been chasing him, he had a cloth bag in his hands. I am guessing that Luke eliminated some sort of evidence from the bag while it was under the water. Luke suddenly walked out from under the dock and acted like there was nothing wrong. He said, "I am going to get out of the water now." I advised Luke that he was going to have to wait until the back-up units arrived. He argued, but didn't get out of the water until two Moline officers had arrived. I placed Luke in handcuffs. Running a background check on Luke through ISP, they told me that he was wanted on a warrant for failing to appear in court. Luke ended up receiving five citations, including reckless operation of a watercraft and resisting arrest. Luke pled guilty to reckless and resisting and was fined $782. A lot of the time, it is more important to get the conviction

55

than a big fine. The money will not be missed a year later. The conviction will usually stay with the offender for life. Even if they get supervision, the truth will be out there somewhere.

MMA, CANNABIS AND POACHING DEER

As a game warden patrols, they should always be looking for both potential violators and potential violation locations. Sometimes, you find these locations when it is off-season or when you are en route to some other complaint. While walking through remote areas, I have found piles of #8 shot shells. If it was not on a range (and the habitat was right), I knew that I had likely found a dove hunting area. When you find these potential locations, you do not always find them when they are being hunted. I always kept a list of potential violation locations and what I wanted to work them for. If I found a spot that looked like it had been a dove hunting area, I would work that area the next year (or season). It didn't always lead to a great arrest, but would generally lead to an opportunity to catch somebody. Then it was just whether I worked the area in the right way and at the right time.

As I was heading toward my house on an early October Saturday, I saw a vehicle parked just inside a field entrance (on Stallion property). This area was about five miles from my house (as the crow flies) and I had not seen a vehicle parked there before. By the way the vehicle was parked, it appeared to be someone archery deer hunting. Returning the following week, I parked approximately a mile away and walked to the Stallion property.

Early in my career, I found that I had to be willing to walk to be effective. If I parked too close to my potential area, it generally led to the potential violator(s) being tipped off. When that happened, I would find myself working the potential area for nothing. As I got better at "wardening", I would try to park a mile or more from the potential area and walk in. If done right, I almost always succeeded in working that location.

As I walked through Stallion's property, I didn't locate any hunters, but I did locate several baited deer stands. The stands were located off a mowed trail that had salt and mineral blocks on or along it. In Illinois, we do not allow people to hunt with the use or aid of bait. It had been that way for my entire career. In 2002, we had the discovery of Chronic Wasting Disease (CWD) in Illinois. CWD is a terminal disease in deer that is believed to be spread through their saliva. Because of this discovery, a new law was passed in Illinois. The new law restricted the placing of food in an area where deer would have access to it. The intent was to limit the ability of a deer with CWD to eat from a bait pile and pass CWD to another deer through the residual saliva left behind. This change made the law easier for us to enforce. With the change, I did not actually have to catch a hunter in the stand over the bait pile. I just had to prove who put the food out.

Having found the bait on Stallion's property, all I needed to do was catch the "bad guy". Even though I could likely have made the feeding deer case relatively easy, I still preferred to catch the hunter in the stand. Sometimes, this is easier said than done. On this occasion, I got lucky. About three days later, I returned to the property and located a female subject (Adrian) hunting in one of the stands. Adrian admitted that she and her husband (later identified as Rocky) hunted on the property. At that time, I did not know who Rocky was. I was not a big mixed martial arts (MMA) follower. Although I had trained in martial arts myself (and liked studying the arts), I never followed MMA fighting. Adrian admitted that she and Rocky had put the bait out together. While checking Adrian's licenses, I saw that she had resident hunting licenses and deer permits. Adrian had Iowa registration on her vehicle and appeared to be a resident of Iowa. When I questioned her about her residency, Adrian claimed that they had recently moved to Illinois. This is a common problem in border counties. After people move to another state, they often maintain their old licenses or ID cards. When doing so, some people keep claiming that they live in the state that they moved from. Because resident licenses are much cheaper that nonresident licenses, this can save people hundreds of dollars every year. Claiming to be a resident of Illinois when you are not is considered to be falsification and is a class A misdemeanor. I decided to give Adrian the benefit of the doubt and just issued her a citation for hunting over bait. I really did not think much else of it at that time. Would I have liked to have caught more people hunting in the other baited stands? Sure. Even though I had only written one of the hunters, I figured that I had taken care of the problem and could mark it off my "list".

During the next few months, I talked with some of the neighboring property owners. As I talked with them, I heard that Rocky was a professional mixed martial artist. Not just a professional, but a highly successful one who was well known. I also heard that Rocky and Adrian were hunting another property located directly across the road (Ian and Myra Hill's property). I figured that although I had cured the problem for this year, I better put Hill's property on the "list" for the following year.

In September of the following year, I went for a walk across the road. Before going on the walk, I looked at a couple of maps of the area. This is common practice. When I first started, I just used paper maps. As I got longer in my career, technology gave me the ability to use aerial photography maps (like Google). While looking at the plat map, I saw that Hill's property was a 20-acre parcel. The aerial map showed that the property had a long driveway that led back to a homestead. Most of the acreage was to the west of the homestead. It was shaped kind of like a lollipop. The stick was the long driveway that led back to the 20 acre "head" of the sucker. The head was then surrounded by larger tracts of land. The aerial map also showed that the Hills shared a driveway with their neighbor to the north. The north neighbor appeared to just use the driveway for access to a rear field.

Parking a mile away, I found a fence line that would take me to the neighbor's field driveway. Once I hit the driveway, I knew that I just needed to circumnavigate the curtilage of Hill's homestead and work my way back into the timber (west of the residence). I figured that if I got lucky, I might actually catch someone hunting early. A little less lucky would lead to finding another baited deer stand.

My plan was going well. I had found the neighbor's driveway and could see that the curtilage of Hill's residence was fenced. That made it easy to keep out of the "protected" curtilage area. I cut to the west. As I was walking through the weeds, I kept sight of the fence line so I would stay out of the curtilage. Getting to a farm field near the northwest corner of the curtilage, I suddenly got blasted with a very strong smell of cannabis. Having made hundreds of cannabis arrests, I was pretty sure of what I was smelling. Then I second-guessed myself. I mean, I was kind of in the middle of nowhere. I took an investigative "deep breath" through my nose. Confirming my initial thoughts, I looked into the wind (toward the curtilage). I could see some big plants near the northwest corner of the fence. Walking toward the fence, the smell of cannabis consistently grew stronger. Nearing the fence, I could see several big cannabis plants growing just inside the fence. Reaching the fence, I could see that some of the plants were staked down with rope (to keep them from falling over). It was obvious that the plants had been cultivated. I took pictures of the plants from outside of the curtilage and backed out of the area.

Reaching my squad, I called the Rock Island County States Attorney's Office and advised ASA Norma Kauzlarich of what I had found. To put it simply, Norma is awesome! She was always a straight shooter, knew her job, worked hard and would help you with anything. Norma was so good that she eventually became a judge. I never got to take a case in front of Norma (as a judge), but know that she would have been fair. You would think that this is always the case, but it is not. Over the years, I had more than one case lost because of a judge that appeared to be "compromised". That would not have happened with Norma!

Norma told me to contact the Quad Cities Metropolitan Enforcement Group (MEG) and get some help drawing up the search warrant. In the Quad Cities, MEG is a multi-jurisdictional drug task force. I called MEG, and yes, left a message. There I am wanting a search warrant, but waiting for a call back. It was like you have something you really want to tell someone but nobody to tell it to.

Hooking up with MEG the next day, Special Agent Matt Russell helped me to pen the search warrant. Or maybe I actually helped Matt to pen the search warrant. Signed by a judge, we had a briefing at the MEG office and were ready to head toward the Hill property. We stopped at the Illinois City Post Office to get all the officers together (about eight in total). My neighbor (Elda Mier) was working at the post office at that time. Mrs. Mier was just finishing her day at the office and asked me what was going on. Although she never would have said anything, I told her that I couldn't tell her. Even though Elda didn't have any information, I'm sure that we were the talk of her and Larry's (her husband) table that night!

Heading to the Hill property, the MEG officers took the contact position and knocked on the front door. Myra Hill was the only one home, but she was expecting Ian at any time. Not wanting to be in the middle of a search and have Ian Hill come pulling in, we decided to stop him at the entrance. Conducting a traffic stop, on a truck pulling into the Hill driveway, we were able to take Ian into custody without incident. Because the cannabis plants that I found were outside of the residence, our warrant was just for the curtilage of the residence and the outbuildings. By the time I made it back to the residence, MEG had located more cannabis plants around the house and some drying in one of the outbuildings. We then also obtained permission to search the residence. As we searched it, we found cannabis or paraphernalia in nearly every room of the house. We also found a hydroponic growing system in the basement and a "grow room". Though it was not being used at the time, it could have been. We ended up seizing 61 plants, over 2,500 grams of sale-ready cut cannabis, .3 grams of cocaine, a digital scale, numerous pipes and about $1,000 in cash. Both Ian and Myra were taken into custody and charged with three felonies each (possession, manufacture and production of cannabis).

Though I had worked cannabis grows before, they had not worked out as good as this one. I really enjoyed working with the MEG unit. I got to work with them on several other occasions after this one. Over the years, I learned a lot when I was working with any specialized unit. One thing from this case that helped me in a future case was the hanging of cannabis plants. Prior to this case I had not realized that growers hung their cannabis plants upside down to dry. This is because gravity helps to concentrate the THC in the leaves of the plant (as it dries).

As I talked about this case with the other officers, I found out that Ian Hill was also a professional mixed martial artist. Reportedly, he and Rocky occasionally trained together (or at least in the same gym). During the search of the Hill property, I did find some deer stands. None were baited. I figured that I wouldn't catch anyone hunting them now anyway. If I had to trade one for the other, I would always take the six cannabis felonies over the bait case.

In fact, I would say that I have always felt proud of the fact that I eliminated all that cannabis from MY community. As I said, this was five miles from my home. Maybe, just maybe, I stopped one of the local kids (or one of my own) from getting started on using cannabis. Both Ian and Myra pled guilty to all their charges and were fined a total of $9,071. Neither received any jail time, but both got two years' probation.

Sean's Catch

I did not hear about either Rocky or Adrian hunting in our area for the next couple of years. On a November evening in 2012, I received a call from Sgt. Sean Butler with the Mercer County Sheriff's Police. Since I was on my regular day off, Sgt. Butler called me at home. Sgt. Butler was always a proactive officer. Proactive officers get into things. Sgt. Butler fit the mold and seemed like he was always getting into something interesting.

Sgt. Butler had conducted a traffic stop on a vehicle driving erratically down Route 17. Upon approach to the vehicle, Sgt. Butler located an uncased gun and a young girl that was not in a child seat. Sure enough, Rocky was driving the vehicle. A subsequent search of the car revealed a bloody knife and arrow in the trunk (along with miscellaneous hunting equipment). Rocky made indications that he had killed a deer. I was asked to come down and assist with the interview of Rocky and his adult son (Robbie).

Getting my uniform on, I headed to the Sheriff's Department. Meeting with Sgt. Butler and Deputy Tony Baugh, we discussed what they had learned during the traffic stop and a subsequent interview. From there, I decided to interview Robbie first. In any investigation, I would try to figure out who is the "weakest" link (if more than one person is involved). That is the person that I want to interview first. The weakest link will give you the most information to start your investigation. They may not give you much, but more is more—and that is good. Once you have gained everything you can from the weakest link, you have more "ammunition" when you interview the other involved parties. Not only do they have to refute what logically happened, but they also must refute the weakest link. Since most people are inherently honest, they generally will have guilt if they are the only one lying (even if they are the "stronger link"). It also opens several other good interview approaches that will help you get to the truth. The reality of any interview or investigation is that the officer really just wants the truth. Yes, it is that simple.

Robbie was brought to the interview room and sat down with me. Having looked at his paperwork, I confirmed with Robbie that he was from North Carolina. Robbie agreed. When questioned about how he got to Illinois, Robbie told me that he met with Rocky in Kentucky. He said that they trained and hunted down there for about a week. Robbie said that Rocky brought him to the Quad Cities. I asked Robbie if he was also an MMA fighter. Robbie proceeded to tell me that he was just getting into MMA fighting. Robbie said that MMA fighting was helping him get to know his dad better. He told me that he and Rocky did not have much of a relationship while he was growing up.

I asked Robbie to tell me about their hunt that day. Robbie proceeded to "paint" a pretty good picture for me. He said that they had gone hunting first thing in the morning on a property near New Boston, Illinois. Robbie said that he hunted with a .308 and Rocky used a .270. Both are illegal for deer hunting in Illinois. I asked Robbie if they had killed any deer. Robbie said that Rocky shot a 10-point buck. Robbie indicated that they were hunting across a field from each other when he heard Rocky shoot. He said that he sent his dad a text message and confirmed with Rocky that he had killed the deer. Robbie said that he walked over and helped his dad recover the deer and drag it part way out.

I asked Robbie if they had any deer bait out. I figured that since Rocky had gotten away with it previously, he would likely do it again. Sure enough, Robbie said that Rocky had a pile of corn near his stand. Robbie told me that after he helped his dad drag the deer a few hundred yards, Rocky decided to go get an ATV. He said that a short time later his dad returned without an ATV. Robbie said that Rocky cut the head off the 10- point buck and took one chunk of meat from the back straps. He said that they buried the remainder of the deer in a creek. Robbie told me that they took the deer parts and drove back to Davenport. I asked Robbie why they had not taken the whole deer. Robbie was unsure why they had wasted the rest of the deer. I asked Robbie what they did with the deer in Davenport. Robbie said Rocky put the meat in the refrigerator and the head in a brush pile behind the house.

I asked Robbie what else they did in Davenport prior to returning to Illinois. Robbie said they picked up Rocky's daughter from school. I asked Robbie if they were hunting when they got stopped by Sgt. Butler. Robbie admitted that they had just started looking for deer and were going to hunt with rifles from the car. I asked Robbie why they were swerving on the road when they got stopped. Robbie said that Rocky's daughter had gotten out of her seat belt and Rocky was trying to get her back into it (while he was driving). I asked Robbie where the bloody arrow in their trunk came from. Robbie told me that Rocky ran the arrow through the rifle hole in the deer. You always hear stories about people doing that, but seldom does a game warden actually run into it. This is especially true in Illinois, since people don't have to check their deer in anymore (at a check-station). Back when hunters had to check their deer in, they had to be wary about running into the game warden at the check station. A rifle hunting poacher would likely have taken more precautions because of that possibility. If the poacher did run an arrow through a rifle hole, they better hope that the game warden only looked at the entrance wound. Usually a high-powered rifle exit wound is easy to distinguish from other exit wounds. Normally the high-powered rifle exit hole is both big and odd-shaped. Although I have seen big exit wounds from arrows (when the deer is shot at an angle), I have never seen an arrow shot deer have fine bone fragmentation. In fact, no other firearm that I have ever seen will cause that same fine bone fragmentation. On a deer shot with a high-powered rifle, you just stick your finger in the exit wound and rub it around a little. It will feel like there is gavel in the exit wound. When you pull your finger out, you will have some very fine bone fragments clinging to your finger. Yes, all of this is out the window if the bullet never hits a bone or for some reason does not exit. But that does not happen very often. I then circled back and asked Robbie about their hunt in Kentucky. Though we do not have jurisdiction in Kentucky, we frequently refer cases to other states. We are also deputized by the Department of the Interior to enforce migratory bird, Lacey Act and other federal violations. Robbie proceeded to tell me that they hunted with a third guy in Kentucky. He said that they drove around and hunted with a .308 out of the vehicle. Robbie admitted that Rocky and the other guy shot at a couple of deer. He said that they missed the deer.

Changing gears again, I asked Robbie if he would go out to where they had hunted and show me where they buried the deer. Robbie agreed. I was feeling pretty good about the information Robbie had given me. Although I knew I did not get everything Robbie had to offer, I felt like I had enough to get Rocky to cooperate.

As we were preparing to go with Robbie, I was told that Adrian had arrived at the Sheriff's Department. I went out with Deputy Baugh and asked Adrian if she would come back and talk with us. She agreed. In the interview room, I asked Adrian if she remembered me. She advised that she did and had learned her lesson. Adrian started off lying about a few things. When I called her on it, Adrian appeared to start telling me the truth. Adrian admitted that she had met Rocky at the house that morning when he returned home with the deer parts. Adrian said that the deer looked like one she had seen while she was hunting the same property. Adrian told me that she had also seen the meat in the refrigerator when she opened the door. I asked Adrian if the deer meat was still in the refrigerator. Adrian said that it was not. Adrian proceeded to tell me that Rocky called her during the traffic stop. She said that Rocky told her to get rid of both the deer head and the meat. Adrian said that she drove the head and meat to Concord Street in Davenport. Adrian said that she threw both into the Mississippi River. Adrian let me look at her telephone, but she had erased all her recent messages. Really, as an accomplice, Adrian had done pretty good for Rocky. Not only did she get rid of the physical evidence, but she also erased the text messages. Adrian later agreed to meet a Davenport Police Officer where she had thrown the deer parts into the river. He was unable to find any of the evidence. I am not sure where the deer parts really went, but Adrian's corroboration of Robbie's account helped me to get ready for an interview of Rocky.

At about 11:00 that night, we finally headed out to where Rocky had killed the deer. Robbie went with us and showed us Rocky's deer stand, a couple trail cameras, the corn, the decapitated carcass and where he had been hunting. We documented the blood trail from where the deer had been shot to where it had died and tried to recreate the crime scene. The carcass had been drug down into a swampy area. They buried it by placing brush on top of it. I dug the carcass out from under the brush and we drug it up out of the swamp. Of course, one of the trail cameras was set up to take pictures of the deer going to bait pile. I seized the deer carcass, the deer stand, the cameras and a sample of the bait.

After we loaded the evidence into my truck, we returned Robbie to the jail. Since we were into the a.m. now, I decided to call it a night. I knew Rocky was still going to be there in the morning, so I wasn't really in a hurry to interview him. When I have time prior to an interview (as I did here), I always try to go over the story several times. I try to think of where the poacher is most likely to lie. When you do that, you also figure out how to debunk the lie and steer them back towards the truth. I guess it's kind of like playing mental chess—only with different pieces every time. My goal is to have thought of every move before they can make it. It's never easy, but it is even harder to get to the truth if they "clam up" and refuse to move their pieces. I was hoping that Rocky was up for a game of chess later that day.

Returning to the Mercer County Courthouse later that morning, I obtained search warrants for Rocky's phone, his car and the trail cameras (that I had seized from their hunting spot). I met with Rocky in the early afternoon, but he refused to talk with me. The chess match would have to be rescheduled—if it was ever to happen. I spent the next day or so searching the SD cards, the car and conducting a necropsy on the deer. The SD cards had a picture of Rocky and numerous deer pictures. I found the bloody arrow, corn and a bloody knife in the car. There was a lot of other hunting equipment in the car as well.

A necropsy is essentially an autopsy on an animal. I took the deer to our District office and very carefully skinned the deer out. The most basic thing to remember about a necropsy is that for a bruise to form, there must be blood pressure. In other words, the animal had to be alive when that injury occurred. If it wasn't alive, the breaking of the blood vessels would not have caused the blood to leach out into the surrounding tissue. As you skin the animal, you are looking for bruises under the hide. On Rocky's deer, the bruised area led me to an eight-millimeter hole. That hole was consistent with a .30 caliber bullet entry wound. On the outside of the hide (at the eight-millimeter hole), I found the normal cut hair. If you picture the bullet (or arrow) entering through the hair, it cuts the hair as it passes through it. When you go to the exit side, the projectile pushes out through the hide. Although you will sometimes get some cut hair, it is totally different. As I said earlier, with a high-powered rifle, if there is an exit wound, it is generally huge in comparison to the entry. Rocky's deer was shot on the left side near the rear of the chest cavity. The bullet broke three ribs as it traveled through the chest cavity and fragmented. Since Rocky had not gutted the deer, I was able to see the bullet had passed through one of the lungs. Following the track of the bullet, I recovered numerous bullet fragments from inside of the chest cavity. The bullet either exited through where Rocky had removed the hide or essentially fragmented into oblivion. Either way, I never recovered an "intact" bullet from the deer. It was not a big deal; I had gotten what I really needed—a confirmation that the deer was killed with a high-powered rifle.

The following morning, I returned to the Mercer County Jail and interviewed Robbie again. I advised Robbie that I had applied for a search warrant for his telephone. Robbie hesitantly acknowledged that he understood. You could tell that he had some concern for what I had told him. When asked, Robbie told me that they had hunted near Ashland, Kentucky. I asked Robbie if I would find any pictures of poached deer on his phone. Robbie sank and admitted that he had poached a spike buck in Kentucky. He told me about killing the deer and where they had stored the back straps. Similar to Rocky's deer, Robbie said that the back straps were all they had taken from his deer. All the Kentucky information was eventually relayed to Kentucky Conservation Officer Glenn Kitchens. Glenn was fun to talk with and had a good understanding of what was going on down there. We were able to bridge Rocky to another MMA fighter who had recently fought in the Ashland area.

Later that morning, I was able to get Rocky's phone "dumped". Protected by a security code, all we could get were photos, videos and saved media. I ended up with pictures of a deer that appeared to have been killed in Iowa the previous year.

I did not end up with any real good information from Rocky's phone. I forwarded what I had to Iowa Conservation Officer Jeff Harrison. I have worked with Jeff many times. When you live in a county on the Mississippi River, you are constantly working with the officers on the other side. Not only was Jeff fun to work with, but he also always answered his phone. That is a rare find and was always greatly appreciated. Jeff advised that he was familiar with Rocky and had investigated him previously.

After getting my search warrant for Robbie's phone and a second one for Rocky's phone (to try a new search), we tried to dump both again. Robbie's was unprotected and was a treasure trove. Robbie's phone corroborated everything he had told me about Kentucky and Illinois. There were also pictures of dead deer on Robbie's phone that he had not told me about.

Completing harvest and license searches on all the people involved in the case, I found that the only person who had purchased any licenses in Illinois was Adrian. Rocky had flown totally under the radar for at least three years. Adrian had bought licenses, but she was still buying resident Illinois licenses. I realized that Adrian had pulled the wool over my eyes the first time I dealt with her.

The next day, I met up with Conservation Officer Jeff Harrison and we went to Rocky and Adrian's house. Meeting with Adrian, Jeff questioned her about the Iowa information. After Jeff got some answers, I asked Adrian to talk with me about hunting in Illinois. Adrian agreed. Adrian said that she remembered our talk about residency (when I caught her hunting over bait). Adrian then admitted to having lived in Iowa for the previous five years. After explaining the residency requirements to Adrian again, I issued her tickets for falsely obtaining licenses and permits in Illinois (for two years). Falsification is one of those violations that will almost certainly catch up with you—if you keep doing it. You can't "hide better" each year when you buy your licenses. All it takes to be caught is a game warden that wants to conduct a records search. In Illinois, with a finding of guilt, it also has a mandatory loss of hunting privileges. Each year that someone commits falsification to purchase deer permits and licenses, they are stealing about $300 from the people of Illinois. If they kill a deer, they may also be stealing an opportunity from a legal hunter—resident or not.

I never did have an opportunity to play "chess" with Rocky. He was released on bond during the investigation and did not speak with me prior to making a plea agreement. Rocky was eventually convicted of hunting with the use or aid of a motor vehicle, hunting after hours, hunting deer with the use or aid of bait, hunting deer with a rifle, possession of protected species and hunting from a roadway. The criminal and traffic violations were dismissed against Rocky. Rocky was fined $3,602 and forfeited his car and his hunting equipment. Since Mercer County made the initial stop, I requested that the car be turned over to them. It was a really nice Nissan and was used by their detectives for a few years. Robbie was found guilty of all the same charges as Rocky (apart from the deer bait offense). Robbie was fined $2,749. Adrian was convicted of two counts of falsification and was fined $230. Bigger than the fines on any of the people involved was the loss of property and the privilege to hunt.

DA BOMB

Routinely patrolling remote areas, game wardens run into some of the most interesting things. Generally, when people are going to do something illegal, they don't want anyone to see them. If they go out to the middle of "nowhere", they don't have to worry about anybody seeing them. Except, that there just might be a game warden, standing behind a tree, with a set of binoculars.

When you think of bombs and game wardens, you most likely think about some guy "fishing" with dynamite. Sometimes, it can be a little different than that. This case happened before the 9/11 attacks, but after the Oklahoma City bombing. There was an awareness of bombs in the policing community, but nothing like there is now. Most Game Wardens were just thinking about apprehending the guy fishing with dynamite.

In early February of 1997, our District office was at Kankakee River State Park (KRSP). I was headed that way to drop some paperwork off for Sgt. Mathis (Fred). Having left Wilmington, I was driving eastbound on Route 102. Just after 5:00 p.m., I reached the stretch of Route 102 that travels along the border of KRSP. As I went past the archery range, I saw a car approaching me from the east. When it passed, I saw there were two male youths (we will call them Tom and Jerry) inside. Tom and Jerry were wide-eyed

and smiling like they were in their own little world. Tom was driving and really appeared to be consumed in whatever he was smiling about. They obviously did not realize that they had just passed
a game warden. For some reason I thought that it was odd and
watched their car in my rear-view mirror after they passed me.

Suddenly, their brake lights came on, and they pulled into
the archery range parking lot. I thought, "What the heck are they
doing at the archery range?" It's cold and it's February. Deer season is over and most everybody is taking a break from sighting
in their archery equipment. On top of that, it was starting to get
dark. Nobody wants to sight a bow in when it's cold, dark and the
season is freshly over. I figured that I had better go back and see
what Tom and Jerry were doing.

Turning around at the next pull-in, I drove back to the archery
range parking lot. The parking lot is shaped like a caption box.
You pull into the "caption box" through the little pointed tip. Then,
as you get into the lot, it opens up. As I pulled into the pointed tip,
I could see Tom and Jerry's car parked on the opposite side of the
lot. Tom and Jerry had exited the vehicle and were quickly walking up into the timber on a mowed path. I stopped at the entrance
and got my binoculars out. Tom was wearing a white t-shirt and
Jerry had on a sweatshirt. In a few seconds, they had disappeared
into the timber. It was 34 degrees outside. What the heck were a
couple of 17-year-olds doing without their coats?

I parked my squad by the road and exited the vehicle.
The ground was sporadically covered with patches of ice. It had
snowed, partially melted and re-froze a few times. I knew that if
I drove into the parking lot, it would make a lot of noise. I didn't
want Tom and Jerry to know that I was there just yet. Dodging the
ice patches, I walked over to their car. I tried to figure out what
they were up to by looking through the windows. I could see a
gunpowder bottle and a small black plastic case (about the size
of a handgun case) inside.

Walking up the mowed path that Tom and Jerry had taken, I hopped from one open patch to the next. When I got about 10 yards into the timber, I came to a "T" in the trail. With my binoculars, I had watched Tom and Jerry go to the right. Looking up the trail, I could see Tom and Jerry standing about 100 yards west of me. When I looked at them with my binoculars, one of them suddenly screamed, "FUCK." I lowered my binoculars and began running toward Tom and Jerry. They didn't see or hear me for the first 60 yards. Tom finally looked at me and said something to Jerry. Jerry looked at me and immediately turned away from me. He then pulled both of his hands in front of his body and his shoulders started going up and down. It looked like Jerry was trying to shove something down the front of his pants. Tom kept looking back and forth between me and Jerry. It looked like he was checking to see who was going to win. Would I make it to Jerry before he got it shoved down his pants... or not? As I closed in, Jerry started to walk away from me, and Tom followed his lead. I yelled for both subjects to stop right there. They complied and turned back toward me. Jerry had won. His sweatshirt was pulled back down over his waist.

Reaching Jerry, I asked him if he had any weapons on him. He said that he did not. I told Jerry that I was going to pat him down. Jerry stood there as I patted the front of his sweatshirt. Under his sweatshirt, I could feel a large, hard, round object. It was sticking up and out of the top of his pants. It could have been many things, so I asked Jerry what it was. He said that it was a "pipe". Jerry told me that it was for his "protection". I lifted Jerry's sweatshirt and pulled the pipe out of his pants. I now had a 1" x 6" galvanized pipe in my hands. It had threaded ends with screw-on caps. It looked like a pipe bomb, but I couldn't see a fuse. Checking it more closely, I found a small hole drilled in the side of the pipe. Like most kids where I grew up, I jacked around with fireworks. In fact, I knew kids who made M80s. I even made some fireworks myself, but never anything like this. When we made fireworks, we would buy fuse and feed it through a hole while we were packing the gunpowder in. This thing didn't have a fuse. Maybe they were cussing because they had pulled the fuse out by accident?

Continuing to pat Jerry down, I felt a hard-flat square object. I asked Jerry what it was. He pulled a 7½" x 6¾ " piece of plywood out of his pants. Examining the plywood, it had a spring activated clothespin screwed onto it. It also had four AA batteries taped together and attached to the board. The clothespin had one of its flat sides placed flat against the board. You could still push the top of the clothespin down and open its jaws. There was a hole drilled through the jaws of the clothespin. A wire was run through the hole in the top jaw and to the positive end of the batteries. There was a second wire that went down through the bottom jaw of the clothespin and out through the bottom of the plywood. A third and final wire was attached to the negative end of the four AA batteries.

As kids, we didn't use anything like this. Tom and Jerry were standing there looking at me while I was staring at the board. I had not received any training in how to identify an electric bomb detonation device. Looking around the area, I found a long string with a piece of plastic tied to one end. Suddenly, it all came together. Or so, I thought it had. What Tom and Jerry had done was lay behind a small log. From there, they set the pipe bomb on the ground about 10 feet away. The detonation device was placed next to it. The piece of plastic on the string was fed between the jaws of the clothespin. This would disrupt the positive charge between the batteries and the bomb until the plastic was pulled out (with the string). When the string was pulled, the electric charge would go from the top jaw of the clothes pin into the bottom jaw. The positive charge would continue down to the wire to the bomb. The positive and negative wires would then go into the fuse hole in the bomb. I figured that when the positive and negative charges met inside of the bomb, they would cause a spark. That spark would cause the bomb to explode. Although I did not have the full picture yet, I was on the right track.

Waving the bomb around like a teacher with a stick, I asked Tom and Jerry what they were doing with a pipe bomb. Jerry said that they just wanted to see if it would work. Tom told me that it didn't. I asked them where they got it. They told me that they made it. Tom said that he had found the instructions on the internet. I asked them whose car was up in the parking lot. Tom said that it was his car. I advised Tom and Jerry that they would need to walk with me up to the parking lot. They complied.

Arriving at Tom's car, I asked him if he had any guns or other weapons inside. Tom told me that he did not and gave me permission to check. The first thing that I found was a one-pound bottle of gunpowder. I then located a series of steel and copper metal fragments. The fragments looked like they were pieces of other exploded bombs. I later found out that it is not uncommon for people (who make bombs) to keep them as little "bomb trophies". Continuing to search the vehicle, under the driver's seat I found a tobacco pipe that smelled like cannabis. When I opened the glove box, I found a plastic eight-ounce bottle with a white power inside. Asking Tom what it was, he told me that it was a flammable substance. Tom said that one of his friends had given it to him. The last thing that I found was a 2" x 6" galvanized pipe with threaded ends. It had caps screwed onto the ends and a hole drilled in the middle. It looked like a big brother of the bomb that I had seized from Jerry. Tom quickly told me that it didn't have anything in it. It was heavy and I wasn't going to unscrew one of the ends to check.

Not sure how I was going to proceed, I decided to write Tom and Jerry "information only citations". They were citations that we would use to record a defendant's personal information. It was a formal piece of paper that we used informally. Those citations would not be turned in to the circuit clerk's office, but would be attached to a field report and turned in to the state's attorney's office. The state's attorney's office would then review the paperwork and file a long form complaint. Times have changed and we can no longer use information only citations. I receipted Tom and Jerry for the evidence and loaded it into my squad. I told Tom and Jerry that they were free to go and would be notified of any court dates.

Continuing my way to the District office, I was excited about what I had found. At that time, our evidence facility was contained in the rear section of our office. When I arrived, I carried all the evidence into the office. Not sure how to proceed, I figured that I should call Fred. He would have some guidance and I could brag a little. I told the story to Fred. When I got to the end, Fred asked me two questions. The first was, "Where are the bombs located now?" My bragging abruptly ended when I told Fred that the bombs were sitting on his desk. He flipped his lid and told me to get the bombs out of his office! I never got a chance to answer the follow-up question. He yelled, "What are you thinking?" My long overdue answer comes in several parts. First, Fred's desk was the only flat surface in our office (at that time). I processed all of my evidence on his desk. He added a second desk later—maybe because of me? Secondly, having messed around with "fireworks" as a kid, I had a natural comfort level with them. Third, I never had any real bomb training. At least, not that I could remember. And finally, if Jerry was comfortable shoving the pipe bomb down next to his "junk", I could surely set it on a desk. My conversation with Fred abruptly ended and I carried the bombs out to a tree east of our building.

Turns out, I needed to call the bomb squad. In fact, the bomb squad would have preferred if I had called them while I was still at the archery range. At that time, there was not a bomb squad in either Will or Kankakee County. The nearest one was in Cook County (Chicago). It was 10:00 p.m. before they arrived. By that time, Fred had arrived as well. He was not mad, but was laughing at my expense. I had to tell the bomb technicians the entire story. I think Fred added the part about how I put the bombs on his desk. If it was up to me, we would have left that part out. After they chewed my butt, I was told that they didn't want me touching the bombs at all.

In short order, the Cook County Bomb Squad had the bombs diffused. The big bomb did not have anything inside of it. The bomb that I pulled from Jerry's pants had 1.3 ounces of gunpowder inside. That would make the bomb a felony violation. In order to get charges, I would have to be able to prove that it was a "viable" bomb. I had no doubts of it being "viable". I had the detonation device and a pipe bomb filled with gun powder. As the technicians reviewed my evidence, they told me that I was missing the igniter wire and insulator. I must have missed them while I was dealing with Tom and Jerry. I was told that in order to prosecute, I would need to go back and find them. Fred and I completed processing the evidence. I figured that I would go back and search for the missing parts the next morning. By the time that I got home that night, it was well after midnight.

Fred lived in the house at KRSP. Early the next morning, he went to the archery range and searched for the "igniter wire and insulator". He found it! It sounds like something extravagant, but it was really just a model rocket igniter. The same thing that we used as kids to launch our model rockets. The rocket igniter should have been stuffed down into the hole with the wires attached to it. If the bomb had worked, the rocket igniter would have made the spark that caused the bomb to explode.

Later that day, Laura, Fred and I met with two Alcohol Tobacco and Firearms (ATF) special agents. Reviewing the case, the ATF agents wanted to speak with both Tom and Jerry. We went to Tom's house first. Meeting with Tom and his dad, we were told that they had contacted their lawyer. Tom's dad would not allow us to talk with Tom. He indicated that Jerry should be our focus anyway. I told Tom's dad that we were concerned about Tom possibly still having other undetonated devices in his possession. Tom's dad gave us permission to search Tom's bedroom and his car. We did not find any evidence in either location.

Leaving Tom's house, we headed into the bordering town of Bradley, Illinois. Fred recalled that Bradley P.D. had recently dealt with some "explosives cases". Calling their department, Fred was told that Jerry had been identified in one of their reports. Stopping at the police department, we met with one of the Bradley sergeants. We were told that about a year earlier they responded to a residence for an explosion-based injury. It turned out that a kid had decided to make a bomb out of a CO_2 cartridge. After the kid partially filled the CO_2 cartridge with gunpowder, he decided to make a different bomb. Needing to get his gunpowder back, he started grinding the top off the CO_2 cartridge. While doing so, the CO_2 cartridge exploded and took three of his fingers with it. During Bradley's investigation of the incident, Jerry was identified in a spin-off report. Jerry was reportedly stealing and selling explosives.

We thanked the Bradley sergeant and continued our way to Jerry's house. Meeting with Jerry and his dad, they agreed to talk with us. Following up on some of the intelligence that we had obtained, we also got consent to search Jerry's crawl space, garage, bedroom and his truck. As Laura and one of the ATF agents interviewed Jerry, I searched the approved areas with the other agent. In the garage, I located some packaging for a set of batteries. It matched the type of batteries that Tom and Jerry had used on their detonation device. During Jerry's interview, he admitted that the batteries from the packaging were the ones that they had used. With all the time between the archery range and our arrival at Tom and Jerry's houses, the battery packaging was the only link that we ever found between the bomb and where it was made. Jerry admitted that he had created the detonation device. He said that he had originally made it to launch model rockets. Jerry had obviously found a different use for it now. Jerry also admitted to purchasing most of the materials for the bomb. Jerry told us that he and Tom had made the bomb together. Jerry said that while at KRSP they tried to set the bomb off several times before seeing me approach them.

When the base investigation was completed, all my evidence was turned over to ATF. It was sent to one of their labs for chemical analysis and device determination. The device was found to be a viable bomb. It's believed that the batteries did not have a good connection, which caused the detonation of the bomb to fail. If the batteries were not touching end to end, they would not generate the necessary voltage needed to set the igniter off.

With the case reports turned in to the Will County States Attorney's office, we had to look at the intent of Tom and Jerry. Here were two 17-year-old kids making bombs. Was it just a hobby for Tom and Jerry or did they have other future intentions? Whether or not they had intended to eventually hurt somebody, Tom and Jerry had created a "trip wire"-style detonation device. After a few meetings with the Will County States Attorney's office, we agreed to charge Jerry with misdemeanor reckless conduct. Jerry admitted to being the primary "bomb guy" and was involved in Bradley's explosives related case. Jerry ended up pleading guilty and was fined $500. He was also ordered to complete 100 hours of community service and was given two years of conditional discharge. Since Tom had a clean record, he was just charged with the illegal possession of cannabis. Tom also pled guilty and was fined for the violation.

Although I was not an explosives expert at the end of this case, I definitely had a better understanding of how the entire process works. In fact, by the end of the year, my entire District had a better understanding of how it works. Because of me, they all had to go through explosives training!

Backpack, Backpack

As the years passed, I dealt with many other people who had some type of illegal fireworks in their possession. Most of the stuff came from roadside stands. About ten years later, I was working on a warm September night. Normally, that time of year, I would be focusing on hunters and getting ready for the upcoming hunting seasons. Because I had a night shift, I decided to see if anybody was fishing along the Rock River at Hennepin Canal State Park (HCSP). My favorite stretch of river in that area was the part between the Steel Dam and Mill Creek. It was really good fishing and people felt comfortable doing illegal things. I'm sure that the comfort level was elevated because it was a brushy area that afforded people cover from their surroundings. Most people didn't consider that it also afforded game wardens cover from them. At night, I would walk in the dark on a path along the river. The only time that I used my flashlight was if I encountered somebody. When I did encounter someone, I would sparingly use the flashlight. I didn't want anybody else to know that I was there until I was ready for them to know it. When it was time to take enforcement action, I would turn on every light that I had. I literally couldn't have enough light. At that point, I didn't want to miss a single hand movement by anybody that I was dealing with.

Sneaking along the riverbank that night, I slowly worked my way to a point where I could watch what the next group was doing. When I figured out "who" I was about to approach, I would decide on the best way to approach them. When I say "who", I am referring to figuring out what types of people are in the group and what they are doing. Sometimes, you are approaching a family with a bunch of kids. If you watch the family for a while, you may see that it's just a bunch of kids that are collecting mussel shells, while mom and dad are trying to catch some fish. Other times, I have found mom and dad passing a bong back and forth with Junior and Little Sissy, while all of their fishing poles are just sitting in a pile on the bank. Obviously, your approach to these groups is going to be a lot different.

Working my way to a couple of fishermen sitting on the bank, I watched them for a while, but didn't see anything out of the ordinary. The fishermen had enough light that when I walked into their area, I didn't have to use my flashlight to conduct a check. During the check, I saw that there were a couple of people (we will call them Mutt and Jeff) sitting by a campfire about 20 yards upstream from us. Although this is not a huge area, it is big enough that most of the people will not fish that close to each other—unless they are together. I asked the fishermen if the people up stream were with them. They seemed offended that I had asked them. They advised that they were not together. I acknowledged that I understood. As I completed my check, Mutt and Jeff shot a bottle rocket out over the river that exploded. The glowing fragments from the bottle rocket fell into the river below. I'm guessing that's why I had gotten such a negative response when I asked if they were together.

Being that we were in a State Park, Mutt and Jeff could not legally have any fireworks. They also could not shoot fireworks out over the river and pollute it. Walking toward Mutt and Jeff, I didn't turn on my flashlight until I was about 15 feet from them. When I turned it on, it was pointed right at Mutt. Mutt and Jeff were sitting next to the campfire. Mutt had a package of bottle rockets in his hand. There were a couple of fishing poles casted out and sitting in front of them. I identified myself to Mutt and Jeff and asked them for their fishing licenses. While they were pulling out their licenses, I was scanning the area around them. After both subjects provided me a valid fishing license, I advised Mutt that he could not legally have fireworks in a State Park. Mutt acknowledged that he understood. I asked Mutt to hand me the bottle rockets. Mutt complied.

When I had been scanning the surrounding area, I saw a backpack sitting in front of Mutt and Jeff. The backpack was open and had a paper bag sticking out of the top of it. Protruding from the bag was a bunch of fireworks. As I reached down and pulled the paper bag out of the backpack, I could see a pipe bomb sitting under it. This one was made from a galvanized pipe that was about a half inch wide and five inches long. It had end caps screwed onto it and a "lightable" fuse sticking out of a hole in the center of the pipe. The fuse was only about a half inch long. I can remember thinking that it was way too short for me to light it!

I asked the subjects who owned the pipe bomb. Nobody answered me. Since Mutt had the bottle rockets in his hand and the backpack was closer to him, I asked Mutt if the backpack was his. Mutt said that it was. I asked Mutt if the pipe bomb was his too. Mutt admitted that it was. Mutt told me that he was going to tie the pipe bomb to a rock and throw it into the river. I told Mutt that he might kill some fish if he did that. Mutt acknowledged that he knew that. Mutt said that he intended to pick the fish up if he killed any. Searching the rest of the backpack, I did not locate any other contraband. I did see a big knife in a sheath that was sitting next to Mutt. I told Mutt that I would be securing the knife and the fireworks. Mutt acknowledged that he understood.

After securing the knife and fireworks, I checked the rest of the area. I didn't locate any other contraband. I told Mutt that he would have to walk with me up to my squad. Mutt asked if he was going to jail. I told him that I would make that determination later. Jeff agreed to bring all the fishing equipment up with him.

It was time to deal with the next problem. My squad was parked on the bicycle path about a half mile away. We would have to walk through the brush and then down a narrow path that was bordered on one side by brush and the other by water. When we got to the Rock River levy, we would have to walk up to the top and then down a bicycle path to my squad. When I said that I was dealing with a "problem", I didn't mean that I had a problem with us walking that far. I had to decide if I was going to carry the bomb up to my squad. I got my butt chewed by everybody the previous time. If I left the bomb there, somebody else might find it before the bomb squad could get to it. Maybe they would get hurt if they tried to set it off. Maybe it just wouldn't be there when the bomb squad got to it. Maybe the bomb squad couldn't even get to it where it was located. Yes, I had talked myself into carrying the bomb up to where I could keep an eye on it.

I told Mutt to keep his hands where I could see them as we started walking up to my squad. Mutt complied. When we reached the edge of the levy, I secured the bomb next to a wooden post. I would be able to keep an eye on the backpack as we continued the rest of the way to my squad. At my squad, I told Mutt to keep his hands on the hood. He again complied. I confirmed with Mutt that he understood that he was under arrest. Mutt agreed that he did. After reading Mutt his Miranda rights, I called the Illinois State Police (ISP). I advised ISP of what I had located and requested for them to send the bomb squad to my location.

With everything moving along, I asked Mutt if he made the pipe bomb. Mutt admitted that he had. I asked Mutt if he used smokeless or black gun powder. Mutt told me that he thought it was black powder. He said that he had purchased the gunpowder in Colorado. I asked Mutt how many bombs he had made. Mutt told me that he made two bombs like the one that I had located. Mutt said, "I'm not a terrorist, I just wanted to make some big booms." I asked Mutt where the other bomb was located. Mutt told me that he had already blown it up. I asked Mutt if he blew it up that night. He said that he had blown it up a few days previous. I asked Mutt if he had any more bombs at his house. Mutt said that he did not. Mutt told me that he did have more gunpowder and fuses.

I told Mutt to stay in front of my squad. As I turned and started to walk back to the passenger compartment, Mutt suddenly told me that he wanted to be handcuffed if he was under arrest. That's not something that anybody else has ever requested. On the flip side, a lot of people have asked me not to handcuff them. I told Mutt that I didn't have to handcuff him just yet. Mutt reiterated that he wanted to be handcuffed if he was under arrest. I accommodated Mutt and placed him in handcuffs. Maybe, in his mind, Mutt needed to be a "formally" arrested.

I retrieved the camera out of my squad and took pictures of the backpack and bomb. About that time, Jeff started bringing the fishing equipment up from the riverbank. When Jeff got done carrying the equipment up, I had him stand by Mutt at the front of my squad. Almost immediately, Mutt began complaining about the handcuffs. He told me that he had previously injured his shoulder and it was starting to hurt. I switched Mutt's handcuffs to the front of his body. So much for "wanting" to be handcuffed!

About an hour later, the bomb squad arrived with their tactical truck. After I got my butt chewed for carrying the pipe bomb around, they dismantled it by blowing one of the end caps off. You would think that it would cause the pipe bomb to blow up, but it doesn't. They gave me the gunpowder and pipe after they had it separated.

Just after midnight, I told Mutt that I would like to make sure that he didn't have any more bombs at his house. Mutt told me that he understood and would cooperate. I talked with Jeff one last time and told him that I would not be seeking any charges against him. He thanked me and left the scene.

Confirming that Mutt lived alone, he agreed to let me search his residence. I called ISP and asked if one of their officers could meet me there. When we arrived, Mutt told me that I might find some "other" stuff inside. Mutt said that he had given "that stuff" up a couple of weeks ago. I asked Mutt what "stuff" he was talking about. Mutt would not clarify his statement.

Two troopers showed up to assist me. I asked one of them to stay with Mutt, while the other assisted me in searching Mutt's residence. Mutt resided in a trailer park. Using Mutt's key, we entered his trailer. It looked like a college bachelor pad. There was clutter all over the place, but all of it had very little "substance". I searched the living room, while the trooper started in the bedroom. I found firecrackers, gun powder, fuse, pipe bomb parts and a cigarette box full of steel ball bearings. The trooper located two heavily used bongs and a bunch of other drug paraphernalia. I took pictures of the evidence and seized all of it.

When we were done, I transported Mutt to ISP headquarters and processed the evidence. I weighed the gunpowder that was recovered from the pipe bomb at .4 ounces. In Illinois, that constitutes a class 3 felony. I'm sure that some of the gunpowder was lost when the end cap was blown off. I explained the law to Mutt and told him that he was going to be charged with a felony. Mutt acknowledged that he understood. At approximately 2:00 a.m., I dropped Mutt off at the Rock Island County Jail.

Mutt was 30 years old when I arrested him. This case obviously occurred after the 9/11 attacks. Like it or not, things changed a little after that. Mutt's bomb was easy to confirm as viable since it was made like a giant firecracker. The thing that really makes this case interesting are the ball bearings that I seized from Mutt's residence. Although there were no ball bearings in the bomb that I had recovered from Mutt, he obviously intended on trying to use them. The only purpose for placing ball bearings in a bomb is to cause physical damage. Not create a "big boom". Mutt never told me what his intentions were for the ball bearings, but he may have been on a path to something really bad happening. When bombs go off, it's hard to control where the shrapnel ends up.

Mutt ended up pleading guilty to a class three felony for the possession of a bomb. Mutt was sentenced to 134 days in jail. He was also given a 12-month conditional discharge and fined $1,067.

Those are my "good" bomb stories. Although I never caught a guy "fishing with dynamite", I did catch one who was going to try it with a pipe bomb. I do not advocate walking around with a bomb in your hand, pocket or backpack. Even if you don't get physically hurt, you will likely get your ass chewed. Although it doesn't hurt as bad, it's not a good feeling either.

SHYSTERS, CONMEN AND SWINDLERS

We all know shysters, conmen and swindlers. I have gotten to know quite a few of them due to my enforcement efforts. In today's world, intentional poachers could be considered shysters in some form or manner. Most of them aren't poaching to "feed their family". That doesn't mean that they don't eat their quarry. Rather that they don't need to poach to survive. They cheat the rest of us out of opportunities in order to make life better for themselves. This chapter will instead be focusing on "business shysters" with a touch of conmen and swindlers. Although all the cases here are very different, there is a mindset that is similar between many of the players, especially the "shysters". As I worked on more and more of these cases, I was amazed especially at what a "shyster" would do to cheat a person out of a buck. They seem to do it without guilt and could rationalize their actions. Most of the shysters that I dealt with distinctly cared about themselves more than anybody else. My cases usually started outdoors and led inside.

On a mid-September Sunday in 2009, I was patrolling on the Mississippi River near Andalusia, Illinois. Traffic on the river generally slows down that time of year. It gets harder to find drunk boaters, so you must focus on hunters and fishermen a little more. Since it was not real busy, I figured I would stop every boat I came across. Stopping the first boat I located (a jon boat), I conducted a safety inspection on it and checked the occupant's fishing licenses. As I completed the check, I saw that the registration was expired. I asked the operator if he had renewed the registration. He told me that he had recently purchased the watercraft and had the temporary registration. I asked him for his paperwork. He handed me his registration application. When a new boat owner purchases a watercraft in Illinois, they retain a copy of their registration application as a temporary registration. They just present it in lieu of their registration until their new stickers arrive. Attached to the application was a receipt from a local license and title business. We will call them Ripoff License and Title (RLT). The receipt showed that the new boat owner had paid $117 in state fees, $20 in handling fees and $7 in miscellaneous tax. Having registered several boats over the years, I was thinking that I had never paid that much. I told the operator that it seemed like he had paid an awful lot to register his boat. He agreed. I told him that I would look into it and let him know if he was charged the correct amount. He thanked me as I issued him a written warning for a minor boating violation.

A short time later, I stopped another jon boat. As I conducted a safety inspection on the watercraft, I saw that it also had expired registration. After the inspection, I again inquired about the registration. The operator handed me a copy of his registration application from RLT. Once again, there was a receipt attached to the application. On the receipt, it showed that the operator had paid $117 in state fees and $20 in handling fees. There was no miscellaneous tax charged. Just as I had done before, I talked with the operator about how expensive his registration was. He agreed. I told him about the previous boat, and we discussed the costs of getting their boats registered. As I wrote him a written warning, I let him know that I would be looking into both of their registration applications. He thanked me as I pulled away.

While I motored down river, I really started to think about the $117 in "state fees". I couldn't figure out how it could be that high. I was wishing that the Springfield office (IDNR HQ) was open on weekends. I had to think about it for a day on my own as I tried to figure out what was going on. I thought that I must be missing something. RLT had been in business for many years. Surely, they would not have screwed up something like that!

The next day, I was able to reach one of our technicians in the IDNR watercraft registration section. I told her what I had found on the RLT receipts. She agreed that the numbers did not match up. She said that the only way it could be that high is if there were trailer registration fees rolled into the costs. I called both boat owners and confirmed they had separate receipts for their trailers. They agreed. Calling back to the technician, we figured out what the costs should have been—$52 for the registration, 6.25% sales tax on the boats (they paid $100 and $300 respectively) and whatever RLT's fees were to do the paperwork (later found out to be $20). When it all boiled out, the boat owners were being overcharged roughly $65 in "state fees".

Wanting to get to the bottom of it, I drove straight to RLT. Walking in, I met with one of the employees. I confirmed she was not the owner. She agreed and told me that the owner (we will call her Cruella) would not be in until the following day. I asked the employee if she had been the one who completed the registration transactions and showed her copies of them. Looking at the handwriting, she agreed that it was her writing. I asked the employee if she could explain the fees to me. She explained it the same way, as the IDNR technician did except that she added in an additional $65 state fee for a title. I asked the employee if their customers wrote checks directly to the IDNR or to RLT. She advised that they generally wrote them to RLT. She said that RLT would deposit them and send the required fees to the state. I asked the employee who submitted the fees to the State. She told me that Cruella submitted the fees by writing a check from their business account. I asked the employee to write me a statement about how they operated. She agreed.

As I was waiting for the statement, I was thinking about their system. RLT could tell their customers whatever "costs" they wanted to. If the check was written to RLT (or the customer paid in cash), the difference between what they had charged the customer and what they had to actually send to the state could be kept by RLT as a "bonus". That bonus money would just sit in their account after the state was paid. After getting the statement, I thanked the employee and left the business.

Returning to RLT the following morning, I met with Cruella. I confirmed that she was the owner of the business. Cruella said that she had only owned the business for a year. I was told that she had worked at RLT for several years prior to purchasing it. I told Cruella I had been there the day before. Cruella acknowledged that she knew I had been there. Cruella said that her employee had been incorrectly charging people for their registrations. She advised that the employee had overcharged some people by $65. She went on to say that they had been correcting the problem. I asked Cruella how they had been correcting the problem. Cruella said that as people came in and complained about it, she would reimburse them. I asked Curella how many registrations she had corrected. She threw out the name of one local firefighter and told me how nice he was. She then stated that she had taken $65 off his next vehicle registration.

I asked Cruella about overcharging people on their sales tax (charging 7%). Cruella said that she rounded the tax to the dollar. I was thinking that if you were "rounding it", it would be $6 per hundred, not $7. She backed up what she was saying by showing me a tax form. The tax form said to round the purchase price to the nearest dollar, not the tax charged. I pointed out her misinterpretation and advised Cruella I would confirm it with the IRS.

I asked Cruella how many more boats she had registered (than the two I showed her) Cruella pulled out a roll of registrations from behind the counter. In a quick look, I found 11 more that appeared to have been overcharged the $65. Cruella quickly pointed out that all the overcharge receipts had her employees' writing. I told Cruella that if she did not return the people's money, she was stealing it. Cruella did not take what I was saying seriously. Kind of like Zsa Zsa Gabor, she said, "Don't say that." I was waiting for the "darling", but it never came. I explained to Cruella that she was taking in $117 from the customers and only sending the State $52. I told Cruella that she was keeping $65 each time. Cruella told me that she was sure she had sent the State the whole $117. I asked Cruella if she had a check register that we could look at to cross-reference her payments made to the State. She agreed and we confirmed she had only been submitting $52 to the State. I told Cruella that the extra $65 must be staying in her account. Cruella did not comment.

I asked Cruella if she had any more boat registration applications. She advised that she did not. Cruella told me that she destroyed all her paperwork every three months. I told Cruella I would be seizing the paperwork that appeared to be incorrect and was going to write her a receipt. I advised Cruella that I would be talking with the state's attorney's office later that day. She suddenly said that I could look at all of her files if I wanted to. Cruella said that she just wanted to get this over with. I confirmed with Cruella that I could have free access to all of her files. She agreed.

I walked out to my squad and filled out a receipt for the files that I had already seized. I tried to call the state's attorney's office, but could not get through to an assistant. I was able to get through to a Special Agent with the Illinois Department of Revenue. The Special Agent was able to confirm some of my suspicions.

Completing the evidence receipt, I returned to RLT. When I walked in the door, Cruella had a big box full of boat registrations sitting on the counter. Cruella again told me that she just wanted to get this done. Cruella asked if I wanted to go through the records in her rear office I hesitantly agreed. I did not have any "Permission to Search" forms with me, so I called Laura and asked her to bring me one. She agreed. Sitting down with the records, I started to separate them into piles. Cruella watched me for approximately 10 minutes and told me that she was going to start working at the front counter again. I agreed. A little while later, Laura arrived with the Permission to Search form. Cruella agreed to allow me to continue going through her paperwork and signed the consent form.

Returning to the back office, I started going through the paperwork again. When I was about two hours into the paper-work, I found a bill of sale for a watercraft attached to some other paperwork. The sales price on the bill of sale was "whited" out. In the "whited" out area, the bill of sale said the sales price was $6,500. Holding the paper up to the light, I could see that it origi-nally said the boat sold for $10,000. I carried the bill of sale up to Cruella and showed it to her. I asked Cruella if she had changed the sales price. Cruella said that she had not. She said that when she told the customer how much he was going to have to pay in taxes, he went outside and came back in with it changed. Cruella proceeded to tell me that it happens all the time. Cruella said that people routinely come in and ask how much their taxes will be. She advised that after she tells them the amount, they leave. She said that they usually return the next day with a bill of sale that shows a lowered sales price.

When I completed going through the box of records, I had found another 146 registration applications that appeared to have inconsistencies. I told Cruella I would be seizing those docu-ments as well. She acknowledged that she understood and asked me what she should be doing differently. Obviously, she was play-ing up the "I didn't know" card. I reiterated the proper charging of tax, advised her to maintain her records for seven years and told her to stop overcharging her customers. Cruella acted like I had told her something that she did not already know. I took the box of records back to the office and slowly went through them again. I separated the records into types of violations.

With this case breaking loose in the fall, I was very busy with "game warden work"–besides working on this investigation. There is no "time out" from your normal workload to work on an investigation of this type. With Cruella's records, I started by investigating the easiest type of violation to prove. I figured it was the overcharging of her customers. This equated to Theft by Deceptive Practice. Around the rest of my workload, it took me about three months to go to 17 of Cruella's customer's houses. At each house, I confirmed that the customer was overcharged and wanted their "overcharged" monies returned. Each customer was willing to write a statement and was fully cooperative in the investigation.

Moving into February, I had gone to the residences of another 10 customers and confirmed they were overcharged by RLT. One of these customers had two tax forms (RUT-75) in their file for the same boat. When the purchaser of a boat applies for registration in Illinois, they must file an RUT tax form with their registration application. RUTs document the required 6.25% in state sales tax that is paid on used boat purchases. One of the RUTs documented the purchase price as $6,000 and the other listed the purchase price as $3,000. This change on the tax form would cause the owner to pay about $187.50 less in state sales tax.

While at the customer's residence, I asked him how much he had paid for his boat. He told me that he paid $8,100 for it. I showed him the first tax form. He agreed that it was his signature on the form. He advised that there was a trailer with the boat that he had purchased. He figured that the trailer was worth about $2,100, which made the boat worth about $6,000. I then showed him the second RUT and asked if it was his signature on the bottom. He said that it was not. I asked the customer if he ever claimed to have paid $3000.00 for his boat. He said that he had not. This is when it started to get a little more interesting. As I talked with more and more RLT customers, I started asking more questions about the "process" at RLT. Most of the customers said that RLT would tell them to just sign the RUT form. They said that the worker would offer to fill in the sales amount and the remaining information. Of course, everybody would accept the offer to complete their paperwork. They didn't have to worry about doing it wrong and they were paying them to do it anyway, right?

As I started focusing more on the tax related part of the case, I contacted Investigator Brian Cooper (with the Illinois Department of Revenue). Brian was fun to work with and a wealth of tax knowledge. Brian eventually became the Criminal Investigations Manager of his division. When I contacted Brian, he told me that they had already opened a working file on Cruella. We sat down and went through what I had uncovered. I had a lot of documents that Brian had not seen. Although I was showing Brian my "cards", he wouldn't show me his. In that regard, working with Brian was kind of like playing blackjack at the casino. He knew what I had and what he had. I only knew what I had. Tax documents and information cannot be freely shared by Revenue Officers.

After reviewing the documents, Brian and I drove to RLT. Walking in, we were greeted by Cruella. We asked Cruella if we could talk with her about her business. Cruella agreed and invited us to the back office. After we sat down, Brian started the interview with questions about tax documents. As he interviewed Cruella, Brian showed her several documents. Cruella admitted to altering and forging them. When asked how many documents she had altered or forged, Cruella did not know. Cruella said there was very little money in the business account when she took it over. She admitted that she was trying to help her business account by altering and forging documents. Cruella agreed she had been keeping money that was required to be sent to the Illinois Department of Revenue.

When it was my turn, I showed Cruella boat and snowmobile registration documents. One person had been overcharged $156.25 and another $112. Cruella admitted that she had completed one of the transactions and that the other had been completed by her employee. I asked Cruella if her employees would have stolen their customer's money. Cruella told me that any missing money was her fault. She said that her employees would not have taken anybody's money. Cruella repeatedly said that she felt bad for overcharging her customers. She admitted that the overcharged money must have remained in her account. She also said that she wanted to "make it right" with everybody. At the end of the interview, Cruella briefly cried and said that she hoped we did not think less of her for what she had done. After that, Cruella refused to write us a statement and advised that she would be getting a lawyer. We thanked Cruella for her honesty and left the business.

At that point, you may think that we just went and filed charges. But it's not that easy if you want to do a good job. You must get a grasp on the gravity of the situation. This is where I came to understand a major failure in the tax and registration systems. When the documents are submitted to the State, they are filed under the purchaser's name. There is not a way to review everything that is submitted by a business for their customers. In essence, we could not ask the State to send us everything submitted by RLT—and then track down their customers. We had to rely on RLT's records to figure out who their customers were. Although Cruella was not destroying all her records every three months, she was not keeping all of them either.

I gave Brian all the tax documents that I had seized. As Brian completed an investigation on our tax documents, I completed working on the theft by deceptive practice cases. I was able to identify 67 cases where there had been money stolen from someone trying to register a boat or snowmobile. The overwhelming majority of those people I talked with in person and confirmed their transactions.

After 16 months' worth of investigation, we went to the Rock Island County State's Attorney's office and obtained a 20-count warrant for Cruella's arrest. Eleven felonies and nine misdemeanors. The charges included seven counts of forgery, four counts of filing fraudulent tax paperwork and nine counts of theft by deceptive practice. We were told that a jury may have trouble following the prosecution if we filed more charges. About eight months later, Cruella and the state's attorney's office reached a plea deal. Cruella plead guilty to three counts of theft by deceptive practice. The remaining charges were dismissed. Cruella was ordered to pay back all the victims of theft by deceptive practice. She was also required to pay the Illinois Department of Revenue the money that she had fraudulently swindled from them. Between fines and restitution, Cruella was ordered to pay $47,966.75. Keep in mind that our prosecution was primarily based on the records that we had obtained from Cruella. There are possibly hundreds more victims and likely thousands (if not tens of thousands) of dollars unaccounted for. Several years later, Revenue worked another case on Cruella. She was again charged with many of the same violations. I believe that she has finally sold the business.

Cruella's methods of stealing money were varied. She would change the reported purchase price, change bills of sale, overcharge on fees and forge signatures on documents. Cruella's "T" was one of the dead giveaways on her forged paperwork. When she crossed the top of the "T", she always had a little "curl" at the end of her top line. It's funny how the little things can trip someone up. I'm glad RLT attached receipts to their registration paperwork!

I don't care who you are, Cruella is a shyster. Although Cruella was good at what she did, she doesn't hold a candle to the guy (Swifty) you will read about later. Cruella was in her 50s during my investigation of her. Swifty, on the other hand, was way ahead of his time. He was only 25 when I started my investigation into his business practices.

The Tire Underground

Over the years, dumping complaints ended up being some of the most common ones that I received. People were reported for dumping everything from grass clippings to shingles. Trying to catch a dumper, after the fact, was sometimes hard to do. Building materials and appliances were usually a dead end. I was a little more successful with deer parts. About 30% of the time I could find an address, or somebody's deer permit mixed in with the parts. Bags of trash were always my best bet. There was usually some form of mail mixed in. Even if the mail didn't belong to the culprit, I could track it back to them.

In June of 2012, I got a dumping complaint from the Site Superintendent (Dave Hahne) of Hennepin Canal State Park. Dave told me that a bunch of tires had been dumped along the Hennepin Canal. He said that most of the tires were at the Lock 32 parking lot. Although the lot is in Rock Island, it's kind of a desolate area. It sits on a long dead-end road and only has a few permanent residences.

It's not uncommon to have tires dumped on State sites. After all, if people don't burn, bury or dump their tires, they must pay to get rid of them. The lowest combined expense, risk and effort comes from dumping tires in a desolate location. The surprising part of Dave's complaint was that there were about 100 tires. I never had that many tires dumped in one location before. I hated to admit it, but I told Dave that I might not be able to solve the case. Tires don't generally have any relatable marks or tags, which will lead you to a particular person. On top of that, we didn't have any cameras along the Hennepin Canal.

A couple of days after getting the complaint, I drove down to the Lock 32 parking lot. There were tires lying in and around the lot. You could tell that the tires had recently been dumped. They were relatively clean and were lying on top of everything. The grass, weeds and brush had not started to grow up through the tires yet. Checking the rest of the canal, I located another spot where an additional 50 tires had been thrown out onto the towpath. Some had even rolled down into the canal.

Like every other time that I had to deal with dumpers, I was frustrated. Frustrated that I had to deal with the tires and frustrated with the thought that I may not be able to solve the case. It's amazing how many people think of the world as their own personal garbage can—from the slobs who leave their fishing trash, to the companies who create illegal landfills. As a kid, I often saw what the fishing slobs had left behind. I never thought of it on a grand scale. I just thought about the spot that I was fishing at. When I became a game warden, I came to realize that we have slobs all over. I got to see everybody's fishing spot. I literally dealt with littering, dumping and illegal landfills everywhere that I ever worked. The commercial ones were the worst. Those guys were making money for polluting our environment. Although I wouldn't be able to change the landscape of the world, I would have to start focusing on catching a tire dumper!

As I checked the rest of the canal, I continued to think about the tires. The dumper would almost have to be a commercial business. Nobody has that many "personal tires". Not only was the quantity ridiculous, but the tires were of all different sizes and brands. On top of that, most of the tires were in really "bad shape". It was actually hard to find a tire with any useable tread left on it. Further indicating that they came from a repair shop was the fact that some of the tires had chalk marks on them. The type of chalk that a repair shop uses when they find a defect in a tire.

That left me with a few types of businesses to look at. It would have to be an automotive repair shop, junk yard, car dealership or tire store. Trying to further narrow my search, I figured that a reputable business wouldn't risk their integrity for a mere 150 tires. Shady automotive repair shops probably wouldn't have that many tires lying around. I ended up focusing on used tire shops. It didn't seem like there were very many of them when I worked in Will County. When we moved to the Quad Cities, I couldn't believe how many there were. It seemed like there was a used tires shop around every other corner. Not only do used tire shops have access to a bunch of tires, but when they're also replacing used tires with better used tires, the old ones must be really bad! Those would be just like the ones dumped at the Lock 32 parking lot. Having driven by the used tire stores hundreds of times, I knew that I had a couple of them within a few miles of the canal.

Driving to the closest used tire shop (Franco's Tires), I parked in their lot. Franco's had been open for about 10 years. The owner (Franco) had started off with a little steel shelter and about 200 tires. He now had two fenced lots with trailers full of tires. Franco was obviously making a good business for himself.

Exiting my squad, I met with Franco and one of his employees (Julio). I introduced myself to both and asked Franco how they disposed of their "junk" tires. Franco and Julio simultaneously said that they paid a licensed hauler to remove them. It sounded like they had rehearsed their response. I decided that I would try to play on their ethical side. I explained my investigation to them. I told Franco and Julio that there were too many tires to have come from somebody's house. They agreed. I paused and waited for a further response, but didn't receive one.

Hesitantly thanking Franco and Julio, I started to walk toward my squad. Just as I reached the door, Julio asked me to wait. He walked over and said that he had some information for me. Julio told me that I should look for a guy named Arnold. Julio said that Arnold had stopped in about a week ago with his cousin (Lou). Julio told me that Arnold offered to take all their junk tires for $1 a tire. Julio said that it normally costs them $3 a tire with the licensed hauler. I got Arnold and Lou's last name and was told they were driving a green Dodge minivan. Julio also gave me descriptions of Arnold and Lou and told me that Lou was wearing an ankle bracelet. Not a decorative "anklet", but a prison release bracelet. I asked Julio if they paid Arnold to take any tires. Julio said that they had not. He told me that Sergio's Tires in Moline was paying Arnold to dispose of their junk tires. I thanked Julio and gave him my number. I told him to call me if he thought of anything else.

Shortly after leaving Franco's, I got a call from Julio. Julio told me that I should also be looking for a guy named Reg. He told me that Reg was reportedly picking up tires from a place called TJ's Tires. Julio said that Reg was being paid the same as Arnold. Julio didn't know Reg's last name, but gave me directions to his house. Hanging up with Julio, I couldn't believe how much info I had gained on my first stop. Two real good leads. I was already feeling better about my chances of solving the case!

Driving to TJ's Tires, I met with the owner (Thomas). I didn't figure that I would have to press him very hard since I had gotten what appeared to be good information from Julio. When I asked Thomas how he got rid of his junk tires, he said that he paid a licensed hauler to take them. Thomas said that he doesn't allow anybody else to take his junk tires. I didn't want to stir the pot too hard. I already had two good leads and didn't want everybody to "clam up". I thanked Thomas for his time and left the business.

Figuring that I needed do a little more "reconnaissance", I ran computer checks on Arnold and Lou. Sure enough, Lou was on federal probation. Both had the same address and were living with Lou's mom (Carla). Driving toward their residence, I saw a "beacon of light" when I turned down their street. There was a stack of four tires on the sidewalk and a green Dodge van parked in front of the house. It was easy to line them up since Lou's house was literally built on the edge of the sidewalk and the sidewalk was literally on the edge of the road. In other words, the three-foot-wide sidewalk was the only thing that separated Lou's garage door from the edge of the street. I ran the plate on the van and found that it was registered to Lou.

Deciding to see if anybody was home, I parked my squad and walked toward their residence. Looking at the "sidewalk tires" as I passed them, I saw chalk marks on their sidewalls. They were similar to the ones dumped along the canal. If there's a hole in a tire's sidewall, it cannot be safely repaired and is considered to be junk. I've had it happen many times with my own tires. It's very frustrating when the tread is like new and you get a sidewall puncture! The only ethical thing to do is replace the tire. As I continued past the van, I saw that Lou had three more tires sitting in the back of it. Those didn't appear to be any better than the ones on the sidewalk.

Reaching the house, I knocked on the door several times. Nobody answered. Walking back to my squad, I grabbed my camera. I took pictures of the tires on the sidewalk and in the van. As I pulled away, I was hoping that Arnold and Lou weren't just sitting inside playing opossum. I always like to have the element of surprise when I went to interview somebody for the first time.

Leaving Lou's house, I drove past Reg's house. Reg's block had an alley, so I circled the house and went down the alley. As I idled up to Reg's backyard, I could see about 15 tires sitting back there. I stopped and took a picture of the tires. When I got back in the vehicle, I figured that I would try to contact the Illinois EPA. I was digging into this tire business a little deeper than I ever gone before. I didn't want to screw something up or miss a violation that I didn't know about.

After I checked on some more used tire locations, I got a call back from Todd Marvel with the Illinois EPA. Todd was the EPA's expert on tire laws. He got me on track with the State's regulations on tire transportation, storage and disposal. There were a lot of Illinois tires laws that I didn't even know about. Over the course of the next couple of months, I talked with Todd many times.

After my July vacation and a bunch of boat patrols, I went to check out Sergio's Tires. I had driven past Sergio's many times over the years. I arrived at the business only to find that it was no longer there. There was a guy next door who was able to tell me where Sergio's had moved to. As I drove toward the new location, I went past a place called Lee's Tire's. I didn't even know that Lee's Tires existed! Turning around, I drove back to Lee's and parked in the lot. Meeting with one of the employees (Frank), I identified myself and asked if he was the owner. He said that he wasn't, but led me into the office. Inside, Frank introduced me to the owner (Lee). Lee didn't speak any English, so Frank translated for us.

I asked Lee how they disposed of their "junk tires". After Frank and Lee discussed it, Frank told me that they had a couple of guys who would stop in and picked them up. I asked Lee if he had any receipts for those transactions. Frank told me that they didn't. As things progressed, Frank just answered the questions without consulting with Lee. Frank proceeded to tell me that the same two guys stop in every week. He said that they take the junk tires for $1 a tire. I asked Frank what the guys looked like. Frank said that they drove a green Dodge van. I asked Frank if he could tell me anything about the guys. He told me that one of them wore an ankle bracelet. I asked him if it was a "prison-style" ankle bracelet. Frank agreed that it was. I asked Frank how long it had been since they picked up tires. He told me that they stopped in the previous day. Frank told me that they paid "the guys" to take

18 tires. I told Frank and Lee about my investigation. They both said that they didn't know who was dumping the tires. Lee actually spoke some English on that response. I asked Frank if he would write me a statement. He agreed. Along with the statement, I got directions to Sergio's Tires.

Going to Sergio's, I walked inside and met with the owner (Sergio). I asked Sergio how he disposes of his junk tires. Sergio proceeded to explain that he buys tires from a guy named Reg. He said that Reg works for Mysterious Auto Center (MAC) in Moline. Sergio told me that he and Reg had worked out a trade deal. He said that Reg always takes the same number of tires as what he drops off. Sergio said that both he and MAC wanted to keep their "tire numbers" correct. Sergio went on to tell me that he also purchases tires from a local junkyard. I asked Sergio if he ever paid somebody else to take his junk tires. Sergio told me that he did not. He said that he wouldn't do anything to jeopardize his business. Sergio seemed sincere and requested that I contact the junkyard and MAC to confirm what he had told me.

Leaving Sergio's, I drove to MAC and met with Reg. Reg had a truck full of tires when I arrived. I explained to Reg that Sergio had directed me to him. I asked Reg to tell me what he was doing with the tires. Reg told me that he sells tires to both Sergio and Ronnie's Tires. I asked Reg if he picks up junk tires. Reg told me that he makes an even trade with Sergio, but doesn't get any junk tires from Ronnie. I asked Reg how he keeps his numbers correct if he doesn't take the junk ones from Ronnie. Reg told me that he just gets more from Sergio. I asked Reg how often he trades with Sergio. Reg said that they trade tires nearly every day. I asked Reg if he would write me a statement. He agreed.

Leaving MAC, I drove to Ronnie's Tires. As I pulled in, I saw a truck full of tires parked out front. There was a guy (Steve) standing at the back of the truck. Parking in the lot, one of Ronnie's employees walked up to Steve. Steve pulled a tire from the bed of the truck and they began inspecting it. I exited my squad and walked over to Steve. Identifying myself, I asked him if he was selling used tires to Ronnie's. Steve agreed that he was. I asked Steve where he obtained the tires. Steve said that he had gotten seven from repair shops and the other eight from a car dealership. I asked Steve if he was taking any junk tires back. He told me that he wasn't. I asked him if he knew who was dumping the tires along the canal. Steve told me that I should be looking for a "druggie" named Markus. He said that Markus was in constant need of a "fix". Steve told me that he had heard Markus was getting paid $3 a tire to take the junk ones from Franco's Tires. I couldn't believe that I had already made a complete loop back to Franco's.

Walking into Ronnie's Tires, I met with the owner (Ron). I identified myself to Ron and asked him what he did with his junk tires. Ron told me that he had a licensed hauler who picks them up. Ron showed me some receipts to confirm his claim. I asked Ron if he had been approached by anybody offering to take his junk tires. Ron told me that two white guys in a green van had stopped in about a month earlier. He said that they offered to take his junk tires for a buck a piece. Ron said that he refused their service. I thanked Ron for his time and left his business.

At this point, I had talked with five tire shops and two guys who were selling used tires to the shops. The "tire undergound" was starting to come into view. The same set of suspects kept coming to the forefront. I decided that it was time to find Arnold and Lou for an interview.

Driving toward Arnold's house, as I turned onto their road, I saw two subjects (Arnold and Lou) standing next to the green van in front of the house. Pulling up in front of the van, I parked my squad and exited the vehicle. Walking over to Arnold and Lou, I identified myself to them. They had a bunch of steel window frames sitting on the sidewalk and were busting the glass out of them. I confirmed with Arnold and Lou that they were scrapping out the steel. They agreed that they were. When I asked if one of them was Arnold, he stepped up and confirmed his identity. I asked Arnold if he would step over by my squad. He agreed. At my squad, I asked Arnold what he was doing with all the tires that he had picked up. Arnold told me that he was not the one picking up the tires. He said that Lou was picking them up. I confirmed with Arnold that it was Lou over on the sidewalk. He agreed that it was.

Arnold was obviously not wanting to get in trouble with his cousin. I could tell that he had a fear of saying anything and would rather just throw the ball into Lou's court. Although I preferred to interview the weakest link first, I figured that I would give the ex-inmate a shot. After all, I'm not the kind of guy to cause a family fight.

Walking back over to Lou, I told him that I wanted to talk with him about the tires. He just said, "What about them?" I asked him what he was doing with the ones that he had picked up. Lou simply pointed to the open "man door" on the garage and invited me inside. Following Lou through the door, there were tires stacked to the ceiling with a narrow path going between them. The path led to the rear of the garage. At the time, I guessed that there were at least 200 tires in the garage. I asked Lou if he had any more tires. Lou asked me to follow him to the "upper" part of the garage. Walking down the path, we went up a short set of stairs and into an old basement area. Up against the west wall was another pile of tires (about 50). Looking back now, it was probably not the best location for me to be in with two other guys. I'm not sure if my radio would have worked and nobody would even hear a gunshot. Then again, I suppose it is just like most of the other game warden stops!

I asked Lou what he was doing with all the tires. He shrugged and said, "You can see what I'm doing with them." I suppose that I should have expected that answer. He probably thought that I was the dumbass! I told Lou that I had talked with several tire vendors. I said that I had reports of him getting a lot more tires than what he had showed me. I told Lou that I expected him to be honest with me. I said that I wanted to know who had dumped the tires along the Hennepin Canal. Lou hesitated and told me that he didn't know. I looked at Lou in disbelief. He again hesitated and said that he does occasionally dump tires while he's out driving around. I asked Lou where he dumps them. Lou said that he usually dumps them in an alley. I asked Lou how long it had been since he dumped any tires. Lou said that it had been a couple of weeks. I asked Lou where he dumped the tires. Lou said that it was a couple of blocks over and pointed to the north. I asked Lou if he would show me where he dumped them. He asked me if he was going to be in trouble. I told Lou that he might end up being in trouble. Lou pointed at his ankle bracelet and told me that he didn't want to go back to prison. I told Lou that I was primarily concerned about getting the tires cleaned up. Lou agreed to show me where the tires were dumped.

Lou followed me out to my squad. After we had a discussion about arresting him, I told him that I would not decide about any charges until I had concluded my investigation. Lou climbed into my squad and directed me to an alley about a block and a half away. Pointing to a pile of tires (5), Lou told me that he had dumped them about a week earlier. Stopping in the alley, I told Lou that we couldn't leave the tires there. He agreed and helped me load them into the bed of my truck.

Driving back to the house, Lou again asked if I was going to arrest him. I reiterated that I would be concluding my investigation before requesting any charges. I told Lou that I knew he had dumped more tires. I again told him that I wanted to know who had dumped the tires on the Hennepin Canal. Lou told me that he was going to tell me the truth. He said that he took two loads of tires out to the Lock 32 parking lot and dumped them there.

Lou said there were about 30 tires in each load. I drew a picture of the Lock 32 parking lot and asked Lou where he had dumped the tires. Lou pinpointed where the tires were dumped. I asked him if he would write me a statement. Lou said that he didn't write very well and asked if Arnold could write it for him. I agreed.

When Lou and Arnold finished the statement, I went and logged the five seized tires into evidence. As I thought about it further, I decided that I needed to get an exact count of the tires dumped on the Hennepin Canal. Driving out to the area, I was able to find 188 tires. A few days after I documented everything, we were able to get IDOT to clean up the tires at a cost of $1,817 to the State of Illinois.

Roughly a week and a few meetings later, the Rock Island County State's Attorney's office gave me a search warrant for Lou's house. The warrant was issued to search for tires and any paperwork related to the acquisition or destruction of them. After we discussed the case, I was also given an arrest warrant for Lou. We charged Lou with three counts of dumping tires and one count of operating an illegal tire storage facility. All of the charges were class A misdemeanors.

Early that evening, I went to Lou's house with Rock Island County Sheriff's Deputy Steve Rusk. Over the years, I got to work with Steve several times. Steve was always a good guy to have around. He was large in stature and was well connected in the community. Not only did he usually know of the players, but he would also be a good back-up if things went south! As we pulled up in front of the residence, I saw that there was a new stack of tires sitting in front of the garage. Walking up to the residence, nobody was home. I called Lou and told him that I had a search warrant for their house. He told me that he understood and would be home in 20 minutes.

About 20 minutes later, Lou's mom arrived with Arnold. I asked them where Lou was. Arnold told me that Lou was at a friend's house. I explained to Arnold and Carla that I had a search warrant for their house. Both advised that they understood. Arnold opened the house, secured the dog and showed me where everything was located.

During the search, I didn't locate any surprises. All the tires in the basement were still there. I took pictures of the tires and never found any records. I told Arnold and Carla that I wouldn't be seizing any evidence from their residence. I explained to them the dangers of having tires stored in their house. Having spoken with the EPA, I also told Arnold and Carla that I was trying to arrange for disposal of their tires.

Completing the search of the residence (about 6:30 p.m.), I asked Arnold where the new pile of tires (in front of the garage) had come from. He said that they were brought home by Lou. I asked Arnold if he could secure them. Arnold agreed and put them in the garage. As Arnold was carrying the tires in, I asked him if he knew when Lou was getting home. He said that Lou would be home by 8:30 p.m. Arnold told me that Lou had to check in with his probation officer at 9:00 p.m. I thanked Arnold for the information and started to leave when he told me that I should be looking into a guy named Reggie. Arnold said that Reggie was the one who had taught Lou how to make money from tires. He went on to tell me that Reggie had the State pick tires up before. I asked Arnold what he meant by "the State" picking up tires. Arnold told me that the State picks up piles of tires for free.

My shift was scheduled to be over before 9:00 p.m., so I asked Deputy Rusk if he could swing by and arrest Lou for me. Steve said that he would get it taken care of. Less than an hour later, Steve called and said that he was en route to jail with Lou.

That night, I thought about "the State" picking up Reggie's tires for free. Calling Todd Marvel the following day, I asked him about Arnold's statement. Todd explained that the Illinois EPA does "Consensual Removal Agreements". He told me that they occasionally get calls from people who have acquired large quantities of tires. Todd said that the EPA will do a "one-time" clean-up if there are less than 1,000 tires. As part of the agreement, the property owner must agree not to accumulate tires on their property again.

I suppose that the premise of the program is good, but it's really kind of a crazy deal. Anybody who wants to make some money can go around, get paid to take tires and let the State clean their mess up. On top of that, the way I read the agreement, it's property-related (not person-related). In other words, if you find another property to stack tires on, you can do it all over again!

About a week later, I drove to Reggie's house. Parking out front, I walked up to the front door and knocked. Reggie answered the door. I identified myself to Reggie and asked him if he knew that I would be coming to visit him. Reggie stepped out onto the front porch and sat down. He was super nervous as he pulled his socks up. Reggie told me that he had heard about Lou. Reggie pushed his socks back down and pulled them up again. He kept doing it as he talked with me.

I asked Reggie if he was with Lou when the tires were dumped on the Hennepin Canal. Reggie didn't answer the question. He told me that he and Lou went to Lee's Tires and picked up a couple of loads. I asked Reggie how many tires they picked up at Lee's. Reggie said that they picked up about 50 tires in total. I again asked Reggie about the dumped tires on the Hennepin Canal. He told me that Lou had admitted to dumping "a lot" of tires out there.

I asked Reggie how many tires he has at his own house. Reggie told me that he has about 40 tires. I asked him if had tires picked up by the EPA previously. Reggie agreed that he had. I asked Reggie if he was in violation of his agreement. He acknowledged that he was. I asked Reggie if he would show me his tires. He agreed.

After Reggie got some shoes on, he led me around to the backyard. There were two large piles of tires in the yard. I told Reggie that it looked like he had about 100 tires. He told me that he was not sure how many tires he had. Reggie told me, "You don't have to turn me in!" He then said that when he gets some money, he will get the tires cleaned up.

Looking at the east side of the residence, I saw there was also a shed on the property. I asked Reggie what was in the shed. He told me that there were some tires in the shed. I asked Reggie if we could look in it. He told me that the shed was locked, and his brother had the key. I told Reggie that it didn't look like it was locked to me. I asked Reggie if we could check the doors. He agreed. Walking over to the shed, we found an open door. Pointing out that there wasn't a lock on it, Reggie opened the door. I counted approximately 100 more tires in and around the shed. I told Reggie that it looked like he had about 200 tires. Reggie agreed. I asked Reggie if I could take pictures of the tires. He again agreed. Retrieving my camera, I photographed the tires. I asked Reggie if he was the owner of the property. He told me that it was his dad's house, but he was responsible for the tires. I thanked Reggie for his cooperation and left the residence.

I eventually charged Reggie with the illegal operation of a tire storage facility. He pled guilty and was fined $361. Lou, on the other hand, had his Federal probation revoked and was sent back to prison. He served out his sentence and was fined $654 in the Rock Island County Court system. It took about a year, but the tires were eventually removed from Lou and Reggie's residences. Although Lou and Reggie weren't swindling the public, they were swindling the State and obviously had no regard for the public domain.

During this investigation, I had a couple of other spin-offs that also led to arrests. To say the least, the investigation was enlightening. Before it, I never really gave much thought to what happens when we buy a new set of tires. I obviously knew that people sold used tires, but didn't have the loop filled in. The reality of the situation is that when we buy new tires, we have to pay the New Tire Dealer to "dispose" of our old ones. That New tire Dealer (or an employee of them) double dips and takes our old tires to a Used Tire Dealer. Again, the New Tire Dealer got paid by us to "dispose" of them and then got paid by the Used Tire Dealer for them. Our good, used tires are then sold again for a profit to somebody else. It's really kind of funny. Everybody makes money from our old tires, but us. A few years after this investigation, I had to replace some tires on one of my personal vehicles. I decided to keep my used tires. I think I had to pay a penalty to the New Tire Dealer for keeping my old ones, but it was the same as the disposal fee. A couple of weeks later, I actually took my used tires to Franco's and made $60! If the tires are still decent, he said that he would pay between $10 and $30 for each tire. Of course, the size and demand for that size are important as well. Franco didn't recognize me, and I didn't mention Lou or Arnold.

Fractured Penis

I will give you a "pre-warning" on this chapter - it may be hard to follow. If it was a snowball, it would have ended up the size of a house!

In April of 2014, I received a call from a local timber buyer (we will call him Tom). In my career, I hardly ever received a call "from" a timber buyer. I almost always received a call from a landowner "about" a timber buyer. Not every timber buyer is a shyster, but I never investigated one that I did not find in violation of something. I would guess that the monetary temptation is just too great. Timber buyers are dealing with a commodity that very few people know the true value of. Until I started in this career, I did not know that a walnut tree is generally worth about 10 times as much as an oak tree. In fact, I have seen a single walnut tree be worth as much as $10,000. It is unlikely that the one next to your garage (the one that you cuss every year when you twist your ankle on one of its nuts) is one of these trees—but it could be. I also did not realize that the market for hardwood timber fluctuates as much as it does.

Tom proceeded to tell me that he had received a call from Swifty about some walnut logs he wanted to sell. Tom said that he told Swifty that he didn't have any time to look at the logs. Swifty offered to bring the logs to Tom. Tom agreed to meet Swifty at 5:00 p.m. (at Tom's business). Swifty and another guy (we will call Loaner) showed up on time with the logs. Loaner is a business owner himself. Loaner ran a lawn care, landscaping, firewood and tree service business. If you needed something done outside, Loaner was your guy. Tom looked at the small trailer full of logs and agreed to purchase them from Swifty for $1,000. After getting paid, Swifty dumped the logs in the storage yard and told Tom that he had some more logs to sell him. Tom agreed to buy a second load. Swifty made an appointment to bring them the following day. Swifty never showed up with the second load of logs.

Two days after the first sale, Tom was having breakfast with his friend (we will call him Dick). Dick is a timber buyer as well. During breakfast, Tom got a call from Loaner. Loaner told him that he wanted to bring the second set of logs to him. Tom agreed to meet with Loaner at his business. When he got off the phone, Tom and Dick talked about Swifty and the logs that Tom had purchased a couple of days earlier. Dick told Tom that he had also purchased some walnut logs from Swifty a few days earlier. Dick said that he had marked his logs with yellow paint, but had not picked them up from Swifty yet.

Leaving breakfast, Tom and Dick met Loaner at the business. Dick was able to identify the logs that Swifty and Loaner had brought to Tom as the same logs that Dick had already purchased (from Swifty). After questioning Loaner about the logs, Dick demanded to speak with Swifty. They couldn't get a hold of Swifty, so Tom refused to buy the second load of logs. Tom proceeded to tell me that Swifty had not only taken the logs illegally, but he had also stolen a backhoe from Dick. I could see that this was going to be an in-depth investigation and I had only talked with the first guy. I got Dick's phone number from Tom and set up an appointment to meet with Dick about a week later. In the meantime, I did a little background on Swifty. Swifty was not a licensed timber buyer in Illinois and it appeared that he had never been one.

Meeting with Dick at my office, I asked him what had happened. Dick told me that Swifty had contacted him a few weeks prior and wanted to sell him some walnut logs. Dick agreed to meet Swifty at the "timber property" to look at the logs. While there, Dick said that he agreed to purchase the logs and marked them with yellow paint. I asked Dick how many logs he had purchsed. He said there were about 12 walnut logs. Dick and Swifty came to an agreement. Dick prepaid Swifty $1,000 for the cut logs and Swifty would deliver them to Dick's business. Dick said that he would pay Swifty the remainder of the log value upon delivery. I asked Dick who had purchased the trees from the timber property owner. That would be the person who is required to have the timber buyer's license. He told me that Swifty had purchased the trees. I advised Dick that Swifty did not have a timber buyer's license. Dick told me that he had questioned Swifty about having a license. Dick advised that Swifty had reassured him he was legal. Dick sprung on me that he believed that the same logs had been sold to a third timber buyer (Harry) as well. Dick told me that he originally met Swifty through Harry. Dick did not have any more details about Harry's purchase of the logs.

I told Dick that I heard there was a backhoe involved in this whole ordeal. Dick told me that he had sold a truck, trailer and backhoe to Swifty. Dick had let Swifty take the equipment without paying for it. Dick said that when everything started to "go south", he told Swifty to return the truck, trailer and backhoe.

Swifty promptly returned the truck and trailer, but claimed that he was too sick to return the backhoe. Swifty told Dick that he would return the backhoe the following day. Weeks later, Dick said that Swifty still has not returned his backhoe. Dick told me that he heard Swifty had sold it. I asked Dick if he knew who had purchased the backhoe. Dick said that he was not sure, but that Harry had been involved in the sale and would know the buyer. Dick said that when he questioned Harry about Swifty, he learned that the backoe had been sold. Dick said that that's when Harry told him he had purchased the same logs and Tom and Dick. I asked Dick if he knew how much Harry had paid Swifty for the logs. Dick said that Harry had reportedly paid Swifty $1,200 for the logs. I got a statement from Dick and asked him to get me copies of any paperwork between him and Swifty. He agreed.

Leaving the office, I drove to Loaner's house. Loaner runs his businesses out of his residence. As I pulled into Loaner's driveway, I saw a small pile of yellow pained walnut logs. Loaner wasn't home, so I called him. After telling Loaner that I needed to talk with him about Swifty, he agreed to drive home and meet me.

Meeting with Loaner, he confirmed that the logs next to his driveway had come from the timber property. I asked Loaner how he had gotten the logs. Loaner said that he was trying to help Swifty. He told me that he had taken them to Tom's, but that Tom had refused to buy them. Loaner said that he didn't know what to do with the logs, so he put them in his yard. I asked Loaner why Swifty did not take the logs to Tom's. Loaner said that Swifty had court. I asked Loaner how he got the logs to begin with. Loaner told me that Swifty had loaded them onto the trailer the night before and dropped them off. I asked Loaner if he purchased the logs. He quickly said he had nothing to do with the purchase. Loaner said that Swifty bought the trees.

I asked Loaner how he was connected to Swifty. Loaner said that he met Swifty about a year ago. Loaner told me that he was trying to "mentor" Swifty. He said that he was not doing a very good job. Loaner told me that he had invested over $10,000 in helping Swifty. Loaner said that he posted $10,000 in bond for Swifty to get him out of jail. He said that Swifty failed to show up for court and his money was forfeited. Loaner proceeded to tell me that besides the money, Swifty had been using his business name to obtain work (without Loaner's permission). Loaner said that he had started getting complaints from people about his business. Swifty had secured some contracts, gotten paid from the customers and never completed the work. Loaner said that Swifty was hurting his business. Loaner ended up giving me a copy of a contract that Swifty had signed with a guy named Walt (short for walnut). Under Loaner's business name, Swifty had agreed to cut some walnut trees for Walt and replace them with another tree. Swifty cut and took the walnut trees, but never finished the job. Before I left Loaner's house, I asked him where the missing backhoe had been taken to. He told me that Harry would know where it went. I took pictures of the logs and asked Loaner to write me a statement. He agreed.

The next day, I drove to the timber property owner's house. Yes, this is where the logs were originally harvested from (and sold 2x from). I met with the son of the property owner (Sam) and asked him what had happened. Sam said that his mom had listed some furniture and walnuts for sale on Craigslist. Shortly thereafter, Swifty contacted Sam's mom and offered to buy some of their walnut trees. Sam's mom and Swifty came to an agreement on price. I asked Sam if his mom and Swifty had a contract. Sam said that they did and was able to provide me with a copy. I asked Sam if the trees had been removed from their property. He said they had. I asked Sam if his mom had been paid. He said she had not.

The question you always must ask while investigating timber buyers is whether (or not) the buyer purchased any trees from their neighbors. Sam said that Swifty had bought some from two of his neighbors. I toured Sam's property, took pictures and counted stumps. Although Sam said that there had been 31 logs stacked on their property, I could only find seven walnut tree stumps. Some of the trees were likely cut into several logs. Some of the stumps were likely covered by fallen treetops. Before I left Sam's, I got the names of two of Swifty's helpers (Shady and Shooter). Sam and his mom agreed to write me statements about the purchase.

Leaving Sam's, I met with his neighbors. One neighbor had a contract with Swifty and sold a few trees to him. He said that he was never paid for the trees. While Swifty was there, the neighbor said that he had also loaned a heavy-duty rope to him. The neighbor made sure to tell me that Swifty had never returned the rope. The other neighbor sold Swifty a large walnut tree and agreed to split the profit. It's not uncommon to sell trees that way. The tree was removed, but the neighbor was never paid his half.

Three days later, I received a call from Harry. Harry told me that he felt like he had been set up by both Loaner and Swifty. Harry said that after he looked at the walnut logs (at Sam's house) he paid Swifty $1,200 for them. He said Loaner was supposed to deliver the logs to him a couple days later. Harry told me that Loaner had called him three times, but never showed up with the logs. I asked Harry where Dick's backhoe had ended up. Harry told me that Swifty had sold Dick's backhoe to a guy named "Lucky". I told Harry that I needed to meet with him and Lucky. We agreed to meet the following week.

In the meantime, I figured I would call Loaner and see if he had gotten the statement done. He agreed that he had it done. Loaner asked if I could get it from him in person. Loaner said that he had some more stuff to tell me. It was a good decision for Loaner, since other people had starting to implicate him. We agreed to meet the following morning. I was really looking forward to hearing what Loaner had to say.

The next day, I met with Loaner at his house. We sat down at the table together. Loaner proceeded to tell me that Swifty had scammed him out of more than $27,000 over the last two years. Loaner said that Swifty claimed to have won a $10.6 million lawsuit settlement. Loaner said that Swifty had been borrowing money from him against the settlement. He said that once he started giving Swifty small loans, he had a hard time cutting his losses. Loaner said that although he was suspicious of Swifty, he was afraid to cut Swifty completely off. Loaner said that he was afraid that he would never see his money again (the money he had already loaned to Swifty). He said that Swifty would make him feel both physically and mentally guilty if he did not help him. So, Loaner just kept giving Swifty money and the hole just kept getting bigger. I asked Loaner what Swifty's "settlement" was for. Loaner told me that Swifty was reportedly having sex with his girlfriend when something went wrong. Loaner said that Swifty ended up having an operation on his penis. The operation did not go right and Swifty had won a giant settlement against the doctor.

Loaner told me that Swifty was very good at being believable. Loaner said that Swifty had set up meetings with him to look at $400,000 houses (for after he had gotten the settlement). While touring the houses, Loaner said that Swifty made a deal with the realtor. He said that Swifty was able to get the realtor to pay him in advance for tree and landscaping work that Swifty never completed. Loaner told me that there were others who had been swindled by Swifty, but he was not sure of their names. Loaner agreed to try to get me more information about the other victims.

The following day, I met with Lucky about the backhoe that he had purchased from Swifty. He told me that Swifty had sold it to him for $4,000. Lucky said that he never got a bill of sale for it from Swifty I told Lucky not to let the backhoe go missing. Lucky agreed and gave me a written statement. I took pictures of the backhoe. Later in the investigation, Dick was able to produce bills of sale for when he both purchased the backhoe and sold it to Swifty.

Leaving the backhoe, I decided to see if Walt was home. Arriving at his house, I was able to meet with both Walt and his wife. We sat down on the deck and had a conversation about Swifty. Walt agreed that Swifty had portrayed himself as working for Loaner. Swifty and Walt had two contracts. One was to cut the walnut trees down and the other was to replace them with quality hickory trees. Swifty got to keep the walnut trees for cutting them down and was paid $1,850 to replace them with the new trees. Upon completion of the job, Swifty was to get another $650. Walt said that Swifty never completed the work. After Swifty sold the walnut trees, he didn't clean up the treetops, fill in the ruts or show up to plant the new trees. I asked Walt who Swifty sold the walnut trees to. Walt said that Harry had come to the property and purchased the trees from Swifty. I got statements and copies of the contracts from Walt.

Over the next week or so, I rounded up some more paperwork, completed reports and met with the timber property owner. Toward the end of the week, I met with Harry. Harry confirmed that he had paid Swifty $1,200 for the logs on the timber property. I asked Harry if he had gone and looked at the logs first. Harry said that he had. He said that when he went to the timber property, he met with Swifty. Harry said that Swifty told him he had purchased the property and wanted to sell the logs. Harry confirmed that the logs were never delivered to him. I asked Harry about purchasing Walt's logs. Harry agreed that he had purchased Walt's logs from Swifty for $2,000. Harry said that the payment on those logs was actually made to Loaner. Leaving Harry, I met with Tom in person. We went through his paperwork, got statements and made copies of what he had. I figured that I needed to start reining in some of the loose ends. What a tangled mess!

As I was starting to understand the gravity of what Swifty was doing, I decided to check local court records to see if Swifty had any civil cases pending. Sure enough, earlier in the year, a lady (who we will call "Ma") filed a small claims suit against Swifty. I drove to Ma's house and was able to meet with her. After introducing myself, I asked Ma if she was familiar with Swifty. She confirmed that she was and said that Swifty owes her over $14,000. I asked Ma to elaborate. Ma told me that she met Swifty when she sold him an $8 insurance policy. Not sure what she meant, I asked Ma if the insurance policy cost Swifty $8. She confirmed that it had. Ma indicated that she should have known better when she had to hound Swifty to get the $8.

Ma proceeded to tell me that she felt like Swifty had played on her and her husband's parental instincts. She said that they had never had children. Ma told me that Swifty started calling her "Mom" and her husband "Dad". Ma said that Swifty had swindled them. Ma proceeded to tell me that they had paid Swifty to do roof and septic work on their house. She said that although they had paid him, Swifty never completed the work. In fact, he never even started it. Ma went on to tell me about giving Swifty money to get a wire transfer. Swifty had told Ma about his settlement. He told her that he needed money to get the settlement transferred to him. Because she would get repaid with "interest", Ma loaned Swifty the money. The only money Swifty got that day was from Ma. Ma said she had helped Swifty try to buy a truck and ended up having to return it when Swifty could not pay for it. Ma told me that it had been really hard on her and Dad's marriage. She said that her and Dad would fight about the money they had given to Swifty and the stuff that still needed to be fixed on their house. Ma said she had filed a police report about Swifty with the Silvis Police Department. She said Swifty had not been charged so she ended up filing a small claims complaint against him. I told Ma that I wanted to get a copy of the police report and would be in touch. Ma thanked me. Leaving Ma's, I confirmed her account with Silvis P.D. and got a copy of their report.

A few days later, I went to Shady's house. Shady invited me inside to sit at the table with him. When we sat down, I asked Shady how he knew Swifty. Shady told me that he had kids with Swifty's sister. Shady said that he occasionally worked for Swifty. Shady told me that Swifty owed him $1,000 for tree cutting jobs. I asked Shady what his rate of pay was. He told me they had agreed on $20 an hour. Shady told me that he had helped Swifty on the timber property harvest. He said they had harvested about 13 logs from the property. He went on to say that Swifty had left some paperwork in his truck one time. Shady said that he looked at the paperwork and found the receipt where Swifty had used Loaner's business name to get the job at Walt's. He said that he was the one who had given the receipt to Loaner and made him aware of what Swifty was doing. When I asked Shady about Swifty's money and payments, he always claimed to have no knowledge. He did, however, keep mentioning Swifty's girlfriend. So I got her name and location from Shady.

I asked Shady if he knew about Swifty's lawsuit. Shady told me that Swifty was awaiting a settlement from a penis surgery. I asked Shady if Swifty had ever really had a penis surgery. Shady told me that he was at the house when Swifty "fractured his penis". Shady told me that Swifty was having sex with his girlfriend when the accident happened. Shady said that Swifty showed him his penis. Shady said that it had swelled up and was "huge". Shady told me that Swifty had surgery on his penis and ended up with 62 stitches in it. Shady said that Swifty showed him his penis after the surgery. He said that it looked like a porcupine. I asked Shady how long ago the accident had happened. He said it had been a couple of years. I asked Shady if he knew who Swifty's doctor was. Shady said it was Dr. Littleguy (okay, maybe that's not the real name). I was also able to get Swifty's lawyer's name (Justice) from Shady.

Over the next week or so, I contacted both Dr. Littleguy and Justice. Dr. Littleguy's attorney told me that Swifty had never filed a lawsuit against Dr. Littleguy. Obviously, there was not any sort of a settlement pending. In talking with Justice, he agreed that he was familiar with Swifty. He told me that he had not represented Swifty in a malpractice lawsuit. He did say that Swifty had failed to pay him for representation in another case.

After chasing down more paperwork over the next ten days, I drove to Swifty's girlfriend's house (I will call her Mary). Parking out front, I was able to meet with Mary. I asked Mary if she was Swifty's girlfriend. She advised that she was Swifty's ex-girlfriend. As we started to talk, a truck pulled up next to mine. A guy identified as Swifty's brother (Bob) stepped out. I was introduced to Bob and explained what I was investigating. Bob immediately told me that Swifty is a "conman". Mary said that Swifty owed her $6,000. Bob said that Swifty owed him about $300. I asked Bob and Mary if Swifty had ever held a "real" job. They said that Swifty is almost always "self-employed". Both agreed that Swifty lied all the time. They said that Swifty had a different vehicle every week. Mary said that she had to return two vehicles to people when Swift failed to pay for them. She told me that the last one was a truck that she had to return to 'Sara".

I asked Bob and Mary if they knew about Swifty's penis surgery settlement. Both agreed that they did. They told me that Swifty did have the surgery. They said that they call Swifty Mr. 27". Bob said that Swifty changed his "pay out" date all the time. He said that Swifty always claimed to be getting paid on the 27th. Bob said that when the 27th arrived, Swifty just changed it to the 27th of the following month. Bob told me that Swifty had been conning people his entire life.

After four months, I thought I had the investigation to where we could prosecute Swifty. Just as I was getting ready to turn the case over to the Rock Island County State's Attorney's office, Sara got a hold of me and requested to be added to the list of complainants. Meeting with Sara, she said that she had been swindled out of about $2,000 by Swifty. Sara told me that she met Swifty when he ran into her Buick. Sara said that Swifty wanted to pay for the damage out of his pocket. They came to an agreement, but Swifty never paid to fix the vehicle. Over the course of time, Swifty worked his way into renting one of Sara's trucks from her. While Swifty was driving the truck, Sara paid him almost $500 to fix a shock pump. Needless to say, Swifty never fixed the pump. Hard to believe, but Swifty got paid to drive Sara's truck!

Swifty refused to ever meet with me. I don't know if I could ever totally complete an investigation of him. Faster than I could chase down leads, Swifty was swindling the next person. In October of that year, the final case report was turned over to the state's attorney's office. You would think that with that many complainants they would be chomping at the bit to prosecute. Not so much. They filed several charges, but ended up pleading the case to a felony timber theft charge. You could tell that Swifty's attorney thought that he had pulled the wool over the eyes of the court. I was thinking that he had too when the Assistant State's Attorney (ASA) told me that I should not expect much of a penalty. They said that Swifty was getting one of the judges who tended to be very lenient.

At sentencing, I had to testify. Ma wanted to, but was not allowed to by the ASA. I think the Judge actually read my entire report between the plea and sentencing (about 100 pages). The Judge ripped Swifty's ass! He told Swifty that he was just a conman. The Judge was seriously mad as he tore into Swifty. When the Judge was complete, he told Swifty that he was being sentenced to three years in prison with one year of supervised released (afterward). Swifty was ordered to pay restitution and a $1,000 fine. The Judge told Swifty that he was to be immediately remanded to custody. That is almost unheard of. Usually, the person gets 30 days to get their affairs in order. After the Judge cooled down (about a week later), he ended up giving Swifty the standard 30 days before going to jail. The big thing was Swifty getting sentenced to three years in prison. The ASA was surprised to say the least.

How did the rest of it play out? Dick never got his backhoe returned. Lucky got lucky. The ASA simply told Dick that he had made a bad business decision. I don't believe that Dick or Harry ever saw the money that they paid for the logs (the ones they never received). I think Loaner helped Walt with his yard and the trees. Ma and Dad were never reimbursed. But last I heard Dad was repairing the house himself. I'm sure that Swifty's brother and ex-girlfriend never saw their money. Loaner just had to write off his losses. I never heard, but am sure that Swifty's old attorney and Sara were never paid. I do think that Sam and his mom were paid for the trees that Swifty had taken from them.

It's amazing to see how Swifty was able to leverage a fake lawsuit "payout" to get money from people. I felt sorry for all the different people that he swindled, especially the people that didn't have any "extra" money. All the people (but especially the ones who bought into the penis lawsuit) must look in the mirror. For many of them, their own greed is what allowed them to be played. In fact, when you look past the schemes, that's what Swifty used against nearly all his victims—their own greed. He would leverage a larger future payout for something minor today. The people who got swindled, thought that they would get Swifty in the end. Instead, Swifty got them in the present!

THE MAFIA

Yes, you read the title right. Growing up in Peotone, Illinois, I spent nearly every day running around the little town until I went to college. About 60 miles south of Chicago, Peotone was not a hot bed for Mafia activity. That said, one of the traditional areas for mafia activity in Chicagoland was always the near south side. Peotone was likely a little far south for the continuous activity, but it was always said that Mafia-related activities had regularly occurred as far south as Kankakee.

Peotone's underground claim to "Mafia fame" is a place that we used to call Capone's. Capone's was built in 1929 as Miami Gardens. The business was important at one point to the Peotone community. In fact, my dad would occasionally talk about Miami Gardens and show us an original menu he had from there. As Peotone lore would have it, the business was built by the mafia and was supposed to be a very fancy "speak easy". We were told that there was an underground garage beneath the business. It was said that Capone could pull his car directly into the basement and park out of sight. We were also told that there were bedrooms on the second floor that Capone and his henchmen could use with their ladies.

By the time I was old enough to be getting into trouble (likely about 12), Capone's had been shut down. The doors were closed and there was not a functioning business at that location. Around the same time, my best friend growing up (Bret Jerkatis) got us permission to go camping out on Lewis' property. I don't have enough paper to tell you all the stories about me and Bret. What I will say is that no matter whatever happened in life, I could always trust Bret to have my back. Bret and I spent 80 percent of our time doing things outdoors. From hockey on ponds to fishing to camping, you name it. Lewis' property was about four miles south of Peotone. On their property, they had a stand of mature white pines. We had a camp in the pines where we made a lean-to and had a fire pit. There was not a house for about a mile around us, so we were always on top of the world when we were hanging out at our camp.

When preparing to hike out to our camp, we would stage from Bret's house. After we rounded up all our supplies, we would walk to the abandoned railroad tracks south of town. Following the tracks took us southeast to Rock Creek, which took us south to the pines. After you got to the creek, if you took a right turn, you were at Capone's. Of course, we were great explorers and not afraid of anything—that we would admit to. So, as we were hiking on one of our trips, we got to talking about Capone's. We talked about all the Peotone lore and how the place was now abandoned (or at least shut down). Since it was just a small detour out of our way, we decided to go have a "look". When we got there, we found that there was the main building and a small house behind it. Since the door on the small house was wide open, we looked inside. It was nothing but an abandoned dirty little house. There was no grand Capone picture on the wall or anything.

Walking around the main building, there was a basement window that was missing. You know, if you are 12 and there is a missing window, you are required to see what is on the other side of the hole. After looking through the window, we somehow ended up on the inside of the old Miami Gardens. As a kid, I felt like Geraldo. I was going to find Capone's Peotone vault. Carefully walking through the building, we didn't find any Capone artifacts. We did find where you could literally drive down into the basement. The ramp leading from the rear garage door was narrow and could likely only handle a small car. There were bedrooms upstairs and what was likely a beautiful business 50 years earlier on the main floor. We left the building as we found it and continued on our journey. Capone's was reopened some years later as Edwin's. The times I went there after it reopened as Edwin's, I was able to sit at the bar with my dad. Somehow, it didn't seem as interesting at 21 as it was at 12.

Moving ahead to October of 1998, I was working between Crete, Illinois, and the Indiana State line. This part of Will County is "water-poor". There are some ponds and creeks, but very little good waterfowl hunting habitat. The people that do have water generally have decent duck hunting. Quite simply, if a duck wants to sit in the water, they don't have many choices on where to go. One creek in this area travels through Batterman property. On the property, the creek has a few wide bends and two duck blinds within 100 yards of each other. Just as the ducks compete for water, so do the duck hunters.

As I completed my check of the guys in the south blind, I asked if there was anyone hunting the north blind. They told me that they had seen one guy up there. Walking up to the north blind, I found one guy hunting in the blind (Anthony). After introducing myself to Anthony, I checked his gun and licenses. Everything seemed to be in order except that Anthony wanted me to leave. As a game warden, this is not abnormal, but Anthony really wanted me to go. Walking from the blind over to the edge of the creek, I found there was corn lying on the mud bank. As I further inspected the area, Anthony had corn halfway around his blind. From the air, it likely looked like half a Cheerio. Questioning Anthony about the corn, he initially said he did not know it was there. Pressing him, Anthony eventually admitted that his friend had put it out a few days earlier. As I continued to question Anthony, he suddenly could not remember much about his friend or when he had been there. It was not alarming, but unusual.

I told Anthony that he would be receiving a citation for hunting ducks with the use or aid of bait. Anthony argued a little and asked me if I was "Petreikis". You always hate to hear that because you know that they are going to ask you for a favor. What made matters worse was that he actually pronounced my name correctly! I told Anthony that I was Petreikis. Anthony asked if I knew Joe Petreikis. I told him that I knew a couple of Joes. I have an Uncle Joe and a second cousin (my dad's cousin) named Joe. Anthony confirmed that he was talking about Joe from southern Illinois (dad's cousin). Having hunted in southern Illinois many times, we (my dad, brothers and I) had hung out with Joe at his tavern on a couple of occasions. Joe always treated me and my brothers like he was our long-lost uncle. He was always happy to see us and treated us like gold. He was the perfect guy to be a tavern owner, everybody liked Joe. When I told Anthony that I knew Joe, he said that they were good friends and I should give him a break. I told Anthony that I did not give breaks for duck bait. Anthony got visibly frustrated as he continued to badger me about getting a break. I always hated being in that position, but stuck to my guns and issued Anthony a citation. As I left, I figured that I would likely not see Joe for a long time anyway. I had stopped hunting in southern Illinois and Joe didn't come up north very often anymore. Joe would forget about it before I would see him again, right?

It was a long workday, and I did not make it home until after dark. After I got out of my uniform, I checked to see if there were any mew messages on the answering machine. Pushing the button, I was greeted by Cousin Joe. Even though he lived in southern Illinois now, Joe still had the south Chicago accent. Joe said, "Tony, this is your cousin Joe. I heard you wrote my friend Anthony a ticket. Give me a call," and he left his number. I had received my share of badgering for the day and didn't feel like getting it again, so I didn't call Joe back. Though I felt guilty, I knew I wasn't going to see Joe any time soon anyway.

In the spring of that year I had taken up turkey hunting. After a tough hunt, I finally harvested my first bird on the last day of the season. Excited, I took it to my parents' house and showed it to my dad. My dad was the one who had gotten me to love hunting, so I knew he would think it was neat too. We talked about it during the year and I convinced dad to hunt with me the next year. I had killed my bird on a small state site and knew we would not be able to draw two tags together there. Dad suggested hunting in southern Illinois since we knew the area. I agreed and we put in for tags in the Shawnee National Forest (Pope County). In about January, the tags came in and we were excited to head south. Dad told me that we could stay at Cousin Joe's trailer. My heart sank. I had to explain to dad the arrest of Anthony and the call that I didn't return to Joe. Dad blew it off and told me that Joe wouldn't care. Then he told me it would be a lot cheaper and Joe would likely cook breakfast for us. Money and food, I agreed.

Arriving at Joe's trailer, we parked, and I let dad lead us in. I was thinking that Joe may have forgotten my failure to return his call. What the heck, it was seven months later. Walking in, Joe greeted us as always and my hopes soared. Then he said, "Tony, Tony, Tony, why didn't you call me back?" I shook my head and told him that I just didn't want to get a hard time for writing the ticket. Joe said, "Tony, maybe you don't know it, but Anthony is connected." He proceeded to tell me that Anthony was in the mob and he knew him from the "south side". If I was not wide-eyed yet, I was when he said, "Anthony was mad, he wanted to put a hit out on ya." I said, "My God Joe, if you would have left that on the answering machine, I would have called you back!" He likely could tell that I was a little anxious. Joe told me not to worry about it. He said that he told Anthony that I was just doing my job. He quickly moved on to some other subject and did not revisit Anthony with me. Joe passed away a few years later. I look back now and wish I had taken the time to ask Joe about the Mafia. I don't know how much he would have told me, but have regretted not taking the time to ask.

That summer, my oldest son (Garrett) was about six months old. He liked to go for walks in the stroller. When I made it about 10 blocks from the house, Garrett would fall asleep and I was ready for a break. I decided I would stop at the Peotone Library while he was sleeping and look at the real old Peotone Vedettes. The Vedette was the local newspaper and had been in Peotone for a very long time—almost as long as my family. I had relatives in the Peotone area as early as the mid-1800s. The old Vedettes were stored on microfish, so I would sit and look at them while Garrett was sleeping. In one of the old Vedettes, my great great great uncle Fred Deininger recalled working out in the country when a big sedan pulled up. He said that the passenger in the rear of the car called him over and asked for directions. Fred assisted the man. When Fred later made it to the post office, he realized that he had given directions to John Dillinger. Dillinger's photo was on the Post Office board.

Where's Croatia?

In September of 2000, I located several baited deer stands northeast of Balmoral Park (near Crete, IL.). Two of the stands were behind a house on a dead-end road. Both of the dead-end stands had corn piles below them and appeared to be set up for archery hunting. Since they were only about 40 yards behind the residence, I knew I would have to be conscious of where I parked and being seen during my approach to the hunters. The other baited stands that I had found in the area were a few miles away. When you find a baited stand prior to opening day, it's kind of like being a kid at Christmas. The poacher looks forward to hunting on opening morning and I always looked forward to catching them poaching. I never had trouble getting up early when I knew that I had a good bait case to make.

That year just happened to contain the final hunting season that my first sergeant (Fred Mathis) was going to work. He was scheduled to retire early the next year. When I got out of the police academy, Fred was kind of hard on me. After a few years, I think Fred figured out that I really just wanted to catch "bad guys". From that point on, Fred didn't ride my back so much. Although he was not my favorite sergeant, I learned an awful lot from Fred. Fred had two real good traits as a supervisor, he would answer his phone and was willing to help. That year in particular, Fred offered to help several times. I had a feeling that Fred wanted to be in the mix of things for his "last hurrah". I didn't really need help with the baited stands, but figured if Fred was willing to drive me from spot to spot, I would be able to cover more baited stands faster. If I had to park and walk to each stand, I would likely have spent several hours walking. Instead, Fred could just stop on the side of the road and drop me off close to the stands. I didn't have to worry about having someone see my squad and I could approach the baited stands from the best possible avenues.

When we got to the dead-end stands, Fred dropped me off on the roadside. I cut east through the timber, crossed a fence and located two guys (Milo and Davo) hunting in the dead-end stands. Having them get down out of the stands, I walked with them up to the driveway. Fred and I wrote them tickets for hunting with the use or aid of bait and went on our way. It was a cut-and-dried case. Fred retired the next year. He and his wife sold a bunch of stuff and retired on a big sailboat in the Gulf.

In December of 2004, I got a call from one of the people that lived on the dead end (I will call them Janet). Janet told me that Milo was still hunting the same property. I told Janet that I was familiar with Milo and explained that I had arrested him a few years earlier for deer bait. Janet said that Milo was now hunting after hours. I asked her how she knew. Janet said that Milo's van was parked in the driveway of the "40-yard house" on moonlit nights when there was snow. She said that the van would stay there real late, but only on those nights.

That is a lot of speculation tied into specific variables. With that said, I was very familiar with Janet. I had arrested her for poaching deer twice and she had become a very good informant. If Janet told me that Milo was poaching, he was poaching. The snow had all but melted and I didn't want to "bust" the information by driving up and down the dead-end road in my squad. I asked Janet if she would be willing to call me when she saw Milo's van parked in the driveway. Janet agreed. Janet told me that it might be awhile, but expected me to come when she called. I told her I would be there.

Sure enough, in the beginning of January, I got a call from Janet at about 5:00 p.m. I was not working at the time. Janet told me that Milo was out hunting and would likely be there long after legal hunting hours. Climbing into my uniform, I headed toward Crete. By the time I got to the area, it was already pushing 5:45 p.m. If Milo was still in the stand, he would be hunting nearly an hour after legal hunting hours. Since it was dark and very cold, I decided to park about half a mile from Milo's stand. When I got out of my squad, I realized how cold it was. My ears literally started hurting by the time I was only 100 yards from my squad. I even started to question Janet's information. I can remember thinking, "Who the hell would sit in the dark when it's this could?" About the time my whole body was cold, I had reached the entrance to the driveway. Looking up the driveway, I could see Milo's van parked next to the timber. At least it gave me something to think about other than how cold I was. The driveway was partially covered in crystalized snow, so it was hard to sneak quietly toward Milo's van. Doing the best I could, I passed the van and continued down a path toward the deer stand. Throughout my career, I almost never used my flashlight while walking in the dark. If I was in the woods, I would usually walk with one of my hands in front of my face (so I wouldn't catch a branch in the eye). I always figured that the flashlight would give my position away to someone who was looking for me. When I got to the tree that I remembered Milo's stand being in, I turned on my flashlight. There was Milo standing in the tree looking at me. Milo had an arrow nocked on his bow. In Illinois, that means you are hunting. I had Milo get down and seized his hunting equipment. Milo didn't act like the cold was bothering him at all, but I couldn't wait to get back to my squad. Reaching my truck, I swear it took 10 minutes to start kicking out heat again. I drove back to Milo and issued him a citation for hunting after hours. Milo was eventually found guilty and had to forfeit his hunting equipment.

When I left Milo on the night that I arrested him, I called Janet and told her that I had made the arrest. Janet was happy and said that maybe the landowner would finally kick Milo off the property. I told Janet that I didn't want to get in the middle of someone losing a place to hunt. Janet told me that the property owner had wanted to kick Milo off the property for a long time, but was afraid to do it. I told Janet that was kind of crazy and asked what she was afraid of. Janet told me that Milo is in the Croatian Mafia and is not a good guy. I told Janet that it would have been nice if she had told me that. Of course, she thought that she had.

With everything going on near Chicago, who ever heard of the Croatian Mafia? Not me, not until Milo. I still don't know if there's actually a Croatian Mafia in Chicagoland. No matter, I never treated anybody any different than anyone else—no matter their affiliation. I didn't "try" to catch anyone "connected" to anything. I would guess that over the years I helped as many "connected" people as I arrested. I can also say that nobody ever actually told me (themselves) that they were "connected".

TICK TACK DOE

When I was trying to catch deer poachers, I often felt like I was playing a game. I was always looking for a new way to stay one move ahead of my opponent. Although I could win the game at hand, there were always hundreds of games going on that I didn't even know about. Think about how many times you have been speeding without being caught. Then think about how many police officers there are. Although "percentage wise" there are fewer hunters than speeders, there are also fewer game wardens than regular police officers. We really don't scratch the surface of what is going on.

As I decided which cases to write about here, I looked for ones where the game got interesting. This case is one where I had to make the final move to get the "win". This case occurred in October of 1998 near Crete, Illinois. The Crete and University Park area is a beautiful part of Will County. There are creeks, ditches and a fair amount of timber in and around the local Will County Forest Preserve properties. People built their homes all around the preserves, which makes for an interesting "game wardening dynamic".

In this section of Crete, the nature preserve has a narrow strip of land between two rows of houses. One of the residents

(Florence) had property that bordered the nature preserve along her rear property line. I am guessing that Florence was about 65 years old at the time. She reminded me of a female Indiana Jones. You could tell that she was adventurous and liked to be in the mix of whatever was going on. Heck, she even kind of dressed like Dr. Jones.

Like most people, Florence enjoyed living on the edge of the timber and having the deer come visit her yard. One of her neighbors had been treating the preserve as if it was a continuation of his own property. Florence saw the neighbor wearing full camouflage while sneaking through the timber behind her house. She said that the guy appeared to be deer hunting in the nature preserve. This was a common problem, but was difficult to fix. When a person can sneak into a nature preserve, right out of their back door, it is hard to catch them. To make matters worse, there was not a good place to hide my squad within a mile of where the guy was poaching.

Over a couple weeks' time frame, Florence figured out that the poacher was primarily hunting on weekend mornings. As the next Saturday approached, I needed to decide what was going to be the best way to catch him. I could either "spot-check" the location or do a "walk-in". If I spot-checked it, I would park someplace close and check it as quickly as possible. I would need to be in the woods before the poacher could get out of them. If I did a walk-in, I would hide my squad about a mile away and try to walk to the woods without being detected. After checking the woods, I would have to walk back to my squad. With my list of other illegal stands growing, I decided not to tie myself down at this location. I would do a spot check. Although they are not my preferred method, I knew it would work if I played my cards right.

At about 6:45 a.m. on Halloween morning, I parked my squad next to the nature preserve on Western Avenue. It was not what I would consider to be an ideal location. Everybody who

136

drove down Western Avenue could see my squad. But with the preserve being such a narrow strip of land, I figured that I could check it quickly and be out of the preserve in less than 20 minutes. Hopefully the poacher would be hunting and not driving down Western Avenue!

I had my backpack ready. When I parked my squad, I grabbed it and hurried down into the nature preserve. Slowly sneaking through the woods, I realized that the timber was a little wider than I had originally thought it was. Just like still hunting, I would walk a little way, stop and look around. When I was about 100 yards into the woods, I heard a shotgun blast behind me. It sounded like a shotgun loaded with a slug. There was only one shot and everything was quiet. Having hunted my entire life, I figured that the shot was about 300 yards away. That would put it inside a block of private property on the other side of Western Avenue. I had set myself up to check the preserve, so I was hesitant to go back and cross the road. After all, it could just be somebody target practicing. I didn't hear any more shots for a couple of minutes and thought, "Who would shoot a single shotgun slug at 7 a.m. on a Saturday morning?" My only good answer was, "A deer poacher." With firearm deer season still a couple of weeks away, I knew that if I caught somebody poaching a deer out of season, it would be a real good arrest. Maybe even better than catching somebody in the nature preserve.

Abandoning the nature preserve, I headed toward the gunshot. When I got back to Western Avenue, I could see a driveway on the other side. It was just north of me and went back into the private property. I would be paralleling the driveway as I walked across the road and into the timber. When I crossed the road, I looked toward the driveway and could see an SUV sitting just inside of the entrance. I pulled up my binoculars and looked at it. There wasn't anybody inside of it. The SUV looked like it had recently been parked there. Continuing into the timber, I made my way to where I thought the gunshot had come from. I couldn't find a deer stand, a hunter or a dead deer. There wasn't even a place for somebody to be target practicing. I did a couple of small circles and still didn't find anything.

Second guessing my decision to leave the nature preserve, I headed back toward Western Avenue. When I exited the timber, I came out next to the parked SUV. I figured that I may as well look inside. When I looked in the back window, I could see an empty 50-pound bag of feed corn. Next to the bag was a bow and arrow case. That instantly changed my resolve. I would be going back into the timber until I found either a guy hunting over bait or a dead deer.

Walking back into the timber, I figured that I would go further than I had the first time. Not 30 yards past where I had done my small circles, I located a dead doe. There wasn't anybody around it. It had been about 45 minutes since I heard the gun shot. I walked over to the doe and knelt next to her. There was a shotgun slug hole in her right front shoulder. The body was warm and there was fresh blood all over the side of the deer. It had obviously been hit good and likely wouldn't have run very far. I was kind of surprised that whoever had shot her had not already recovered her.

Backing off to a nearby tree, I found a spot to hide. I decided that I would just wait for the poacher to come and get his deer. After about 10 minutes, I was starting to get antsy. I couldn't believe that I wasn't at least hearing somebody who was looking for the doe. Then I thought, "What if the poacher had seen my squad parked along Western Avenue?" If he had walked back to that parked SUV, he might have seen it down the road.

I really didn't want to leave the dead deer in order to move my squad, so I decided to try calling Laura. Without a phone (we didn't have any back then), I had to call the Illinois State Police (ISP) on my portable radio. Thank goodness I was only 200 yards from my squad. Much further than that, and my radio would not have worked. Since anybody could monitor our radio frequencies, I didn't say why I needed my squad moved. ISP was able to get a hold of Laura and she was en route. Grabbing my spare keys, Laura drove to Florence's house. Florence gave her a ride over to my squad and dropped her off. After about a half hour, Laura had my squad moved.

Within five minutes of Laura moving my squad, I began to hear voices. As the voices got closer, I could hear two subjects (John and Wayne) talking about blood spots and tracking a deer. One of the subjects said, "There it is!" As I laid down behind a tree, the subjects came into view. I realized that I had picked a tree that was way too close to the deer. Hunkering down, I watched as John walked over to the deer and started looking at it. Wayne continued past the deer and walked directly toward me. He obviously knew something was up.

When Wayne spotted me, I stood up and identified myself to the subjects. I asked them who shot the deer. They looked at the deer and told me that they didn't shoot "that" deer. John said that he had shot "a" deer. He said that this one didn't look like the one that he had shot. John told me that "his deer" was bigger. I told John that we could follow the blood trail to his stand. John quickly admitted that it must be the one that he had shot. I told John that I had heard him shoot the deer. I said that it was obviously shot with a shotgun. John said that he had heard the shotgun blast too. John said that it was on the neighboring property to the east. John told me that if "this deer" was shot with a gun, then it was not his. John started rambling about the problems that he had with his neighbors. John said that it might have been shot already when it came in front of his stand. John and his brother went on to profess that they only hunted with bows. After a few minutes of arguing about it, I asked John for his hunting license and deer permit. John told me that it was in his car. I asked John if his car was the SUV parked along the driveway. He said that it was. I asked John where his deer stand was. Both subjects said that it was "over here" and began to walk to the north. I told Wayne that my questions were only for John. Wayne said that he understood and needed to make some phone calls. As Wayne walked toward the house, I called ISP and asked them to have Laura pull my squad up to the house.

While I walked with John over to the stand, I tracked the blood on the ground. It led from the doe over to a spot near John's stand. As I got close to the stand, I could not find any more blood. I asked John if he shot the doe out of that stand. He said that he had. I asked him where the corn was located. John pointed at the fence that was about 10 yards away. I told John that I would need to see the corn. John led me over to a big pile of cracked corn. I took a sample of it as evidence. As we walked and talked, John continued to profess that he was just an archery hunter.

Returning to the doe with John, I helped him carry her down a trail that went to the house. When we reached the trail entrance, I told John that I would be seizing the doe as evidence. I explained to John that I could not allow him to keep an illegally taken deer. John acknowledged that he understood. When we set the doe down, John told me that I could drive my squad over and pick it up.

After meeting with Laura, I walked with John over to his SUV. Checking his licenses and permits, John had everything that he needed. On my way back, I was thinking about the situation. John had done a good job of giving me excuses. In my heart, I knew that John had killed this deer with a shotgun. A tiny part of me was wondering if the deer could actually have been shot before it got to John. Although I was 95 percent sure that I had found the only hole in the deer, I had to wonder if there couldn't be another one. I didn't want to write something that I couldn't prove, so I decided to write John the bait citation and follow up on the hole in the deer. When I issued John the citation, I left him with the thought that the investigation was complete. Loading the doe into my squad, Laura and I left the residence.

After I drove Laura back to her squad, I stopped and gutted the deer. I was able to track the entrance wound through the body to the exit wound. In doing so, I was able to clearly see what damage had been done to the deer by the projectile. Both the entrance and exit wounds were perfectly round. There were no blade marks from an arrowhead cutting through the hide or meat. The hole measurements matched that of a 12-gauge slug, and I was able to find several larger bone fragments. When I cut the hide away, I found more bone fragments and a ton of trauma under the skin. Searching the carcass, I couldn't find any other injuries. Everything I found confirmed that the doe had been killed by a shotgun slug.

I took the doe to Quality Meat Locker in Peotone. Whenever I seized deer, I would drop them off there. The Koehne's had owned Quality Meats for many years and would donate the deer meat to a local food pantry. When I showed the deer to Jeff (son of the owner), he agreed with my assessment. Jeff skinned the deer for me, and we confirmed that there were no other injuries.

Heading back to John's house, I met with him again. He was obviously surprised to see me. I knew that I was going to have an interview advantage this time. Since John was not expecting me to return, he had not continued to rehearse his story. He also did not have Wayne boosting his confidence. Shortly after I explained to John how I knew that he had killed the deer with a gun, he admitted to it. John told me that he was frustrated because everybody around his property was poaching deer. He said that they had hardly seen any deer in the last couple of years. John said that he was also concerned about having a deer suffer if he shot it with a bow. I asked John if I could see the gun that he had killed the deer with. John complied. I seized a Browning shotgun from

John and issued him a citation for taking a deer with a firearm out of season. Before I left, John admitted that they had seen my squad parked along the road. He confirmed that they were waiting for me to leave before they recovered the deer. A few months later, John pled guilty to both charges and was fined $300. His gun was eventually returned to him.

It's funny to think about this case years later. If Laura hadn't moved my squad, would John have ever tried to recover the deer? If I had left the doe in order to move the squad myself, would John or Wayne have seen me leave their property? If they had, would they have bothered to come looking for the deer at all? I could have walked south and circled back to my squad on the other side of Western Avenue. If they pulled the doe out before I got back, I still could have made the case. It just would have been a lot harder to make. The game was really over when they came looking for the deer. From there, I just had to tie up the loose ends. The last big piece to move was my squad.

Scanning Mode

Six years later, I was working in Rock Island County. The hunting laws and hunter values are roughly the same, but there's a difference in hunter mindset. A big part of the difference comes from property ownership. Property was expensive in Will County. Most of the hunters couldn't afford to own hunting property. That meant that they were always at risk of losing the ability to hunt somebody else's property

In Rock Island County, there are a lot more landowners that hunt their own property. For many of those people, it is as important to hunt the family farm as it is to harvest a deer. Many property owners and extended family members hunted together on their property for several generations. Often, a few of those generations would be hunting the family farm at the same time. People tend to hunt differently based on who owns the property.

Long before becoming a game warden, I saw this difference myself. I grew up hunting in Will County. We always dealt with hoping to get permission again the next year. As my brothers and I graduated into deer hunting, dad took us to the national forests in Southern Illinois and Wisconsin. It was fun to see different places and meet different people. During those years, we hunted both Federal ground and continued to rely on people for permission. A couple of times, we even got to hunt on my uncle's properties. Having seen and lived both mindsets, I grew up wanting my own property to hunt. I wanted to make sure that my family would have the ability to hunt together without having the fear of losing that opportunity.

When it came to becoming a game warden, all those experiences did something else for me. It gave me the ability to quickly recognize what hunters were doing and why. If I hadn't done it, I had thought about doing it or had seen someone else do it. Whether they were hunting their own property, public ground or someone else's property, I had been there.

Since moving to Rock Island County, I had always worked out of my squad or from an ATV during firearm deer season. I would drive from location to location and walk from where I had parked. On opening day (Friday) of this year, I had cleared my list of "locked" violations. Those were the cases where I had a confirmed illegal activity and just needed to catch the poacher. An example of that would be a baited deer stand. I knew where it was and just needed to catch a guy hunting out of it.

As I put together my game plan for Saturday, I decided to try something different. I was going to put my jon boat on the Mississippi River and patrol by water. I had effectively done some of those patrols in Will County and figured that I could do even better on the Mississippi River. The Mississippi River in Rock Island County has over 4,500 acres of huntable public land consisting of islands and river frontage. By contrast, the rivers in Will County were mostly bordered by private property.

On the water at sunrise, I decided to take my little scanning walkie-talkie with me. When we used them as kids, they didn't scan. You could change channels, but you could only monitor the one that you were on. With the scanning feature, I could monitor all the channels at the same time. When somebody keyed up on any of the channels, my radio would automatically switch to their channel. As I idled downstream, I had three good ways to find hunters—looking for blaze orange clothes, listening for shots to chase and hoping to hear somebody talking on the radio. After a couple of hours on the water, I hadn't had any luck.

At about 9:00 a.m., I was approaching the Andalusia Waterfowl Refuge. Although it's illegal to enter the refuge during deer season, I had caught several people hunting in there over the years. As I started paralleling the refuge, I heard the radio "key-up". I cut the engine and let the boat start drifting. I didn't want to miss anything that was being said. If I could clearly hear the "broadcaster", I had to be within a half of a mile of them. If they were further away, I might be able to hear them, but it would be mixed with static. A voice (who we will call Frank) came on the radio and said, "Sammy, I have a deer down and I'm way in the refuge." Sammy quickly responded by asking if it was a buck. Frank confirmed that he had an eight-point buck down. Sammy told Frank that the eight-pointer had passed by him with a 10-pointer. He said that he thought he may have hit the 10-pointer and was going to check. Sammy went on to tell Frank that he "shot at" a doe, the eight-pointer and a 10-pointer all in a row. When Frank didn't respond right away, I started my boat back up and quickly beached it on the bank. After tying it off to a tree, I stepped out into the refuge.

Waiting a couple more minutes, the radio stayed quiet. When the guys stop talking, I don't know what they are doing, and it gets harder to find them. If they keep talking and I'm getting closer to them, their radio traffic will sound clearer. Obviously, if I get further away, I get more static mixed in with the transmission. If I could keep the guys talking, I could gradually zero in on where they are. I had figured out a trick to break the silence years earlier. All I had to do was key-up my own mic. Whenever I got radio traffic, I would lock my radio in on their channel. If they stopped talking and I keyed-up my mic, they would hear my static come over their radio. Inevitably, one of the guys would ask the other if he had said something. It was funny because it would usually start a whole new conversation between the other two guys. That conversation would give me an opportunity to continue zeroing in on them.

As I walked into the refuge, I still hadn't heard anything, so I keyed-up my mic. Sure enough, a few seconds later, I heard Sammy ask Frank if he had said something. Frank said that he had not. Frank then directed a third guy (Dean) to bring the ATV over and help him move the deer. Frank advised Dean to get the sled and gave him directions on where to get it. My radio signal was strong and steady, so I knew that I was going in the right direction. When I heard an ATV in the distance (south of me), I cautiously made my way toward it. I didn't want the hunters to see me before I saw them.

The ATV was running intermittently and wasn't getting any further away. After about five minutes, I heard the ATV starting to get closer. A few minutes later, it was close enough that I decided to find a tree to hide behind. As the ATV came into view, it turned to the west and drove down into the refuge. Getting up my binoculars, I watched Dean drive over to Frank. Dean parked the ATV, got off and started talking with Frank. After a brief conversation, Dean and Frank secured the deer on the sled and put their uncased guns in a rack on the ATV. Jumping onto the ATV, Frank and Dean took off to the south. I was still 60 yards away from them. I couldn't see a tag on the deer, their guns were illegal, and they were in the refuge. I started running toward them, figuring I had a good set of violations. They never looked back, and I couldn't run that fast. I lost sight of Frank and Dean as they drove south through the timber. Thank goodness I could hear the ATV.

About 300 yards into my foot pursuit, I was huffing and puffing pretty good. I'm sure that I was a little out of shape, but I was also running through brush with about 35 pounds of gear on. Slowing to a fast walk, I could hear the ATV going "up" and caught a glimpse of it climbing a hill. When I say hill, I mean a 60-degree grade that goes up about 75 yards. When I got to the base of the hill, I couldn't hear the ATV anymore. I knew there was a garage on top of the hill and was hoping that the ATV had stopped there. I wish I could say that I ran up the hill and caught them, but I had to pause before I tried to climb the hill. I likely paused a couple more times on my way up. By the time I could see the crest of the hill, my legs were burning. I could hear Frank and Dean talking.

Walking over the crest, I found Frank and Dean still sitting on the ATV. Dean was driving and Frank was seated behind him. The uncased guns were on the front gun rack and there was an eight-point buck tied to the sled behind the ATV. When Frank and Dean looked at me, I identified myself to them. As I closed the gap between us, I could see that there wasn't a tag on the buck. In Illinois, a deer must be tagged before it can be field dressed or moved. When Frank turned off the ATV, I asked them who had killed the buck. Frank said that he did. I asked Frank why he had not tagged it. Frank said that he forgot to. I told Frank and Dean that I needed to check their licenses and permits. Frank and Dean dismounted the ATV. Dean handed me his paperwork, while Frank said that his deer permit was in the garage. Obviously, Frank couldn't have tagged it when he didn't even have the tags with him. I asked Frank why he had been hunting without his permit on him. He told me that he had forgotten it in the garage.

I asked Frank and Dean who owned the guns on the ATV. They each claimed one of them.

I asked Frank and Dean how many more deer they had down. Dean told me that he had a doe on the ground over by his stand. I asked him if he had tagged it. Dean said that he had not. Dean told me that he was waiting for his son to come over so he could teach him what to do. I told Dean that I would like to look at his deer. Dean agreed to show it to me. I advised Frank not to move anything until I returned. He agreed.

Dean led me over a small hill and toward his deer. As we walked, Dean told me that Frank was a really good guy. He tried to tell me that Frank had just made a couple of mistakes. We were about 25 yards away from Frank, when I heard my radio key up. It was Frank. He told Sammy that the "Ranger" is here. I looked at Dean as Frank was talking. Dean huffed and shook his head in disbelief. Frank told Sammy to come up to the garage on the east side of the hill. He said that the "Ranger" was on the west side of it. Frank said, "We are already in a world of shit." He advised Sammy to put his tag on the deer that Joey had shot. Sammy questioned what Frank was telling him. Frank again told Sammy to put his tag on Joey's deer. Frank said that it would be easier that way. Sammy acknowledged what Frank had told him to do. I looked at Dean and told him that his friends were conspiring to break the law. He just shook his head and didn't say anything. I asked Dean why they had not tagged the eight-point buck before they pulled it out of the woods. Dean said that they just wanted to get it out of the refuge.

When we reached Dean's doe, I checked its wounds. Dean had made a good heart shot. The doe hadn't travel far before it collapsed. Dean had not moved, or field dressed the deer. When I finished checking the deer, I told Dean that we could walk back to the garage. As we crested the hill on our way back, Sammy called Frank on the radio. Sammy told Frank that he had forgotten his deer tags in the garage. He asked Frank if somebody could run his tags down to him. Frank agreed. I watched Frank walk into the garage and come back out with a set of deer tags in his hand. He looked at me and quickly put his hands into his pockets. I really just wanted to laugh at that point!

Reaching Frank, I showed him my portable radio and told him that I had heard everything. I told Frank to have Sammy bring the deer up to the garage. Frank called Sammy and told him to bring the deer up. Sammy confirmed what Frank had said. Frank then told Sammy that he had better tell the Ranger the truth. Frank told me that the deer Sammy was bringing up was a spike buck. He said that he had shot it earlier in the morning. Frank said that after he shot the spike, he saw the eight-pointer coming toward him. Frank said that the eight-pointer had been shot in the leg, so he shot it again. Frank advised that he didn't kill the eight-pointer when he shot it the first time. Frank told me that he got down, chased it into the refuge and killed it. Looking at Frank's permits, I told him that he only had one either sex (antlered) deer permit. I told him that he could not legally kill two bucks. Frank agreed and said that he had made some mistakes.

While I had been talking with Frank and Dean, two more hunters walked up. Neither one of them was Sammy. After I checked their licenses and permits, Joey asked me if he could go down the hill to check on his son. I agreed and advised him that I would go with. As we walked down the hill, we ran into Sammy and Joey's son coming up on an ATV. They had the untagged spike buck behind the ATV. On the rear rack of the ATV was an uncased gun. Shaking my head in disbelief as I asked them whose gun it was. Sammy said that it was his. He told me that he had forgotten to put it in a case. I asked Sammy why he didn't have his deer permit on his person. Sammy said that he had forgotten it in the garage. Pulling the gun off the ATV, I told all of them to go up to the garage. I advised them that I was going to get my ticket books and would return. They acknowledged that they understood.

It was about a half mile to my boat from the garage and I really didn't like leaving the hunters by themselves with the evidence. Yep, I called Laura. She wasn't too far off and agreed to meet me at Frank's garage. Throughout my career, if I caught somebody with illegal fish or game, I generally always seized them. Figuring that I was going to be seizing Frank's deer, I really wasn't looking forward to dragging them a half mile through the brush back to my boat. The hunters wouldn't be obligated to assist me in any way. If Laura could get to the garage, I could just throw them into the back of her truck until later.

After walking to my boat, I returned to the garage with pen and paper. Laura was already there. I issued Frank, Dean and Sammy citations for having uncased weapons on a vehicle. Frank received two additional citations for his deer hunting violations. I also gave Frank a few written warnings. I did end up seizing Frank's deer and donating the meat to the Sportsmen Against Hunger Program (local food pantries). Looking back now, I can remember thinking that some "strings" got pulled during the plea deal on this case. Frank pled guilty to one charge and was fined $214. Dean and Sammy plead guilty to their charges and were fined $75 each. Frank put the property up for sale a couple of years later.

Laura left with the deer and I returned to my boat. Continuing downstream, I saw some deer swimming across the river. It appeared that they had been pushed off an island. When they made it to the main bank and ran into the woods, there was a bunch of shooting. The radio came in handy again, as it led me to two more hunters. I snuck through the woods and caught one of them tagging the other hunter's deer. I ended up seizing three deer in about five hours. That's a pretty good day for a game warden working out of a boat during deer season.

Some game wardens will say that I shouldn't give poachers my secrets to catching them. With texting taking over, I don't think that this one will hurt much. The funny part will be for the hunters who still use their radios. If they happen to read this, they will have to wonder every time they hear somebody key-up. Was it their buddy or was it a warden trying to find them?

Just a Motorist Assist

The first firearm deer season in Illinois always falls on the weekend before Thanksgiving. It's a very busy weekend for game wardens. Some officers will write more citations that weekend than they will in the following month. The first firearm deer season in 2005 was no different. I had been busy all weekend and was down to my last ten minutes of legal shooting time. Having cleared all my pending cases, I was driving down the back roads in Henry County. I was trying to find my last check for the weekend. I just needed to find a vehicle parked along some timber.

That's not always as easy as it sounds. A lot of people were done hunting for the weekend and Henry County is sporadically timbered. It has "timbered fingers" that follow the geographical features cutting across it. When you get away from a ridge, creek or river, the land generally turns into flat farm ground. Without much timber, most of those flat areas are not very good for deer hunting. Somehow, I had put myself on the farm ground between the timbered areas.

Trying to get to the next section of timber, I was driving north on Route 82. I had started up the next hill and was approaching some timber when I saw two vehicles in the roadway ahead of me. The rear vehicle was a pickup truck with its hazard lights on. I really didn't want to stop for a motorist assist. Not because I didn't want to help someone, but because I was hoping to catch one last poacher. It was going to be my last chance before the weekend was over. As I got closer, I could see that the two vehicles were slowly moving up the hill. When the hill got steeper, the vehicles suddenly came to a stop in the road. The lead vehicle had been trying to tow the truck behind it.

Reaching the vehicles, they were parked in my lane. They were just before the crest of the hill and were going to be a hazard. Pulling up behind the truck, I turned on my emergency lights. Looking at the bed of the truck, I could see deer legs sticking up out of it. Parking my squad, I walked up to the bed of the pickup truck. There was a huge bodied buck lying in the bed. Its antlers had been cut off. As I looked at the deer, a guy (Greg) walked back to me from the front vehicle. I identified myself to Greg and asked him what he was doing. Greg told me that he was towing the truck to his house so he could repair it for one of his friends (Mike). I asked Greg whose deer was in the bed. He told me that it was Mike's deer. Greg told me that he was going to take it to the butcher shop for Mike.

Reaching over the side of the truck, I looked at the tag on the leg of the deer. The tag had been issued to a guy named Bobby. Bobby's tag was only valid if it was used in Fulton County. I didn't see many Fulton County tags in Henry County. It was over an hour away. I asked Greg where Mike lives. He told me that Mike lives in Henry County. I asked Greg if Mike was the one who actually killed the deer. Greg told me that Mike was. Greg went on to say that Mike had killed it on his own property in Henry County. I asked Greg if he had a telephone number for Mike. Greg said that Mike lived with his parents and he would try calling them. Greg was unable to reach Mike, but did get a hold of Mike's mom (Alice). As Greg was talking with Alice, I asked him if I could talk to her. He agreed and handed me the telephone. I identified myself to Alice and asked her if Mike had killed a deer today. She agreed that he had. Alice told me that Mike killed a "big one". I could tell that Alice was elderly, but was still excited about how big the deer was. I thanked Alice and handed the phone back to Greg.

When Greg got done talking with Alice, I asked him if he needed any help with the vehicles. Greg told me that he did not. Greg said that he was just having some trouble getting up the hill. I told Greg that I believed Mike's deer had been killed illegally. I advised Greg that I would be seizing it as evidence. Greg acknowledged that he understood. I turned my truck around and we off-loaded the deer from the bed of Mike's truck into the bed of mine. I told Greg that if I was wrong, I would contact him and get the deer back to him. Greg acknowledged that he understood. As I pulled away, I could see that Greg was able to pull the truck up the hill. Like I said, it was a BIG buck. I must have lightened his load just enough!

By the time I arrived at Mike's house, it was dark. There were two driveways at the property. One went to an old set of barns behind the house and the other went to the old farmhouse. I pulled up to the farmhouse and parked my squad. Exiting the vehicle, I walked up to the front door and knocked. I could see the TV going and could tell there were people inside. Nobody would come to the door. After knocking several times, I walked back to my squad. I figured that Greg must have gotten a hold of Mike and told him that I was coming.

As I was deciding what to do, Mike came walking out from behind the house. I exited my squad and identified myself to Mike. I told him that I wanted to talk with him about the deer in the bed of my truck. Mike looked at the buck and told me that his friend (Bobby) had killed it in Fulton County. Mike went on to say that Bobby had dropped it off when he was on his way home. I asked Mike how many deer they had killed on their property this weekend. Mike told me that his father (Sam) had killed a buck. With Mike being about 60 years old, I told him that I would like to talk with his dad. Although some 80+-year-olds still hunt, not very many really do. Mike agreed and led me into their house. Quite often a family will use grandpa's tag on a deer that they killed, but didn't want to tag themselves. Usually, grandpa's tag will go on a buck that was killed early in the season, a small buck or a doe. The reason, quite simply, is the desire to kill a big buck. Hunters in Illinois can only take two bucks unless they are in a special hunting area. Some hunters will only get one buck tag. Nobody ever wants to be done "buck hunting" because you never know when the deer of a lifetime will walk over the hill.

When we got inside, I was introduced to Sam and Alice. I asked Sam about the deer that he had shot this weekend. Sam told me what sounded like a rehearsed story. I didn't believe him, but he stuck by his story. I asked Sam if he had his licenses and permits. Alice said that she would get them and walked over to the desk. Alice grabbed a couple of envelopes and said, "Here they are." Stepping over by Alice, she showed me the contents of one of the envelopes. I asked her if I could see the other envelope. She agreed and handed it to me. Opening it, I found half of Sam's used archery deer tag inside. Sam didn't look like the kind of guy who could still pull back the required 40 pounds. I asked Sam if I could talk with him in the other room. He agreed and walked with me into the living room. I told Sam to level with me. I told him that I didn't believe that he had killed a deer with a bow this year. Sam told me that I was correct. Sam said that his grandson had killed the deer. I asked Sam if it was a buck or doe. Sam told me that it was a doe. I told Sam that he couldn't allow other people to fill his deer tags. Sam said that he did not know that.

Walking back out to Mike and Alice, I told Mike that I would like to talk with him outside. Mike agreed. I followed Mike outside and told him that I didn't believe most of what he had told me. I asked Mike where his "dad's deer" was located. Mike told me that the head was up by the barn. He asked if I wanted to see it. I told Mike that I did. Mike led me up to an open lot between the barns. There were four vehicles parked in and around the barn lot. Walking over to a small tree, Mike showed me an old dried-out deer head hanging on a branch. I told Mike there was no way that the head had come from a deer that was killed this weekend. Mike agreed and told me that he didn't know where his dad's deer head had gone. Hearing something creak in the middle of the barn lot, I shined my light at a vehicle parked over there. I saw a guy (Peter) standing near the rear of it. Peter was taking off his hunting clothes. I walked over to Peter and identified myself to him. I asked Peter what he was doing. Peter said that he had just gotten done hunting. I asked Peter if he killed anything. He said that he had not. I asked Peter where his gun was. He told me that he had given it to "some kid". Literally, as Peter finished saying that, I heard the cycling of a shotgun's action behind me. The hair on the back of my neck stood up! It was pitch black in the barn lot. Turning around, I shined my flashlight behind me. About 30 yards away, there was a kid (Oliver) standing at the corner of a pole barn. Oliver was hunched over and appeared to be trying to unload a shotgun. I asked Peter if that was the "kid" that he had given his gun to. Without looking, Peter said that he didn't know. I asked Mike who the kid was by the barn. Mike said, "What kid?" I advised him the kid at the corner of the barn. Shining my light back at the corner of the barn, Oliver was gone. I walked over to where Oliver had been standing, but couldn't find a trace of him. To say that I was a little uncomfortable was an understatement. I could see adults pulling this crap, but not little kids.

Walking back to Mike and Peter, I separated them. I started off questioning Peter. Peter told me that Mike and Sam had killed two deer that day (a big buck and a doe). Cross-referencing Peter's story with Mike's, they didn't match. I went back and forth a few times between Peter and Mike until I had both locked into their stories. I then had Peter and Mike talk with me together. I told Mike that I believed the deer in my truck was the one that he had killed that morning. Mike told me that I was right. He said that after he shot it, he put Bobby's tag on it. Mike said that Bobby was not going to be able to hunt, so he had given him his tag to use. I asked Mike about the deer that had been tagged with his dad's archery tag. Mike told me that he killed it the week before and used his dad's tag on it. I asked Mike about the doe that had been killed in the morning. Mike said that he killed the doe too. He said that he put his son's tag on it. Mike said that his son was from Georgia, but had already gone back. Mike told me that his son wasn't going to use the tag. I told Mike that I needed to see his deer tags. He said that they were down at the house. I walked with Mike down to the house. When he went inside, I drove my truck back up to the barn lot. I wanted more lights around me!

Parking behind Peter's car, I turned on my brights and all my takedown lights. As I looked at the vehicles around the lot, I saw that one of them was from Georgia and a second was from Arizona. Besides the kid that was hiding with a shotgun, I figured that there had to be a couple more people around there. Still needing to locate deer, people and weapons, I called Laura and explained to her what I had going on. She said that she would be there in about 20 minutes. I didn't want to leave Mike and Peter to go searching for Oliver. Stories can change, things might come up missing or something bad could happen.

Mike walked up a few minutes later with his deer tags. After seizing the tags, I told Mike that he was under arrest for the illegal taking of three deer. Mike said that he understood. I read him his Miranda Rights and confirmed everything that he had previously told me. Mike filled in the dates and times for all three deer that he had killed. I asked Mike about the out-of-state vehicles. He said that the Arizona one was his brother's and the Georgia one belonged to his son-in-law (Jack). I asked Mike if Jack was the kid who had ran from me. Mike told me that Oliver (Jack's son) was the kid who had ran from me. I asked Mike if his brother was hunting there this weekend. He said that he was not. Mike told me that his brother had gone back to Arizona. I asked Mike where the gun was that he killed the buck and doe with. Mike retrieved it from the back of his truck and turned it over to me.

As I started to work on my paperwork, a truck with three occupants pulled in next to me. Exiting my squad, I walked over to the truck. There was an untagged whitetail doe lying in the bed of the truck. The driver (Tiger) exited the truck and walked over to me. I identified myself to Tiger and asked him if he killed the untagged doe. Tiger said that he had. I asked Tiger why he had not tagged the deer. Tiger said that he was bringing it to Mike's house to call it in. I asked Tiger for his license and deer permit. He said that they were at his house. After I seized the deer from the bed of his truck, I asked Tiger to go get his paperwork. He left Mike's residence and returned a short time later with his paperwork.

When I started on my paperwork again, another truck pulled in. I exited my squad and walked over to the bed of the truck. There were no deer in it. The driver exited the vehicle and identified himself as Peter's dad. He was immediately argumentative and questioned if his son had done anything wrong. I told him that I was still looking for Peter's gun. I explained that Peter had let "some kid" leave with it. I asked Peter for his deer permits and hunting license. Peter showed them to me. Peter only had a landowner deer permit. Landowner deer permits are only valid on the land that you live on, own or lease for farming. There are some other loopholes, but those were the original intentions of the free landowner deer permits. I asked Peter whose property he was hunting on. He said that he was hunting on Mike's property. Walking over to Mike, I asked him why Peter was hunting on his property with landowner deer tags. Mike told me that Peter's family didn't own good hunting property. Mike confirmed that Peter did not lease any property from him. When I pointed out the violation to Peter's dad, he didn't argue any more.

About five minutes later, another truck pulled in. It was Laura. I explained to her where the new trucks in the lot had come from. I told Laura that I couldn't find Oliver and Jack. I asked her to see if she could locate them. She agreed. As I started back on the paperwork, Oliver and Jack came walking out of a barn. They admitted to being from Georgia and hunting without licenses or permits. Laura also located Peter's gun. When she handed it to me, I unloaded three slugs out of it. That would mean that somebody was hunting long after legal shooting hours.

With everybody rounded up, I issued Tiger a citation for failure to tag his deer immediately upon kill and seized his deer. Peter's dad got a citation for allowing his son to hunt on Mike's property without a valid permit. Peter turned out to be 15 years old, so I just gave him a warning. I issued Mike three citations for tagging violations and seized the illegal deer and meat from him. Mike had given the rack from the giant buck to Bobby. Since Bobby lived out of town, I had another officer swing by and seize it for me. Laura ended up issuing Jack two citations for hunting without valid deer permits (him and Oliver) and one for hunting without a license.

Tiger and Peter's dad both pled guilty and were fined $75 each. Mike pled guilty to all three counts and was fined a total of $1,350. Jack also plead guilty to all three violations and was fined $900. All the meat was turned over to the Sportsmen Against Hunger program and went to local food pantries. As part of a plea deal, the firearms that I had seized were returned to the hunters.

With what we had uncovered during this investigation, we could have issued "The Bunch" a lot more tickets than what we did. That said, I feel like we accomplished our goal. Mike was obviously the "ringleader" and took most of the blame. When I checked on him in the IDNR system a few years later, he had not recorded any more deer harvests. Mike was held accountable for what looked to be years of indiscretions and hopefully corrected some of his behavior. At a bare minimum, "The Bunch" knows that game wardens really do exist.

The following year was the start of one of the longest cases in my career. It wasn't because I didn't know where to find the poacher. It was because I couldn't figure out when to find him. He kept me guessing for over two years.

A Long Time in Coming

At the beginning of deer season in 2006, I received a call from a landowner (Archie) south of Milan, Illinois. Archie told me that he thought that one of his neighbors (Elmer) had been deer hunting on his property. Archie only allowed one guy to hunt, and it wasn't Elmer. While walking his fence line, Archie found a deer stand on his property. He also found areas where his fence had been compromised. Like humans, deer prefer to take the easy path. If there's a fence and you cut the top strands or tie them down, deer will eventually find the low spot and cross there. Hunters commonly set up their stands next to the low spot in hopes of getting a shot. Archie had horses and was concerned that they may either get shot or escape the compromised fence. He wanted the culprit caught.

As Archie was complaining about Elmer, I remembered a previous complaint about him. A few years earlier, another neighboring property owner had the same complaint as Archie. That neighbor just wanted to "vent", but wouldn't file a formal complaint at the time. Without being willing to appear in court (if necessary), there wasn't much that I could do for him. Many people would rather allow themselves to be taken advantage of than face the consequences of holding a neighbor accountable for trespassing. The bullying and "ill-will" from the guy next door can be miserable for a landowner to live with. Archie talked with the other neighboring property owner and they agreed this time. Elmer was no longer hunting on either of their properties.

While out on Archie's property, I worked my way over to the side that bordered Elmer's property. Elmer only owned a couple of acres of grass with his house on it. When I reached the border,

I saw that Elmer had mowed out a spot in some tall grass. The mowed patch was about 20 feet from Archie's fence and had one small tree in it. As I got closer, I saw a camera on the tree facing to the west. Five feet in front of the camera was a pile of corn. I always like it when hunters put a camera facing their bait pile. It helped me to find it. I always tell people that if they are going to bait, use a nice big white salt block. I always appreciated the ease in finding those too!

As I completed my tour of Archie's property, I was amazed at how easy it was going to be to catch Elmer. Archie and Elmer lived in neighboring subdivisions with separate access roads. I could park in front of Archie's house and Elmer couldn't see my squad. I was able to walk through Archie's gate and out into his timber without being detected. Even better was that Elmer's bait pile and stand were within a few hundred yards of the gate. I could almost drive to Elmer's stand and catch him!

Like the old saying, "When something seems too good to be true, it probably is." I went back and worked Archie's property several times that year. I never caught Elmer in the stand. Normally when that happens, the game warden has been "busted out". In other words, the poacher knows that the warden is trying to catch him. If that was the case though, Elmer would have quit putting corn on his pile. Every time I went back, the pile of corn had been replenished. I had to assume that Elmer didn't know I was after him.

When the 2007 deer season was approaching, I went back and checked the area. The deer stand on Archie's property was gone. Checking the mowed patch on Elmer's property, it had gotten bigger. Elmer put a ground blind in the mowed area with a salt block and corn sitting in front of it. I figured that I had him now! There was no way that Elmer knew I was in hot pursuit. I checked that deer blind at all the "hot times", including opening days, weekends and during the rut. Coming to the end of deer season,

I was very frustrated. Elmer never showed up to hunt. As the 2008 deer season approached, I went back and found the same set-up as I did in 2007. I wasn't going to get my hopes up and only sporadically checked Elmer's ground blind during the early season. I didn't bother checking it on opening day of firearm deer season. On the second day of firearm deer season, I had cleared all my other pending cases. There was only about an hour and a half of hunting time left, so I decided to check Elmer's ground blind. I figured that if Elmer wasn't hunting, I still might hear a shot that I could chase on one of the neighboring properties.

Parking on Archie's road, I went through the gate and walked toward the fence by Elmer's ground blind. The windows on the ground blind were open! I snuck all the way to the fence only to find that there was nobody inside of the blind. There wasn't enough time to go anywhere else, so I decided to stand next to a locust tree by the fence. The next 10 minutes were really slow. There were only a few shots in the surrounding mile.

From the locust tree, I could see Elmer's house. When there was about an hour left, I saw Elmer walk out of the back door of his house and into his garage. He had full camouflage on. Still, I was skeptical at best. Who would walk out to their blind with only an hour left to hunt? Then Elmer walked out of the rear door of his garage and toward the bean field behind his house. After he got to a mowed trail, Elmer turned and started to walk toward the ground blind. Looking at him with my binoculars, I could see that Elmer was carrying a gun with a scope and a spotlight. As Elmer got closer, I realized that I had picked a tree that was way too close to the blind. It was too late to move to another tree and the one that I was standing behind was barely as wide as my body. I stood as straight as I could behind the tree. Thank goodness there was a branch up by my head. If I stood on my tippy toes, I could see through a "V" in the tree and still maintain some cover.

When Elmer got to the mowed area, I could see that he was carrying a rifle! Of course, we don't allow the use of rifles in Illinois. You always hear about guys shooting deer with rifles, but don't catch very many of them. I pulled my head back and started looking through the "V" in the tree. Elmer walked up to the blind and closed the window facing the bait. He then walked around to the door on my side of the blind. With Elmer's back to me, I watched him pull a pair of rattling antlers and an orange vest from inside of the blind. Elmer put the antlers on his shoulders and stuffed the orange vest into his coat pocket. After Elmer zipped the door shut, he stepped to the back of the blind and looked to the south for a couple of minutes. I knew that I couldn't move at all. If Elmer turned around and looked closely at my tree, he would surely see me. I was only 30 feet away from him.

When Elmer turned toward the fence, I pulled my head behind the tree. Elmer walked over to the fence, paused and started to walk along the fence to the west. As he walked away from me, he came into my field of view. Elmer stopped at a small tree and began messing with a scent bottle hanging in it. I slowly stepped around my tree so it would stay between us. When Elmer finished straightening the bottle, he slowly continued to the west. He would walk a few steps, stop and look around.

Elmer continued "still hunting" out into his neighbor's property. It was the neighbor who had not wanted to file a formal complaint years earlier. Staying on Archie's side of the fence, when Elmer got about 30 yards ahead of me, I started to quietly follow him. As Elmer got to the crest of a hill, I ran into a giant briar patch. I knew there was no way I could get through the briars without making a bunch of noise. I let Elmer cross over the hill before I climbed onto his side of the fence. Quietly following Elmer's trail up the hill, I stopped when my head could just see over the crest. I started scanning the field and brush ahead of me, but Elmer had disappeared. I had let too much distance get between us. I really didn't want to go up on the crest of the hill because I knew that Elmer would be able to see me.

As I was considering my options, Elmer's cell phone rang! I looked into the brush about 30 yards ahead of me. Elmer was talking on his phone as he stood next to a tree along Archie's property line. When Elmer stopped talking on the telephone, he put it away and set his gun down next to the tree. Elmer started looking at the ground around the tree. After looking all around the tree, Elmer rattled his antlers. He rattled for about 20 seconds, stopped and looked down into Archie's property. He was on a hill that had a perfect view down into Archie's timber. Elmer pulled up his spotlight and scanned it through the timber.

I started to slowly work my way toward Elmer. I was able to get within five yards of Elmer without him hearing or seeing me. Just shy of yelling, I identified myself to Elmer. He was noticeably startled and jerked his head around to look at me. I told Elmer not to touch the gun. He told me that he was not touching anything and raised his hands. I asked Elmer what he was doing back here. Elmer advised, "I'm deer hunting." What a perfect confession! I asked Elmer why he was deer hunting with a rifle. Elmer looked down and said that he had screwed up. I told Elmer that he "really screwed up". I asked Elmer why he wasn't wearing any orange. He told me that he had it "right here" and pulled it out of his pocket.

Picking up the rifle, I unloaded two rounds from it. I advised Elmer that he was also illegally feeding deer. Elmer said that he didn't know what I was talking about. I told him that I had been following him since the ground blind. I told Elmer that I knew about the salt block. Elmer told me that he had put that out back in the summer. I asked Elmer for his hunting license and deer permits. Elmer told me that they were back in the house. I got Elmer's driver's license and seized all his hunting equipment. I told Elmer that I was going to be seizing the salt block and would meet him at his house. Elmer agreed.

After seizing the salt block, I walked to my squad and drove to Elmer's house. Meeting with Elmer, he said that it was all his fault and apologized for what he had done. I ended up issuing Elmer citations for hunting with a rifle, hunting without any blaze orange, hunting without permission, and making food available for deer. I also gave Elmer some written warnings. If I had waited another 20 minutes before I approached him, I could have arrested Elmer for hunting after hours too.

Elmer ended up pleading guilty to all the violations and was fined $600. He also forfeited all of his hunting equipment. Although Elmer's penalties were not incredible, some very valuable lessons are told in this case. The obvious one is that nothing is as easy as it appears. The more important lesson brought to light something that I believed I was already doing. That was simply to think outside of the box. For two years, I checked that blind and stand with no success. It seems obvious now, but I was not checking it outside of legal shooting hours. Perseverance made the case, but it was a long road to go down. I don't know that the last one is really a lesson, but it is important, nevertheless. Elmer obviously exhibited knowledge of the laws and intent to break them. In the end, he owned his mistake. I would always write that in my reports. If somebody doesn't admit that they made a mistake, maybe they don't believe that they did. If they own their mistake, the legal system generally looks at it favorably and will be more lenient in sentencing.

EINSTEIN

The best part of being a game warden is the people that you have an opportunity to meet. I truly believe that everybody has a "story" to tell. The question becomes whether or not you have the time to listen to it. For almost my entire career, our agency was understaffed. When that happens, the calls for assistance don't go away, you just spend more time working on them. If I wasn't responding to one of those calls, I was trying to catch the next "bad guy". Early in my career, I found myself feeling guilty if I spent too much time talking to a "legal person". I knew that I was missing an opportunity to catch a "bad guy". After all, that's what I was getting paid to do.

As I got older, I came to believe that things happen for a reason. I spent more time talking with people. I enjoyed listening to their stories. Sometimes, I even got to tell one of mine. Either way, when I got done sharing a story, it seemed like I would catch another "bad guy". I often thought that if I hadn't stopped to talk, I wouldn't be in the right place at the right time.

Late in my career, I wished that I would have kept a journal about the people that I had met. Although they wouldn't all have been arrest stories, they would have been interesting, nevertheless. Sometimes, the best part of an arrest story has nothing to do with the arrest, but rather the story behind the people involved.

I have told this story so many times that Laura is sick of hearing it. It's kind of funny because either you really like it or you don't have any interest in it. I happen to love it. In April of 2013, I was contacted by the Illinois Secretary of State Police (SOS). They asked me to assist in the investigation of Embezzlement License and Title Service (ELTS) in East Moline, Illinois. The business was similar to Ripoff License and Title, but the players were not as "refined" as Cruella.

After agreeing to investigate the DNR violations, I received and reviewed the records that had been seized by SOS. I found that there were in excess of 75 boats and snowmobiles that had not been registered. Figuring that each registration was well over $100 with taxes and fees, there was likely several thousand dollars in just DNR registrations that were unaccounted for. Like always, I needed to "find the money". Complicating matters, the SOS agents who initiated the investigation decided to take transfers south. Although they completed their investigations, getting any criminal prosecution would be largely dependent on me.

I contacted the owner (Laurel) of ELTS and set up an interview with him. When Laurel and I sat down, he quickly tried to absolve himself of any culpability. Laurel said that he had become a "hands-off" businessman. Laurel took the business over from his parents in 1994. After about 14 years of running it, Laurel began having trouble making ends meet. A job opportunity at a local factory presented itself, so Laurel decided to switch professions. Laurel admitted that he should have just closed the ELTS doors. Instead, Laurel turned to the guy next door (Hardy). The neighboring business where Hardy had worked closed, so he came to work full-time for Laurel.

Laurel was working long hours at the factory, so he pretty much turned the reigns over to Hardy. Hardy was tasked with running almost every facet of ELTS. He was paying the bills, making deposits and even paying himself. They had agreed that Hardy was to be paid $350 a week. After we discussed how the business accounts were run, I asked Laurel if he ever took cash out of the register. Laurel said that he may have taken $20 one time in the last year, "but that was it".

I showed Laurel a list of the missing DNR registrations. I explained to him that somebody had stolen their money. I told Laurel that I intended to figure out where the money had gone. He asked if I knew how much was missing. I advised Laurel that I was still working on it. Laurel told me that he would like to pay the money back. I asked Laurel if he knew where the money had gone. Laurel said that he was not sure. Laurel told me that he was trying to keep the business afloat by putting his own money into the account. He said that he had deposited a couple thousand dollars only a few weeks earlier.

I again showed Laurel the list of missing DNR registrations and told him that all of these "victims" had money stolen from them. I then asked him if the people in those papers should be considered "victims". Laurel agreed that they should. I asked Laurel what should happen to the thief. A thief that had stolen thousands of dollars from the victims. Laurel was not sure. I asked him if the thief should go to prison. Laurel again said that he was not sure. That was not the answer that I was hoping for. Laurel proceeded to tell me that the victims should have their registrations "take care of". I told Laurel that there was one problem. I explained to him that his "business bond" would not pay for the DNR registration thefts. The bond was only for the SOS registrations. All the people on my list would have to pay for their registrations again. Laurel acknowledged that he understood. Laurel did not admit to doing anything wrong during our first interview. He was adamant that Hardy was in total control of the business. Laurel wrote me a statement. Before he left, I told Laurel that I would be in contact.

I met with Hardy the next day. I started off by asking Hardy about his history with ELTS. Hardy said that he had worked there part-time for about six years. Hardy told me that he never received any formal training. He said that he learned "on the job". I asked Hardy if he had a title. He said that he did not. Hardy said that he was essentially a "Title Clerk". Hardy was already greasing the wheels for an "I didn't know" defense.

Before the interview, I had drawn up a diagram. I wrote "Truthful" on the left side of a piece of paper and "Lying" on the right. I told Hardy that I would be asking him some tough questions. I set the diagram in front of him and wrote his name in between the words. I explained to Hardy that he had a choice to make. I told Hardy that he could go to the Truthful side or the Lying side. I advised Hardy that I expected him to be on the Truthful side as I pointed to the word. I got a head-nod confirmation from Hardy.

I started off by talking with Hardy about how he had run the business. During his explanation, Hardy told me that he deposited money almost every day. Hardy said that he would generally deposit between $500 and $1,000. I asked Hardy if he had days where he did not deposit any money. Hardy said that he did, but it was very seldom. I asked Hardy if he had days where he deposited $2,000. He said that depositing that much would also be rare.

I told Hardy that I wanted to focus on the last 16 months. He acknowledged that he understood. I asked Hardy if he paid himself. He said that he did. I asked him if he paid himself by check. Hardy said that he paid himself in cash.

I then showed Hardy the victim stack of DNR registrations. We talked about the frequency at which he sent them into the DNR. Hardy admitted that he sent the SOS registrations in on a regular basis. He said that he would wait a few weeks to send the DNR ones in. I explained to Hardy that each set of papers represented a human being. A human being that came in to get a boat or snowmobile registered by him. I explained to Hardy that each of those people was a victim of theft. I told him that they had their money stolen from them. I asked Hardy why their registrations had not been sent in. Hardy told me that he did the best that he could. I told Hardy that some of them had not been turned in for over a year. Some already had the checks written out and literally just needed to be put in the mail. Hardy explained that those were just an oversight on his part.

I told Hardy that I was now going to ask him the hard questions. Hardy acknowledged that he understood. I showed him an envelope marked "Bank Records". I didn't really have any records in it, but I did have it packed full of paper! I told Hardy that I would figure out exactly how much money ELTS had been paid through the receipts. I then explained to Hardy that I would tally up his deposit receipts and subtract all the business expenses. I went on to tell Hardy that the nice thing about numbers is that they are exact and cannot be altered to equal something that they don't. Hardy agreed. I told Hardy that when I finished, I would know if the numbers matched or if there was any unaccounted-for money. Hardy shook his head in agreement. I confirmed with Hardy that he was supposed to be paid $350 a week. He agreed. I once again directed Hardy to my diagram and drew a line down the middle. I told Hardy that I expected him to be on the "Honest" side of the line. Hardy shook his head in agreement. I asked Hardy how much "extra money" (above his $350) he took from the business every week. Hardy told me that for a while he had to take some "extra money" to meet personal bills. He explained that he ran into some tough times. I acknowledged that I understood. I then directed Hardy to a new sheet of paper and again told him that I was only concerned about the last 16 months. I drew a timeline on the paper that started in January of 2012. Hardy claimed that for the first six months he had stolen about $200 a week. Hardy said that after six months, he was getting caught up and only took an extra $100 a week for the remaining 10 months. When we were done, we added it all up. Hardy admitted to having stolen approximately $9,400 from ELTS. I asked Hardy if he understood that it was wrong and illegal to steal. Hardy advised that he did. I asked Hardy if he had ever written himself checks or used the debit card. Hardy told me that he only took cash.

After confirming the amounts, Hardy asked about Laurel. Hardy told me that Laurel had made up a fake Purchase Agreement in order to get $30,000. Hardy explained that Laurel's brother (Fran) was wealthy and wanted Laurel to sell the business. When Laurel approached Fran for the loan, he agreed to give him the money, but under one condition. Laurel would have to sell ELTS. Hardy said that Laurel wrote up a fake Purchase Agreement for ELTS and had it notarized. Hardy told me that Laurel had forged the buyer's signature (Ollie) on the document. Ollie was a past employee of ELTS, which made it more plausible. Hardy said that Ollie had gotten a copy of the Purchase Agreement and still had it. Hardy told me that he and Ollie had grown up together. He said that Ollie would likely cooperate with my investigation. I told Hardy that I would look into what he was telling me.

I got a statement from Hardy. In his statement, Hardy admitted to stealing the money. He explained that he had trouble keeping his house after his mother had passed away. He said that he needed the extra money to make ends meet.

About 10 days later, I drove to Ollie's house. Ollie was surprised to see me. I figured that Hardy would have told him to expect me. I told Ollie that his name had been brought up in the investigation of ELTS. He seemed a little frustrated that he had become involved. Ollie ended up providing me a copy of the forged Purchase Agreement. I asked Ollie how he had gotten it. Ollie told me that he received a call from Fran about the sale of the business. During the discussion, Ollie told Fran that he was not buying the business. When Ollie was told that there was a

Purchase Agreement, he asked Fran to send it to him. Fran forwarded it in a fax. Ollie saw that someone had forged his signature on the document. Ollie went on to confirm that Laurel had used the Purchase Agreement to get a $30,000 loan from Fran.

I ended up meeting with Laurel a few more times. During the next interview, Laurel admitted to making the false Purchase Agreement in order to obtain a fraudulent loan. He also admitted to forging Ollie's name on the Purchase Agreement and getting it notarized. Speaking with the Notary, she didn't remember putting her stamp on the document. I eventually got most of the bank records and found some inconsistencies in the deposits. The problem with getting "most" of the records is that I couldn't come up with a definitive number for missing money. That was made more difficult with the amount of cash going through the business. I counted one year's cash intake to be in excess of $100,000.

Laurel was eventually charged with forgery and Hardy was charged with theft. Both charges were class 3 felonies. They both pled guilty in plea agreements. Laurel had to go to an Offender Initiative Program and was fined $800.36. Hardy was fined $1,909 and was given 24 months of conditional discharge. Not much of a penalty for two guys who were responsible for admittedly "stealing" almost $40,000. I would guess that if we added up how much it cost to complete all the vehicle, boat and snowmobile registrations, it was much more than that. Although the investigation of ELTS is interesting, the reason I wrote about this case is because of another person. During the interview of Hardy, he said that people would regularly come in and complain about not getting their boat registrations. He claimed that all he had to do was tell them that it was the DNR's fault. Of course, everybody believed him. The DNR had always been slow at completing their paperwork. Hardy had the perfect scapegoat built right into his Ponzi scheme. One of the first people to call me after the investigation started was Lois Esterlein.

Lois and her husband Robert were two of the victims in this case. Like so many others, they had gone to ELTS to register a boat. Almost a year after paying ELTS to register it, they still hadn't received their registration. Also like many others, Robert and Lois wanted to file a complaint. Talking with Lois on the phone, I made an appointment to meet with her.

On 05-03-2013, I drove to the Esterlein residence. Knocking on the door, I was greeted by Lois. I identified myself to Lois and told her that I was there to talk with her about their watercraft registration. Lois invited me inside and again gave me the quick verbal version of what had happened. It was the same as all of the others. They paid Hardy $72 and didn't get anything for it. Lois told me that she had stopped at ELTS several times and was always told the same thing. "The DNR is running behind."

When Lois got done telling me about their ordeal, I asked if she would be willing to write me a statement. Lois agreed. As I handed Lois a statement form, she asked if she could type it instead of hand-writing it. Lois proceeded to tell me that although she had really nice handwriting at one time, age had made it difficult to read her writing. Lois was likely about 80 years old at the time. I told Lois that I understood and that a typed statement would be great.

Lois told me that I could talk with her husband (Robert) while she was writing the statement. I agreed. Prior to walking into the living room, Lois told me that Robert had recently had a stroke. She said that he didn't get around very well, but was as sharp as a tack. I told her that was not a problem.

Following Lois into the living room, she introduced me to Robert. I walked over and shook Robert's hand. Lois offered for me to sit down, so I took a seat across from Robert. As Lois exited the room, she told Robert to tell me about the time that he had met Albert Einstein. I was immediately all ears!

Shortly after World War II, Robert had obtained a job at a place called Sperry Corporation. Robert said that Sperry Corporation was a manufacturing company that made gyroscopes. I knew what a gyroscope was, but was not sure what they were used for. Robert explained that gyroscopes are used in torpedoes. He said that he figured it out when he accidentally walked into a restricted area. Robert said that he saw people working on a "huge torpedo". If I remember correctly, Robert quickly exited the area before he was caught.

Robert went on to tell me that he worked in the testing division. Him and several other employees were tasked with testing the gyroscopes before they could be used. One day, Robert's supervisor told them that Albert Einstein was going to be visiting their facility. During his visit, Einstein would be making a stop in the testing division. A few days later, when Robert was testing gyroscopes, he looked up and saw Einstein with his supervisor. They were watching Robert and his coworkers conducting tests. Robert told me that he just kept working.

As Robert was testing a gyroscope, he was approached by his supervisor and Einstein. Robert said that Einstein walked up, shook his hand and introduced himself. After the introduction, Einstein asked Robert why he was testing the gyroscopes both forward and back. Robert said that if they worked properly both ways, he was confident that they would function properly when used. Einstein told Robert that he was the only tester who was checking them both ways. Einstein advised Robert that he was doing a good job and to keep up the good work. As fast as he appeared, Einstein left the testing division.

I probably asked Robert 20 questions about Einstein, Sperry Corporation, gyroscopes and torpedoes. Lois completed their statement and brought it out to me. After talking a little more, I thanked Robert and Lois for their time and left their residence.

After leaving their house, I thought of a hundred more questions that I wished I had asked Robert. How many times do you get to meet somebody who actually talked with Albert Einstein and shook his hand? Then I thought, "Ya know, I shook the hand of a guy who shook the hand of Albert Einstein." How many people can even say that? Pretty cool!

A couple years later, I was fishing at Dogtooth Lake Resort in Kenora, Canada. It happened to be the year that we finally figured out how to catch the big walleyes. When we arrived in camp, a rumor was going around that Babe Winkleman was going to be filming a show there later in the week. I was looking forward to seeing their set-up. After Winkleman and his crew got a day of fishing in, they offered to have a meet and greet with the rest of the people at the resort. Like everybody else, we lined up to get pictures and autographs. Even though my kids did not know who Babe Winkleman was, they understood that they were getting to meet a legend in the outdoors community. As we were lined up to get the autographs, I got to thinking about the fact that Babe was giving us a memory as a family. We would be able to talk about that year forever. When it was my turn to get an autograph, I handed Babe a fillet knife that I had purchased at a garage sale. It was a really nice knife that I couldn't have afforded to purchase when it was new. Babe looked at it and said, "A fillet knife. You know, I think this is the first fillet knife that I have ever autographed." It was neat that I was the first to come up with that idea. When everybody was done, I stepped to the side with Babe, shook his hand and told him that I wanted to thank him. I told babe that he had given my family more than just a picture and an autograph. I told him that he had given my family a memory that we would have forever. I then told Babe that I felt compelled to give him something. So, I told a shortened version of Robert's story to Babe. When I got done, I told Babe that he could forever tell people that he had shook the hand of a guy who shook the hand of a guy who shook the hand of Albert Einstein. I'm sure that my wife rolled her eyes while Babe and I chuckled.

METH

I arrested a lot of people for drugs in the first 10 years of my career, but never caught anybody with meth. Moving to the Quad Cities changed that for me. It seemed like I found people cooking or using it almost every year. I know that other drugs ruin a lot of lives, but meth is particularly horrible. I have arrested people for cocaine who thanked me for helping them break the habit. Not meth. I don't wish it upon anybody or their families. I've met people who claimed to have tried it once and quit, but don't remember ever meeting an addict that got off it. I'm going to try to show you both the arrest and human side of meth.

On a warm Thursday in September of 2013, I was working along the Mississippi River near Muscatine, Iowa. Being that it was the middle of the month and the middle of the day, things would normally be a little slow. For some reason, my gut was telling me that things would be picking up. I know it sounds a little cliché, but I really did have a "gut feeling" that day. I figured that I just needed to keep working hard and I would find something. I decided that I needed to check every nook and cranny from Muscatine, Iowa, to Keithsburg, Illinois.

Starting just north of the Muscatine bridge, I had been slowly working my way south along the bank of the Mississippi. I figured that I would just drive or walk down every road and path for the next 20 miles. Sooner or later, I would find somebody doing something.

When I left Muscatine Boat Club, I took the next road to the south. This road is about four miles long with just a few houses on it. Once you get past the houses, the road cuts up onto the Mississippi River levy. The levy is made of sand and is elevated about 25 feet above the surrounding properties. Like other levies, this one holds the flood waters of the Mississippi River back. It helps keep the river from flooding the farm fields and homes on the other side. During normal water levels, the actual bank of the Mississippi River is about 200 yards west of the levy. During flood times, the levy is the bank.

About 300 yards south of where I drove up onto the levy, there's a dirt road going down the west side. I slowed to a stop as I reached the dirt road. I could see fresh tracks on it going toward the river. Following the tracks down the levy, I continued on the road as it wound through a grassy strip toward the riverbank. Just before I got to the actual bank, I came to a silty hill. It's not very big, but is high enough that I couldn't see what was on the other side.

As I crested the hill, I could see a black Jeep Cherokee parked about 15 yards in front of me. There was a male subject (Fred) standing outside of the driver's window. When Fred stepped back to look at me, I could see a bottle in his hands. The female (Wilma) in the driver's seat and the guy (Barney) in the right rear passenger seat looked at me too. Wilma immediately bent over and reached behind her seat. It looked like she was trying to hide something behind it. Barney opened his door and stepped out of the vehicle.

Parking my squad, Fred turned his body back toward the Cherokee and hid the bottle between him and the side of the vehicle. Exiting my squad, I walked up to the subjects and identified myself to them. I asked the subjects what they were doing.

Fred said that they weren't doing anything. Looking at the bottle in his hands, it appeared that Fred was holding a "shake and bake" bottle. "Shake and bake" is a method of producing methamphetamine. The ingredients are put into the bottle and shook up. As the ingredients interact, they produce lots of pressure. If the guy shaking the bottle doesn't keep letting the pressure off, the bottle will explode. It will send the caustic ingredients flying all over.

Wilma leaned forward again as she continued trying to move something between or behind her seat. I asked the subjects if they were cooking meth. Of course, they all said that they were not. I told Fred to put the bottle down and put his hands on the hood. After he set the bottle on the roof, Fred stepped up the front of the vehicle. When he put his hands on the hood, I told him to keep them there. Fred agreed. I told Wilma to put her hands-on top of her head. She began erratically moving them all over. I again told Wilma to put her hands on her head. She literally did not appear to understand what I was saying. As she continued to flail her arms all over, I pointed at my head and told Wilma to put her hands-on top of her head. She finally got what I was saying and complied. I told Wilma to keep her hands there. She agreed.

Looking past Wilma inside of the Cherokee, I could see a pill bottle sitting on the inside of the front passenger door handle. There was also a soft-sided cooler on the front passenger floor. I again told everybody to stay where they were. As I stepped toward the front of the vehicle, I saw that Fred had a knife in his pocket. I pulled the knife out of Fred's pocket and checked him for other weapons. He did not have any.

Walking around to the passenger side of the Cherokee, Barney was standing next to the back door. I asked Barney what he was doing. He said that he wasn't doing anything. I told Barney to step up to the front of the vehicle and put his hands on the hood. Barney continued to be mouthy, but complied. Looking through the front passenger window, I could see into the open cooler. There was a funnel and a pop bottle with a white substance inside. There was also a plastic bag wadded up between the front passenger seat and the center console. It was in the area where Wilma had been reaching.

I asked the subjects whose pill bottle was on the door handle. Fred hesitated and told me that it was his. He said that it had acid inside. Moving the pill bottle to the dashboard, I opened the front passenger door. Looking in the cooler, I asked the subjects what the white stuff in the pop bottle was. Fred said that it was salt. I pulled the plastic bag out from between the front seat and center console. There was an unraveled battery inside. Closing the passenger door, I again began to walk around the vehicle. Before I passed Barney, I saw that he too had a knife in his pocket. I secured the knife from Barney and told him to stay where he was. He agreed.

Continuing around to Fred, I placed him in handcuffs. Looking at Wilma, she had pulled her hands from her head and was reaching toward the floor with her left hand. I told Wilma to put her hands back on top of her head. She hesitated. When I finished handcuffing Fred, I walked over to Wilma and again told her to put her hands back on top of her head. When she complied, I told her to keep her hands there.

Walking over to my squad, I got my second set of handcuffs. Returning to Wilma, I opened the driver's door and told her to step out of the vehicle. She complied. I placed Wilma in handcuffs and had her walk over to the front of my squad. I advised Wilma to stay there. She complied. Looking at the floor of Wilma's vehicle, I saw a cloth bag where she had been reaching. I asked Wilma what was in the bag. She said that it was not hers. As I began opening the bag, Wilma told me that there was a pipe in the bag. I got the bag open and pulled a glass drug pipe out of it.

Walking back over to Fred, I searched him. I didn't locate any other contraband or weapons. I asked Wilma to pull her shirt up high enough for me to see her waistband. She complied and didn't have any visible weapons either. Wilma then began to cry. She told me that she had shoulder surgery and neck problems. I uncuffed Wilma and mover her handcuffs to the front of her body.

Returning to my squad, I called the Illinois State Police (ISP) and ran driver's license checks on Fred, Barney and Wilma. I advised ISP that I had a meth lab and requested that they contact MEG. MEG is the drug task force for the Quad Cities. Not only do they catch bad guys, but they are also the best at prosecuting drug arrests. On top of that, I would need them to clean up the lab. I have never been trained to do it. I was told that MEG would be en route. Being in the middle of nowhere, I knew that "the crew" and I would be hanging out together for a while.

As I was sitting in my squad, I was glancing at the bottle on the roof of the Cherokee. I kept thinking about how easy it would be for one of them to throw it into the river. Exiting my squad, I walked up to the Cherokee and pulled the bottle off of the roof. It had so much pressure built up inside that it felt like a rock. I set the bottle on the driver's floor of the Cherokee. Fred immediately asked if I could release the pressure from inside of the bottle. He told me that he didn't want it to explode inside of their vehicle. Fred said that it would destroy the vehicle. I told Fred that "I" wasn't releasing anything. Fred asked if "he" could release the pressure. I asked Fred if he could do it with his handcuffs on. Fred said that he could. I really didn't want to allow it, but succumbed to Fred repetitive requests.

Agreeing to let Fred release the pressure, he stepped over to the driver's window. I placed the bottle in his hands. I didn't want Fred running with the bottle, so I stayed next to him. When Fred unscrewed the lid, I could hear the gasses escaping from inside. I should have held my breath, but wasn't thinking. On my next inhale, my lungs started burning and I started coughing. All

I could think was. "You dumbass, you should have left the damn bottle in the Cherokee!"

When Fred was done, I put the bottle back in the Cherokee. I told him that we wouldn't be releasing any more pressure. Fred said that he understood. I walked back to my squad and got my camera. I took pictures of the scene and all the subjects.

As we continued to wait for MEG, everybody started to complain about how hot it was. I had all them sit on the ground in the shade. Wilma kept going in and out of crying spells. After about 45 minutes of crying on and off, I had Wilma get up and walk over to my squad.

Securing Wilma in the front passenger seat of my squad, I got in driver's side. When I sat down, Wilma began uncontrollably crying. Thinking that she was simply getting too hot, I turned up the air conditioning. As Wilma continued to cry, she said that she needed to get her kids out of school at 3:00 p.m. I explained to Wilma my constraints with handling meth. I told her that we would have to wait for MEG to arrive.

At 1:16 p.m., I read Wilma her Miranda Rights and asked her if she understood. She agreed that she did. I asked Wilma how she knew Fred and Barney. Wilma told me that she had been married to Fred for about a year. She went on to say that Barney just lives in their neighborhood. Wilma would not admit to cooking meth, but did admit to using meth. Wilma also admitted to doing meth with Fred. Wilma told me that she didn't have any drugs in her vehicle. I asked Wilma if anybody else had drugs in her vehicle. She advised that she was not sure. I helped Wilma exit my squad and had her sit back in the shade.

At about 1:27 p.m., I had Fred sit in the front passenger seat. Sitting in the driver's seat, I read Fred his Miranda Rights. After he agreed that he understood, I asked Fred if I had to worry about the bottle exploding anymore. Fred said that it should be "OK" now. He told me that he would need to shake it to increase pressure again. Fred told me that he normally must let air in and pressure out. I asked Fred how many times he has "cooked" meth. Fred said that this was just his second time. Fred advised that it didn't work the first time that he had tried. He went on to tell me that he had learned how to cook meth from the internet. I asked Fred if uses meth. Fred told me that he does, but prefers to smoke cannabis. Fred proceeded to tell me that he was waiting for his unemployment check. He said that he needed money because he had bills to pay. I asked Fred if he had any other drugs in the Cherokee. Fred told me that he did not. I asked Fred if all the meth-making materials in the Cherokee were his. Fred admitted that they were. He verbally gave me his ingredients list and a brief lesson on how to make meth. I thanked Fred for his honesty and had him sit back in the shade. Reflecting on my conversation with Fred, I should have asked him how much he would get for the finished product.

Almost an hour and a half had passed since I discovered Fred, Barney and Wilma. As I was getting ready to have Barney walk over to my squad, the MEG unit arrived. Since Barney was the argumentative one, I had intentionally saved him for last. As it turned out, I didn't need to interview Barney at all. I always considered it a favor when MEG came to assist me with my investigations. Like several other cases, I turned the prosecution of Fred, Barney and Wilma over to the MEG unit. Fred ended up getting charged with five felonies. They were for the possession of methamphetamine precursors, the manufacture and possession of methamphetamine itself. Wilma was charged with three felonies. Hers were for conspiring and the manufacture of methamphetamine. Barney was charged with four felonies. His charges were similar to those of Fred's. All three subjects ended up pleading guilty to the attempted manufacture of methamphetamine. Fred also plead guilty to the possession of methamphetamine and its precursors. Fred and Wilma were both sentenced to 180 days in jail with 48 months' probation. Fred was fined $4,112 and Wilma was fined $4,526. Barney was sentenced to 60 days in jail with 48 months probation. He was fined $2,451.

Besides getting drugs and their makers off the street, this case had extra importance to me. I made this arrest about 10 miles from my home. Barney grew up living within two miles of us. He had ridden the same bus to school as my own children. One can never be sure who lives down the street.

Hard Habit to Break

The roads along the Mississippi River near Muscatine seemed like "Meth Alley" for a while. In April of 2009, Laura and I were out patrolling on a Sunday night. Sometimes, a Sunday night can be very productive. A cold one in the middle of April is usually not one of them. We had struggled for a couple of hours trying to find anybody out and about. As we drove northeast of Lock and Dam 16, we located a truck parked between the road and the Mississippi River. In that area, there's a wing dam that extends out from the riverbank. Wing dams are just walls made of crushed rock that the U.S. Government has dumped into the Mississippi River. They help in maintaining the commercial navigation channel. By putting these rock walls near the bank, it forces the river to send more water through the main channel. That increased flow helps to keep sediment from settling in the main channel. For fishermen, wing dams are awesome. For boaters, not so much. Quite often, the wing dams are just below the surface of the river. Although you can see the disturbance on the surface, many people have lost lower units by hitting one. At low water levels, some of the wing dams will be exposed. This particular wing dam was exposed on that night.

Stopping on the road, we looked toward the river and saw that there was a guy (Louis) standing out on the wing dam. Louis was about 20 yards out from the riverbank. Parking my squad, Laura walked over to check Louis' truck. As I walked down the bank toward Louis, he saw Laura's flashlight up by his truck and yelled at her. When I had reached the wing dam, I identified myself to Louis. Louis had fishing poles in the water, so I asked him for his license. Louis said that he didn't have one. I told Louis that he would have to walk with me up to my squad. Louis agreed.

Reaching my squad, I called ISP and ran a driver's license check on Louis. Sure enough, Louis was wanted on a warrant. Louis had violated the terms of his probation. Exiting my squad, I placed Louis in handcuffs. He had about four layers of clothing on, so searching him was a bit of a chore. In the belly pouch of Louis' inner sweatshirt, I located a soft vinyl case. Opening the case, I located four hypodermic needles. When questioned about them, Louis said that he wasn't diabetic and didn't inject anything. He told me that he was just getting rid of the syringes for his friend. I asked Louis what his "friend" would inject with them. Louis told me that his "friend" would inject all sorts of stuff. Louis refused to tell me what his "friend's" name was.

I secured Louis in my squad. Although he was an adult, Louis asked if we could turn all his belongings over to his parents. We agreed. Calling them, we transferred everything when they arrived. Relaying Louis to the Rock Island County Jail, he was charged with the possession of hypodermic needles and fishing without a license. I relayed the needles to the lab where they tested positive for methamphetamine. Charges for the methamphetamine were never filed, but Louis ended up pleading guilty to the other charges and was fined $635.

Almost two years later, it was nice warm April day. At about 6:30 p.m., I was driving south on the same road. After I passed the dam, I saw there were two vehicles parked along the road up ahead. They were facing the wrong way on my side of the street. The front vehicle was a truck with wood extensions going up from the bed sides. The vehicle parked behind it was a passenger car.

As with Louis, it's not uncommon for people to park along the road and walk down to the river. Approaching the vehicles, I could see a subject (Winston) in the front passenger seat of the truck. Nosing my squad up to the front of the truck, I exited the vehicle. Walking toward the open passenger window, I identified myself to Winston. When I reached the window, I asked him what he was doing. Winston told me that he was just sitting there. I didn't see anything illegal in the truck, so I continued past Winston. Walking along the passenger side of the truck, I had limited visibility behind it. The wood panels on the truck bed were high enough that I couldn't see over them. All I could see was the very rear of the vehicle parked behind the truck.

When I reached the back corner of the truck, I could see two subjects sitting in the car behind it. They immediately looked at me and their eyes got huge. They were obviously thinking "Oh shit!" I recognized the guy in the front passenger seat as Louis. The driver (Vigo) and Louis immediately looked down at the center console and started to move stuff around.

I quickly walked toward Louis' partially open window and identified myself to the subjects. When I reached the window, both Louis and Vigo sat straight up and looked straight forward. It was like their mom had just caught them with a Playboy. I asked Louis what they were up to. He told me that they were just "hanging out". Louis had a lighter clenched in his left fist and wouldn't look at me. Vigo had his right hand against his right hip and his left hand buried in his crotch. Both of them were frozen in place. There were a few $20 bills sitting on the seat next to Vigo's right leg. It was almost funny to see how good they were at sitting still. I asked Louis what they were moving around in the center console. Louis said, "Nothing". He just sat still and didn't say anything else.

While staring at Vigo and Louis, I walked around the front of their vehicle. Reaching Vigo's door, I found that his window was completely rolled down. I asked Vigo what they were up to. Vigo told me that they were just "hanging out". I asked Vigo if it was his car. He told me that it was his wife's car. Vigo said that his wife

didn't know that he had taken it. I asked Vigo if he had any identification. He got very excited and told me that he didn't. I asked
Vigo his name. He repetitively started saying, "Don't do this". In
between Vigo's continuous plea, I was able to get his name and
date of birth. I confirmed with Vigo that he didn't have a driver's license.

I asked Vigo to step out of the vehicle. He immediately
said, "Don't arrest me, let me go home". I again asked Vigo to
step out of the vehicle. As he began to open the door, Vigo excit-
edly pleaded with me not to arrest him. When Vigo stepped out,
two baggies of meth fell from his lap. One landed just inside of
the door and the other fell to the ground. Vigo closed the door
behind him. I asked Vigo to step to the rear of the vehicle and put
his hands on the trunk lid. Vigo started jerking his arms all around
and began continuously pleading with me, "Don't arrest me, don't
arrest me." I repeatedly told Vigo to put his hands on the trunk. As
he continued to shuffle toward the rear of the vehicle, his arms
never quit moving. I finally yelled at Vigo and told him to calm
down. I told Vigo to step up to the driver's door and put his chest
against the side of the vehicle. Vigo hesitated but complied. I told
Vigo to put his hands behind his back. He again cooperated but
started getting upset. I placed Vigo in handcuffs.

As I had Vigo step toward the rear of the vehicle, I told him
that I had seen the baggies of meth fall off of his lap. Vigo began
screaming and quickly walking in circles. He then yelled at me
that I was going to send him to prison for 15 years. I tried to calm
Vigo down, but he just kept screaming. This was one of very few
times that I ever requested routine assistance. I could not get Vigo
to settle down and still had two other people on scene. I moved
Vigo up to the front of his vehicle and told him to put his chest on
the hood. He continued screaming, but cooperated.

Searching the driver's area of Vigo's car, I didn't find any
other contraband. I walked around to the passenger side and

asked Louis to step out of the vehicle. He complied. I searched Louis but didn't find anything. I had Louis go up and sit on the bumper of his truck. When I started searching the passenger side, I glanced up and saw Louis reaching into the bed of his truck (over the tailgate). I again told Louis to have a seat on his bumper. Luis complied and told me that Winston had tossed a phone out of the back window to him. I told Winston to close the window. He complied. I then told Louis not to move again. Louis agreed. Under the front passenger seat, I found a glass meth pipe.

Completing the search of the car, I had Louis and Vigo move up to the front of my squad. Pulling Louis off to the side, I confirmed that he was the owner of the truck. Louis gave me permission to search it. During the search, I located drug paraphernalia and two containers of cannabis. As I completed the search, a Rock Island County Sheriff's Deputy arrived on scene and assisted in securing the subjects. Vigo had calmed down quite a bit.

I field-tested the cannabis and meth. Both tested positive. I was able to issue Louis a bond sheet and release him on scene. Once again, Louis couldn't lawfully drive his vehicle. This time, I had to call his sister to come help. Since Vigo was going to jail, he gave all his personal belongings to Louis.

While I was transporting Vigo to the Rock Island County Jail, he began crying in my squad. Vigo told me that he was on a 15-year deferred probation for possession of methamphetamine in Iowa. He said that he knew he was going to prison for 15 years. Vigo said that he had stopped using meth for seven months. He told me that his grandfather died last week, and he started using it again. I asked Vigo how long he had been using meth. He told me that his sister's boyfriend introduced him to it when he was 14 years old. Vigo was now 45. I asked Vigo if he had continuously used meth for the last 30 years. He agreed that he had. All except for the seven months prior to his grandpa's death. I asked Vigo how much he had paid for the two baggies of meth. Vigo told me that he had paid $300 for them. I asked Vigo how long the two baggies of meth would last him. He told me that they would last about a week. I told Vigo that he could have paid a house off with the money that he had spent on meth. Vigo agreed. He told me that he was glad that he had not tried to run from me, run me over or take my gun. Vigo admitted that he had thought about doing all three. Vigo said that he was a meth addict who had made a mistake. A short time later, Vigo was dropped off at the Rock Island County Jail.

Vigo eventually pled guilty to the illegal possession of methamphetamine and was fined $2,235. He ended up getting 24 months' probation in Rock Island County. Although I talked with Vigo's probation officer in Iowa, I never heard if his probation got revoked. The charges against Louis were dismissed.

Both Vigo and Louis were roofers. Louis lived in my community. I eventually got to know his family. They are good people. Louis was not the type of guy that likes to have in-depth conversations. He had not reached the same point as Vigo. Vigo was finally starting to understand where he had been and where meth was taking him. I don't know if either of them was ever able to kick the habit.

Hope

Although I can tell several more meth stories, I am going to finish with a short one. It's more about the person than the arrest. On an early August evening in 2015, I was patrolling Blackhawk State Historic Site. Having seen only one vehicle parked in the east lot, I decided to see who was in it.

As I approached the parked car, I could see there was a female (Dana) in the driver's seat and a male (Peter) in the front passenger seat. It was almost dark, so my headlights illuminated the interior of the car as I pulled my squad up by the driver's door. Parking my squad, I exited the vehicle and walked toward Dana's open window. Both subjects looked at me. Peter said something to Dana and she looked down between her legs. Dana quickly began moving something around.

I identified myself to the subjects as I reached the window. I asked the subjects what they were doing. Dana said, "Nothing." Dana was wearing skin-tight "shorty shorts". Looking down at where she had been reaching, Dana had little scabs all over her legs. Although Dana's left foot was sitting on the floor, she had pulled her right leg up and extended it across the car. Her calf was resting on Peter's lap. On the seat between Dana's legs was an open folding knife with a three-inch blade, two red straws and a small black case. Sticking out from under Dana's right leg was the end of a small glass drug pipe.

I advised both subjects to put their hands on their heads. They complied. I told them to keep them there as I stepped back to my squad and got some rubber gloves. When I returned to Dana's car, I opened the driver's door and pulled the loose things off Dana's seat. I then told her to hand me the glass pipe. Dana complied. I secured the evidence and asked Dana for some iden-tification. She handed me a valid driver's license.

I told Dana that I would be searching her and her vehicle. She acknowledged that she understood. I asked Dana to exit the vehicle. As Dana lifted her right leg from Peter's lap, she reached down below it with her right hand. I told Dana to stop moving her hand. Dana said, "Here" and handed me a small baggie contain-ing crystalline rocks. I had Dana exit the vehicle and checked her for weapons. She didn't have any, so I had her move up to the front of the vehicle. I asked Peter if he had any weapons and some identification. Peter handed me a razor knife and an Iowa ID card.

I told Dana that she was under arrest and read her Miranda Rights to her. After she acknowledged her rights, I asked Dana if the baggie contained meth or crack rocks. Dana admitted that it was meth.

Moving around to the passenger side of the vehicle, I searched Peter. He didn't have any other weapons or contraband. I asked Peter to step up to the front of the vehicle and put his hands on the hood. Peter was compliant. Searching the interior of the vehicle, I sifted through what seemed to be all of Dana's worldly possessions. The only other contraband that I found was a pill bottle with three pills. Dana said that they were her ex-boyfriend's.

The crystalline rocks field tested positive for meth. I handcuffed Dana and told her that she would be going to jail. She seemed unfazed by what I was telling her. Peter agreed to take care of Dana's car and belongings.

About an hour after the stop, I started transporting Dana to the Rock Island County Jail. We had not made it very far when Dana started getting upset. I asked her how much she had paid for the baggie of meth. Dana told me that she only had $40. She said that she had given it all for the baggie. Dana went on to tell me that she was homeless. She said that she had been kicked out of where she was living. Dana confided that she had not always done meth. She told me that she started doing meth after her three-month-old daughter died. Dana was only 22 years old when I arrested her. I asked her what happened to her daughter. Dana told me that she always slept in bed with her daughter. She said that she got drunk one night. Dana said that when she woke up the next morning, her daughter was dead next to her. Dana told me that it was ruled to be a SIDS death.

I felt horrible for Dana. I tried to give her a life "pep talk" on the rest of our ride together. It's really hard to do in one 10-minute session. Dana was initially found guilty for possession of methamphetamine and fined $1,232. She was entered into a two-year Offender Initiative Program (OIP). During the OIP, Dana had to routinely submit to drug testing. When she completed the program, all the charges against her were dismissed. About the time that Dana completed the OIP, I saw a picture of her on the internet. She looked nice and had graduated from a junior college program.

If you read into what I have written about meth cases, there's a lot going on in them. There's my own community connection to some of the people involved, the long- and short-term effects of the drug on its users and the dangers involved with meth as a police officer. The danger of dealing with both the substance and the user who doesn't want to go to jail. I don't live in a "druggie community". It's just a typical Midwest American town—the same Midwest America that many of you live in. Meth, in some form or another, will be here forever. Don't ever take for granted what's going on around you and within your community. Be curious, educate your kids and be willing to be the "bad guy". That's the one who doesn't let their kid hang out with somebody they don't trust. It's also the one that makes a positive difference in their community by reporting the things they see. It's easy to hate a game warden if you get a ticket for poaching a deer, but having a game warden in your community is not necessarily a bad thing!

BUSINESS INSPECTIONS

Over the years, many people have asked me what my favorite part of the job is. There are so many parts of the job that I thoroughly enjoy that it can be a hard to answer the question. Thinking broadly, I would have to say that I love the challenge of the job. The challenge of catching someone who is intentionally breaking the law. Can you beat them at their "game"? Even if they get away with the act, will they let their guard down later? If so, can you figure it out and still make a case? As far as areas of enforcement go, fishing, hunting, drug arrests and business inspections would be my top four. Business inspections can be really special. Not only do you have an opportunity to catch the business owner, but you also have an opportunity to catch everyone that they do business with. No matter what type of business it was, I always tried to figure out the "quirks". Where will the owners and/or customers try to cheat?

My favorite type of business inspection was always taxidermy inspections. I think I came about it naturally. My dad had an interest in taxidermy when I was a kid. Although he never learned how to do it, I think his desire rubbed off on me. I always liked looking at mounted fish and animals. Every time I caught a big fish, I would ask dad if it was big enough to have it mounted. Over the years, dad got one fish and a deer head mounted for me. When I got hired with the DNR and started doing taxidermy inspections, I got the best of both worlds. I got to look at the taxidermist's artwork, while challenging myself to catch bad guys through their business. Late in my game warden career, a local taxidermist (Gary Finch) taught me how to do fish taxidermy. Gary not only taught me a trade but became a good friend. I will forever be thankful for both. Now I find myself mounting just about everything that my kids ask me to!

Even though I had only been a game warden for three years, by 1997 I was getting decent at doing taxidermy inspections. I had been averaging about 10 a year. Although I had seen other officers look for paperwork violations during their inspections, I was looking for poachers. In December of that year, I was having trouble catching one of my taxidermists at home (we will call him Jeb). Finally, on Christmas Eve, I went to Jeb's house and found him at his house. Jeb's work area was inside of the house, but the rest of his business had consumed the garage behind it. In the business of taxidermy, Jeb was somewhat of a pioneer. He was likely one of the first guys to develop foam deer forms. Years before I met Jeb, he created fiberglass molds that he filled with spray foam. After trimming them up, a taxidermist would be ready to start mounting a deer head. Early in his career, I think Jeb sold more deer forms to other taxidermists than he taxidermied animals. The big businesses eventually caught up with Jeb and left him in the dust. By the time I met Jeb, he was still making forms for himself, but was not selling any. He had primarily returned to simply doing taxidermy work.

On this day, I met with Jeb and advised him that I needed to inspect his taxidermy business. Jeb agreed and explained the layout of the business. After we looked in his house, Jeb led me out to the garage. As Jeb showed me the layers of stuff inside, I saw that he had a freezer along the rear wall. I told Jeb that we would need to check the freezer. He agreed and started to clear the stuff off the top. When Jeb finally opened the freezer, I could see several untagged items. Taxidermists are required to have all the items in their shop tagged. The tags must be coordinated with their logbook. The logbook is then required to have the hunter or fisherman's information. For migratory waterfowl, there are some extra regulations (the Feds have inspection authority as well).

Pulling out one of the untagged items, I was able to identify it as a wild turkey. Besides not having a business tag, the turkey did not have a harvest tag on the leg. If a hunter had legally harvested the bird in Illinois, it should have a leg tag. I asked Jeb where he got the turkey. He told me that he had gotten it from his ex-wife (Martha). Jeb proceeded to tell me that Martha was also a taxidermist. He said that Martha had opened a business of her own in the Chicago suburbs, which was quite different than the remote area where Jeb was operating. Jeb proceeded to tell me that a guy had come into Martha's business with four turkeys. Reportedly, the guy only wanted two of the turkeys taxidermied. He gave the other two turkeys to Martha to eat. One of them eventually made its way to Jeb's house.

After completing the check of the freezer, we went back into the house and checked Jeb's work area. Looking through it, I asked Jeb if he had any animals in his kitchen freezer. Jeb opened the freezer and pulled a hen pheasant from inside. There are several ways to legally have a hen pheasant in Illinois, but none of them are real common. I asked Jeb where the pheasant had come from. Jeb told me that he had found it dead along the road. I explained to Jeb that he could not legally possess the pheasant under those circumstances. Jeb acknowledged that he understood. I ended up seizing the two illegal birds from Jeb and advised him that I would be back in contact with him after I investigated the turkey. Jeb acknowledged that he understood.

Martha's business was in a section of Chicago that I was not real familiar with. Having trained up there with CPO Stan Camlic, I figured that I would just call Stan and he could help me. I had a lot of fun when I trained with Stan. Stan was very nonchalant in his approach to the job. If I screwed something up, Stan didn't get too stressed out about it. In fact, Stan never got too stressed out about anything during training. I was really looking forward to going back and working with Stan now that I was an officer. Making the call, Stan was happy to help me. We agreed to meet about a week later.

Arriving at Martha's place of business, we walked through the front door and met with her. After introductions, we told Martha that we were going to do an inspection on her business. Martha's business was the exact opposite of Jeb's. It consisted of two big rooms in a strip mall setting. One of the rooms was loaded with exotic full-body mounts. As we talked with Martha, she told us that she had made a lot of money renting the mounts out. Apparently, people would call her when they were making commercials in Chicago or if they had an event where they needed one for display.

During the inspection, we located undersized yellow perch and untagged deer heads. As I was looking through Martha's logbook, her phone rang. Going into the other room, Martha returned in short order. When she came back, Martha told me "those are the people that you need to arrest". Surprised at her comment, I asked Martha what she was talking about. Martha proceeded to tell me that some guy just called her and asked how to mount a hawk. Martha explained that a hawk's head is bigger than its neck (unlike a game bird). I was really surprised at what Martha had just told me. What are the odds of this call coming in while I was standing there? In 1997, I don't know that "caller ID" was even available. If it was, hardly anybody had it. But in the months before this, there was a new phone option that had become available.

After you got off the phone, you could lift it back up and dial *69. It would tell you the telephone number of the last person who called you. I asked Martha if I could try it on her telephone. She agreed. Dialing it in, it actually worked! I got a telephone number to follow up on.

Completing the inspection, I asked Martha where the receipts and paperwork for the turkeys was located. Going into the other room, Martha returned with the paperwork. She had removed it from the regular logbook. I asked Martha what happened. She told me that two guys (we will call them Laurel and Hardy) brought two tagged turkeys in for full-body mounts. While they were there, they asked Martha if she wanted two others to eat. Martha said yes. Laurel and Hardy walked out and came back in with two more untagged turkeys. Martha said that they just wanted the tails and beards mounted on the untagged birds. They told her that she could eat the meat. I asked Martha where the mounted turkeys were located. She told me that both full-body mounts and one tail fan had been completed and returned. The remaining tail fan Martha turned over to me as evidence. Martha provided us a statement and we told her that we would stop back later.

The following day, Stan and I met up again and drove to Laurel's house. Knocking on his door, we met with Laurel. We told Laurel that he was not under arrest, but that we would like him to meet us at LaGrange Police Department for an interview. Laurel agreed. This is a tactic that I did not normally use. I will call it "city boy" interviewing. I didn't mind people being a little more comfortable while they were talking with me at their house or out in the field. I guess my method was a little more "hillbilly". A lot of officers really liked the "home turf advantage" that talking with someone at a police department gave them.

When we sat down with Laurel, I asked him if he knew why we had asked him to come to talk with us. Laurel said that he had no clue. Yea, right. I asked Laurel what happened when he went turkey hunting. Laurel told me that he and Hardy had gone turkey hunting and killed two turkeys. I asked Laurel how they had taken four turkeys to Martha. Laurel immediately admitted that he and Hardy had killed four turkeys. He told me that he killed three of them. After reading Laurel his Miranda Rights, I asked Laurel to give me the full story. Laurel explained that he and Hardy had gone deer and turkey hunting at Rock Cut State Park. As they sat in a ground blind together, a flock of turkeys came in. Laurel said that he shot at three of them. He told me that two of the birds ran off over a hill and the third fell in its tracks. Laurel said that he went out and recovered the turkey and they went and checked it in. After lunch, Laurel and Hardy returned to the blind. At about 1:00 p.m., another flock came in. Laurel did not have a shot, so he handed the gun to Hardy. Laurel told me that Hardy wounded one of the turkeys and it ran down over the hill. Laurel advised that when they went to recover the wounded turkey, they found three dead birds in the same spot. Laurel said they tagged one of the birds, checked it in and left. Laurel wrote me out a statement. We went back to Laurel's house and seized the untagged turkey tail fan and beard.

I was not familiar with Rock Cut State Park. It is in north central Illinois (not my district). Calling one of the officers that works that area, I asked him about the turkey hunt. I was told that the hunt was only for disabled hunters. He said that disabled hunters could take a "helper" with them, but the "helper" could not obtain a permit to hunt on that site.

Driving to Hardy's house, we knocked and met with him. Hardy invited us into his home. Stepping inside, I explained to Hardy that we could issue him a citation and read him his Miranda Rights. Hardy acknowledged that he understood. I asked Hardy what happened during the turkey hunt. Hardy's story was the same as Laurel's. I asked Hardy if he had a permit. He advised that he was the helper and did not have a permit. Hardy knew his violations and wrote a statement for us. We seized his full-body turkey mount and issued him citations for taking a turkey without a valid permit and the illegal possession of a turkey. Returning to Laurel's several days later, he received matching citations. It was noted that the permit violation was for taking over the limit. Both subjects received several written warnings and a mandatory court date.

Stan and I were feeling pretty good about our turkey caper, but now we needed to think about the hawk telephone call. Using the prefix for the telephone number, we were able to figure out that the call had come from Oak Lawn, Illinois (a Chicago suburb). Contacting Oak Lawn Police Department, they advised that they did not have a way to search their in-house system for telephone numbers. We tried calling the telephone company. They would not tell us who the number was registered to. A search warrant was not going to be attainable with what little information that we had. After talking about it for a while, Stan and I decided that we would just call the number. As a general rule of thumb, you do not want to do interviews over the telephone. It's too easy to lie when you are not looking at someone. You also don't want to alert anybody to the fact that you are investigating them. They get too much time to develop and rehearse their "story". We called the number when it was likely that nobody was home (daytime on a weekday). We were hoping to get an answering machine with a last name on the recording. Sure enough, after five rings or so, it went to the answering machine. The answering machine said, "You have reached the 'Smitty' residence, please leave your..." Needless to say, we didn't leave anything but had gotten what we were hoping for.

Going back to Oak Lawn Police Department, we asked them to punch Smitty into their computer. They came up with a guy (who we will call Scott Smitty) who had the same telephone number as the hawk caller. We were able to get and address and check on Smitty's background. When we ran Smitty through the DNR system, we found that he was not a licensed taxidermist in Illinois.

Later that day, Stan and I went to Smitty's house and met with him. Smitty admitted to doing some taxidermy, but would not admit to having a hawk. We asked Smitty to show us his facility. Smitty agreed and led us out to his garage. Smitty had a work area at the back of the garage and was conducting a taxidermy business without a license. Although he was not doing a lot of items, he admitted to knowing that he needed a license for what he was doing. While in the garage, we asked Smitty more about the hawk. Smitty would not break. We knew he was lying to us, but he just kept doing it. Every angle we tried with Smitty, he deflected. He would not admit to having or knowing where the hawk was. Finally, we just asked Smitty if he would meet us at Oak Lawn Police Department. Since my "hillbilly" method of interviewing Smitty was not working, we were going to try Stan's "city boy" method.

Leaving Smitty's house, Stan and I went to Oak Lawn P.D. We really didn't talk about our approach or how to get a confession out of Smitty. We primarily discussed our frustration with Smitty continuously lying to us. At Oak Lawn P.D., we were told that we could use one of their meeting rooms. I have to say that I was a little curious to see if Smitty would show up. I am sure that he was just as frustrated with us as we were with him. Smitty arrived in short order and we headed up to the meeting room. There was a big meeting table in the room. Stan and I sat on one side of the table and Smitty on the other. We went through the "rules" of the interview with Smitty and told him that he was free to go at any time. When we started the interview, Smitty stuck to his guns. He did not have a hawk and was just curious about how to mount one. Going from one interview method to the next, Smitty held it together. I couldn't tell it, but Stan's frustration level had obviously reached the top floor. I was about to get my first lesson in "city boy bad cop".

Stan leaned forward in his chair and said something to the point of "This is fucking bullshit! You're fucking lying!" He went on from there as I sat in disbelief. Heck, I had not heard an officer crack a whip like that with on a suspect. I stood up and told Stan that we had better step outside. As I moved him toward the door, I felt like Stan was a boxer taunting his opponent at the weigh-in. I was just the manager moving him out the door. When we got out into the hall, Stan carried it on until the door closed and both of us started laughing. I think he was as surprised as I was at what he had said. I told Stan to stay in the hall and I would go in to see if Smitty had a change of heart. He agreed.

It was probably good that we had not rehearsed what Stan did. If Smitty looked at me during the rant, he saw that I was just as shocked as he was. When I went back in and sat down with Smitty, I started to explain that it was frustrating to talk with a liar. Smitty cut me off and said that he wanted to be honest. As he started to tell me the truth, I told Smitty to hold that thought. I went out and got Stan. Stan came in, sat down and looked like an angry parent listening to his kid's line of BS. Smitty proceeded to tell us that he had a friend from Michigan who had picked up a hawk. As we anticipated, Smitty wanted to mount it for the guy. Smitty wrote us out a statement. Since the remainder of the case would be in Cook County (and Michigan), Stan completed the investigation. If I remember correct, there were tickets issued for operating a taxidermy business without a license and possession of a bird of prey.

Yes, the "city cop" method worked good for the situation that we had. I still preferred to use field interviews, but was enlightened on the use of a formal setting. I never got to work with Stan after that. We were always in different Districts. Laurel and Hardy were found guilty of taking turkeys illegally. For some reason the circuit clerk would not tell me what their fines ended up being. Losing the full-body turkey mount likely cost Hardy over $300 by itself. Jeb and Martha got some warnings for their business practices and Jeb got a citation for his pheasant. All in all, a fun taxidermy inspection.

Online Dating

Being a relatively urban area, when I was in Will County, I dealt with many nuisance animal complaints. There is always someone complaining about raccoons getting into their garbage, deer eating their plants and groundhogs burrowing under their shed. If the complainant cannot legally kill the animal by normal hunting means, they can request a nuisance permit from a biologist or a Conservation Officer. A nuisance permit can be written to allow a complainant to use otherwise illegal means to take the animal. It can also be issued during a time of the year when the animal cannot otherwise be legally taken. With this kind of a permit, the complainant is required to do all the work in order to remove and dispose of the animal.

If someone has a problem with nuisance wildlife, but is not a hunter or trapper, they can try option number two. Option number two is to hire a licensed nuisance trapper. Licensed nuisance trappers are commercial businesses licensed by the IDNR to remove nuisance species (from a complainant's property). Upon fielding the complaint, a nuisance trapper will survey the situation and come up with a remedy for removal of the animal(s). A nuisance trapper will commonly set traps on the premises until the animal is captured. Because the animal is considered to be a nuisance, it's required to be destroyed and burned or buried. There are always exceptions to the destruction rule, but that is the standard protocol. There's no sense in moving a nuisance animal to somebody else's property—just to turn into a nuisance there. The exceptions generally occur when the nuisance animal happens to be a deer, turkey, waterfowl or on the endangered species list.

Sometimes, an animal becomes a local celebrity and is spared the destruction fate because of public interest.

Animals taken by a licensed nuisance trapper cannot be kept or sold even if the nuisance animal is taken with lawful means and during an open season. As a young officer, I often thought that it would be hard for a nuisance trapper to pass on the ability to "double dip". They've been paid to catch and kill the nuisance animal, why not get paid to sell the hide too? Of course, the nuisance trapper would risk losing their commercial license. But all the nuisance trapper would have to do is skin the animal and add it to their "sportsmen's" pile. Unless we caught the nuisance trapper with green hides out of season, we would likely never know the animals had been taken with the use of their commercial permit. That is, unless the nuisance trapper never purchased a "regular" trapping license.

In mid-September of 1999, I received a call from a complainant in Romeoville. Talking with the complainant, I was told that there was a skunk caught in a live trap next to a house. The skunk had reportedly been in the trap for five weeks. I was told there was also a second live trap at the rear of the property. Responding to the area, I drove past the residence and could see the skunk on the north side of the house. It was caught in a live trap and was still alive. I drove back to the residence and parked in the driveway. Walking up to the front door, I knocked and ended up meeting with an elderly lady (Barb). When I asked Barb about the traps, she told me that she was having problems with critters around her house. Barb advised that she had hired a nuisance trapper to take care of the problem (we will call him Pepe). Barb said that she got Pepe's number from the city's public works department. She said that Pepe came out and set two traps for her. I asked Barb how long the animals had been stuck in the traps. Barb said that they had been in there for almost six weeks. I told Barb that the traps are required to be checked every day. Barb told me that she has called Pepe every week. She told me that Pepe had not come back to empty the traps. I got Pepe's name from Barb and asked her if we could look at the traps. Barb agreed. Following Barb to the trap behind the house, there was an opossum in it. Looking at the opossum, I could see cat food that had sifted to the ground underneath the trap. I inquired about the cat food. Barb told me that she was feeling guilty about the animals being stuck in the traps for so long. Barb said that she started feeding them. Looking closely at the trap, there was not a name tag on it (as required). I took the opossum with the trap and told Barb I would get in touch with Pepe. She thanked me. Before I left, I looked at the skunk in the other trap. I couldn't see a tag on that trap either. When the skunk spun around on me, I decided to just leave it in place. I didn't feel like being sprayed and figured that Pepe would have to deal with that one.

Leaving Barb's house, I drove to Pepe's residence. Walking up to the front door, I knocked. Pepe eventually came to the door and met with me. I advised Pepe that I needed to talk with him about some nuisance trapping. Pepe said that he had not taken on any new jobs in two months. I asked Pepe if I could see his logbook. Pepe agreed and retrieved it from his van. As I paged through the book, I found a contract with Barb's name on it. The beginning service date was three months earlier. I told Pepe that I had been called to Barb's house because the traps had not been cleared. Pepe indicated that he had forgotten about Barb's traps.

Following my gut instinct about nuisance trappers, I asked Pepe where his dead animal freezer was located. Pepe shot to a "10" on the nervous scale. He hesitated and told me that he did not have one. I asked Pepe if I could see some of his traps to cross-reference them with the one that I had seized. Pepe agreed. At this point in the investigation, I was just trying to keep Pepe engaged. I followed Pepe into the backyard where he showed me some of the traps. They were secured in his van and stacked in a breeze way behind the house. The traps matched the one that I had seized from Barb's house. I could smell a faint odor of skunk in Pepe's backyard. I asked Pepe if he had any dead animals in his garage. Pepe said that he did not. I asked him if we could look. Pepe agreed.

When Pepe opened the door, the skunk smell was very strong. What I could smell outside was definitely coming from the garage. Stepping inside, I could see a freezer along the back wall. There were boxes stacked up to my waist everywhere. Along the walls, the boxes were stacked even higher. It was the perfect "hoarder's garage". I asked Pepe if there were any dead animals in the freezer. He said, "Yes...I mean no!" I tipped my head down, looked at Pepe and asked him if we could look. Pepe lowered his shoulders and said, "Yes".

Making our way down a path to the freezer, Pepe moved a bunch of stuff from the lid and opened the freezer. It was full of bags containing animal hides. I asked Pepe if he had a regular trapper's license. He said that he had not gotten one in 10 years. He quickly added that he did not sell hides. I confirmed with Pepe that he had taken the animals under his nuisance trapper's license. Pepe agreed. Going through the freezer, I found 14 dead skunks, 15 raccoon hides, a grey fox and a whitetail deer fawn hide. Pepe said that the fawn was a roadkill. I asked Pepe if he had gotten a confirmation number or tag for it. In Illinois, the law has changed several times over the years. Generally, people have had to get something to show that they registered the deer. Pepe advised that he did not have one.

As we walked back toward the front door, I saw another door that went to a different section of the garage. I asked Pepe if he had anything in that section. Pepe agreed that he did. I asked Pepe if we could look. Pepe said, "Yes" and led me into another small room. The room was full of old mounts and animal parts. As I asked Pepe where the things had come from, he would give me an explanation. When I got to a bunch of skunk parts, Pepe told me that he had not bought any of those. I asked him if he had gotten all of them from nuisance trapping. He agreed that he had. Pepe told me that he had an affinity for skunks. He said he liked them so much that he would tan the hides and make stuff out of them. Seeing a big dog carrier, I looked inside and saw three live raccoons. Pepe said that he had caught the raccoons in a nuisance trap earlier in the year. Knowing he could not keep them, Pepe offered to euthanize the raccoons. I agreed that he would have to. I asked Pepe if he would also euthanize the opossum from Barb's house. He agreed. I seized six skunk skin hats and everything from Pepe's freezer.

After Pepe euthanized the animals, I issued him five tickets for his trapping and possession of animals violations. I could have written him a citation for each animal, but figured it would be overkill. I also told Pepe that he was responsible to take care of the skunk at Barb's house. He agreed. I photographed the dead animals and hides and took them to Peotone Animal Hospital. I knew that Peotone Animal Hospital had an incinerator and would help me out in the destruction of what I had seized. They did and cussed me afterward. They said that as soon as they started the incinerator the dead skunk smell permeated their entire business. Apparently, it took a week to get rid of the stench! They told me that they would not be incinerating skunks for me in the future.

You would think that story ended there, but no. Just before I went to court for Pepe's trial, I got a call from Pepe's wife (Flower). Flower was obviously upset and was crying on the phone as she talked to me. Flower told me that she thought Pepe had gotten into drugs. She said that Pepe left her for another woman (Sugar Momma) that he found on the internet. You must keep in mind that although this kind of stuff is common now, it wasn't back then. Half of the people didn't even have a computer. The ones who did had a really slow one. Apparently, Sugar Momma was wealthy and had sent Pepe money so he could travel to the east coast (to be with her). I was wondering what all of this had to do with me. Well, it had significantly warmed up that January. Everything had been melting and Flower was stuck with cleaning up the mess that Pepe had left behind. That included their garage. Looking to see what she could get rid of, Flower went out into the garage and started opening boxes. To her surprise, almost all the boxes in the garage were filled with dead animal carcasses. When I was there it had stunk really bad, but I just attributed it to what I was seizing from the freezer. As Flower continued talking, I couldn't help but wonder why the hell Pepe was storing animal carcasses in boxes! Flower eventually asked if I could come clean out the garage for her. I agreed to clean it out if I could seize everything that was animal related. Flower agreed to my terms. I ended up seizing two 55-gallon garbage cans full of dead animal carcasses (about 50 animals in total). I use the term "animal carcasses" loosely. The carcasses were tied in plastic bags and had literally turned into a watery puree "slop" with some hair and bones. The species of animal could not even be identified in some of the bags. I found a business that destroyed yard waste. They agreed to get rid of this batch of slop.

A week or so later, we were scheduled for trial. Prior to going to trial, we had a meeting with Pepe's defense attorney. The new evidence was disclosed. With that, Flower had become our "trump card". Having returned from his adventures, Pepe pleaded guilty to disposing of dead animals improperly. He was fined $619. The other charges were dismissed. I never did get an answer as to why Pepe was storing animal carcasses in his garage. Kind of fun turning two animals in traps into what the case ended up being.

Quail Talons

I would have to say that 1997 solidified my love for taxidermy inspections. In the "game wardening" business, February has traditionally been a slower month. Looking for things to keep busy,

I knew that if I did a taxidermy inspection I would find something to investigate. Laura and I decided to inspect one of my "favorite" taxidermists (Eddie). Eddie was nice enough, but that wasn't why I liked inspecting his business. It was because Eddie did a great job of mounting deer heads. At the time, Eddie was way ahead of the other local taxidermists. He had better definition in his mounts and took extra time with the most minor details. If you were looking at one of Eddie's mounts, you felt like it was alive. I looked forward to inspecting Eddie's facility—just to see his work.

Going to Eddie's house, we met with him. Eddie didn't do a lot of customer work. It was more of a hobby business for him. Something to fill his time and make a few extra bucks. I advised Eddie that we were there to conduct an inspection on his business. Eddie told us that he had not purchased a license yet this year. He said that he was getting out of the business. I asked Eddie if he was still completing customer work in his shop. Eddie admitted that he was. I advised Eddie that if he was conducting business, he would be required to be licensed. Eddie agreed and led us out to inspect his facility.

Eddie lived in a ranch style house with a detached garage. As we followed Eddie into the rear door of the garage, we walked directly into his workshop. The wall between the workshop and the remainder (front) of the garage also had a door. Only the workshop was heated. I told Eddie that I needed to check his records. Eddie told me that he didn't have all his records together. He said that he would need some time to get it done. Acknowledging that I understood, I advised Eddie that we would need to check his work. Eddie agreed and led us to the cold side of the garage. Eddie had two freezers. A chest freezer and a refrigerator (with a freezer on top). Checking the chest freezer, Eddie had several untagged items. Without records, we had no way to cross-reference the items and confirm that they had been legally taken. As we located violations, we mentioned them to Eddie.

Moving to the refrigerator freezer, Eddie handed me a bag of untagged bluegills. Then he handed me a zipper bag full of birds. Eddie pointed at the first bird and said, "This is a blue bird." Pointing to the next bird, Eddie said, "This is a redbird." Eddie said that he thought the third one was a wren and the last one was a "skinned quail". I knew that Eddie's identifications were wrong. It really didn't matter much because Eddie couldn't legally have any songbirds. I looked more closely at the fourth bird. It was wrapped up tightly in a plastic bag. If it was a quail, it was definitely the biggest damn quail that I had ever seen. It was about 12 inches long. Unwrapping the feet, I could see that they were raptor talons. Showing them to Eddie, I told him that I had never seen a quail with feet like that before. I am pretty sure that I heard him swallow hard. I unwrapped the head and found a sharp curved beak. Eddie sighed and told me that it was a "sparrowhawk". He quickly added that all the birds had flown into his windows. Eddie told us that he had them in his house freezer. He said that his wife must have moved them out to the garage. Yes, wives get a lot of blame in this business. Eddie knew that he could not have any of the birds. After completing the freezers, we checked the workshop. We found a few more untagged items.

Completing a check of his facility, we talked with Eddie about the illegal birds. He indicated that he was going to mount them for display in his house. We told Eddie that we were going to be seizing the birds. Eddie acknowledged that he understood. Laura and I walked back to the squad, filled out a receipt and gave a copy to Eddie. Eddie asked if we wanted the carcass of the sparrowhawk (it had been skinned out). We told Eddie that we did. Eddie looked around, but couldn't find it. It seemed like Eddie was stalling us. Eddie said that he knew the carcass was around the shop somewhere. He advised that he just needed more time to find it. I told Eddie that if he found the carcass, he could call me. He acknowledged that he understood. We told Eddie that after we had positively identified the birds, we would come back. Eddie agreed.

As we were about to leave, Eddie again reiterated that he had not killed any of the birds. We told Eddie that we would be having them x-rayed. Eddie advised that he wanted to "help" his situation. Eddie said that he knew a guy who had poached a red-tailed hawk (we will call the guy Bif). Laura and I were all ears at that point! Eddie was hesitant to tell us Bif's name, but proceeded. Eddie said that Bif shot the red-tailed hawk while he was goose hunting. Eddie told us that after Bif killed the hawk, he called Eddie and asked him to mount it. Eddie said that he kept refusing to do the mount. Eddie told us that he didn't want to get caught with the hawk. He said that it would have been different than having one that flew into your window. We asked Eddie how long it had been since Bif killed the red-tailed hawk. Eddie said that Bif killed it during goose season (a few months previous). We asked Eddie if Bif would still have the hawk. Eddie said that Bif asked him to do the mount several times. Eddie was pretty certain that Bif would still have the hawk. He said that he would try to get the red-tailed hawk and call us. We agreed.

The following day, Eddie called me and said that he had found the sparrowhawk carcass. I advised Eddie that I would stop back in a few days to get it. Eddie agreed. I asked Eddie if he had called Bif. Eddie said that he was working on trying to get the red-tailed hawk. Eddie was not real confident that he could close the deal. In a single day, I had gone from confident myself to doubtful.

Although Laura and I felt pretty good about our identification of Eddie's birds, we wanted to confirm it. Taking the birds to a local expert, he confirmed that we had seized an indigo bunting, cardinal, ovenbird and a sharp-shinned hawk. When I left the expert, I drove back to Eddie's house. Meeting with Eddie, I got the sharp-shinned hawk's carcass. I told Eddie what his birds actually were. Eddie and I talked about Bif again. Eddie assured me that Bif was still in possession the red-tailed hawk. He just wasn't as confident that Bif would bring it to him.

The following day, I took the songbirds and the sharp-shinned hawk carcass to Peotone Animal Hospital. Being friends with the owners, I asked them to x-ray the birds. They agreed. Reviewing the x-rays, the veterinarians could not definitively tell me what had killed any of the birds. They were confident that none of the birds had any metal fragments (or BBs) in their bodies. Good news for Eddie!

About 10 days later, Eddie finally called me. I had almost given up on getting the second hawk. Eddie told me that one of Bif's friends (we will call him Boof) had brought the red-tailed hawk to him. I drove to Eddie's house and met with him in his workshop. Eddie had the red-tailed hawk wrapped up in a plastic bag. As I opened the bag and looked at it, Eddie told me that he had confirmed (with Boof) how the hawk was killed. Eddie said that Boof was goose hunting with Bif when Bif shot it. I asked Eddie if he would write me a statement. Eddie agreed.

Laura and I went back to Peotone Animal Hospital the next day. X-raying the red-tailed hawk, there were several birdshot BBs in the carcass. It was pretty easy to confirm how the red-tailed hawk had been killed. I think the veterinarians were as excited as we were to find the BBs. It really seemed like they had fun being a part of the investigation. It was kind of like being the "Quincy" of animals!

A couple of days later, Laura and I went to Boof's house. Meeting with Boof, we asked him to meet us at the New Lenox Police Department. Boof Agreed. Yes, we were "city copping" it. When we all arrived, we went through the rules of the interview with Boof. He acknowledged that he understood and agreed to talk with us. We told Boof that we knew about the red-tailed hawk. Boof told us that he had not killed it. Boof said that he was hunting geese with Bif. Boof said that Bif was blowing on his goose call when the red-tailed hawk flew over. Boof said that Bif shot the hawk twice. Boof said that the hawk was dead when it hit the ground. Bif reportedly ran out, picked the hawk up and shoved it into his backpack. Boof was on a roll and we let him keep talking. Boof proceeded to tell us that Bif took the hawk home and put it in his freezer. He said that Bif would also have about 16 ducks in his freezer and a live goose in his garage. Boof told us that Bif had decided to throw the hawk out, so he (Boof) took it and was going to have Eddie mount it. Boof agreed to write us a statement.

Leaving New Lenox P.D., Laura and I drove to Eddie's house. As we were talking with Eddie, Boof pulled into the driveway. He walked up to the door and told us that Bif knew we were coming. He said that Bif was planning to tell us that the redtailed hawk was already dead when he "found" it. Boof was obviously playing both sides of the field. Nobody else could have called Bif. Boof just made our job a little harder. Although Boof appeared to have been honest during the interview, giving Bif a "heads-up" could make our interview of Bif much harder.

Driving to Bif's house, at approximately 7:30 p.m. we parked in his driveway. Bif lived near some power plants on a large piece of ground. The property consisted of several gravel strip pits with very few trees. It was a great place for waterfowl hunting. There was always open water on the power plant cooling ponds and the Illinois River was a natural flyway (only a couple of miles away). Walking up to the house, we knocked and were met by a female subject. Identifying ourselves to her, we asked if Bif was home. She told us that he would be back in five minutes.

Waiting in our squad, Bif pulled in on time. Exiting our squad, we identified ourselves to Bif and asked him if we could talk with him. Bif agreed. Bif led us to the house. Inviting us in, we had seats on opposing couches. Bif led off with, "I cannot vouch for all of the hunters that hunt out here." He went on to say that he had found the dead hawk outside. We immediately tossed the ball back into Bif's court. We told Bif that we knew he was going to use that excuse. We further explained that we knew he had killed the hawk while he was goose hunting. It took a while, but Bif eventually admitted to shooting the red-tailed hawk. Bif said that he was calling geese first thing in the morning and saw the bird coming in. Bif claimed that he had low light conditions and misidentified the bird. Bif said that after he shot it, he took it into possession. He said that he didn't know it was illegal to have it. For some reason that is a common theme amongst poachers - "I didn't know." It really didn't matter what Bif's excuse was; we had the confession!

I asked Bif if we could look in his freezer. Bif agreed and led us over to a chest freezer. Opening the top, it seemed like there was an awful lot of "open" freezer space. Inventorying the contents, we found a couple of deer hides and an exact limit of ducks and geese. Bif told us that he had taken a taxidermy class and was thinking about taking it up as a hobby. I asked Bif if he had a live goose in his garage. Bif agreed that he did. He said that when he found the goose, it was injured. Bif told us that he had been nursing the goose back to health and was going to take it to a rehabilitator. Bif showed us a goose with an injured leg. We let Bif hold onto the goose so he could take it in.

The day after our investigation, I got a dumping complaint. I was told that there was a bunch of bird carcasses dumped on the side of the road near what used to be Joliet Army Ammunition Plant. Responding to the area, it looked like someone had taken a bunch of birds (in plastic bags) out of their freezer and thrown them onto the side of the road. It was literally five minutes from Bif's house. We could not prove that the birds were Bif's, but I don't believe it was a coincidence.

Since Bif had killed the red-tailed hawk and Boof was a willing partner, we submitted a request for Federal prosecution on both of them. USFWS agreed with our assessment and filed the charges in Federal court. Bif was charged with the illegal killing and possession of a red-tailed hawk. Boof was charged with the illegal possession of it. Both subjects pled guilty in December of that year. Bif was fined $1,200 and Boof $600.

In the end, Eddie didn't think that we had given him a break. We gave Eddie a lot of "breaks". Eddie had about 30 State and Federal taxidermy violations (tagging and records). He also had a minimum of four Federal violations (for the birds in his possession). We only charged Eddie with one state violation—the illegal possession of a bird of prey. Eddie didn't come to court. He had his lawyer come for him. Eddie's lawyer walked up to me before court and showed me a picture of Eddie with a black eye. He told me that he wanted me to know that Eddie had gotten beat up because he had helped us. I asked the lawyer if they had filed charges on the assailants. I was told that they hadn't and were not pursuing it. The lawyer had Eddie pled guilty. Eddie was fined $200.

While I was conducting another taxidermy inspection in the spring of that year, a different taxidermist said that he knew a guy who wanted to give me some information. He said that the guy wanted to remain anonymous. The taxidermist said that he was told about a guy who was poaching ducks. He proceeded to explain that the poacher had a pole barn out by the cooling lakes. He said that the floor of the barn was covered in all different kinds of ducks during opening weekend of Teal Season. In Illinois, Teal Season is an early duck season. During the season, hunters can only kill Teal. As we talked, I figured out that he was talking about Bif and his buddies.

We were still prosecuting Bif and Boof in the Federal hawk case when opening day of Teal Season came around that fall. Since Bif's property was in Grundy County, I talked with CPO Mark Simon about the information that I had received. We decided to set up a detail on Bif's property. I asked Laura and Sgt. Mathis to help us. Sgt. Mathis acted as a driver for the rest of us. He dropped us off at different locations around Bif's property. Sneaking in, we each watched different blinds and buildings around the property.

All of us were at our posts about an hour before legal shooting time. We were able to watch four different guys shoot at ducks before legal hours. Bif was one of the early shooters. We also caught Bif and one of his buddies killing wood ducks out of season (they killed three of them). We didn't get the "mother-load", but we did seize three ducks and issued six tickets. Four for hunting before legal shooting hours and two for taking wood ducks out of season. The prosecution was not so good on this case. We got convictions, but the hunters were only fined $50 each.

No matter what kind of business inspection I conducted, I enjoyed the thrill of the chase. Sometimes, I was chasing the business owner and other times it was their customers. When it was customers, I would always be looking for "anomalies". Over the course of years, I was able to identify several standard anomalies that I would specifically be looking for. Those anomalies did not always guarantee that a law had been broken, but it would identify people that I needed to scrutinize more closely. It really works. You don't always get lucky and find a hawk in somebody's freezer.

GRETA THE PSYCHIC

I hired onto the IDNR in June of 1994. I was lucky enough to go back to my home area and was placed in Will County. Will County is part of District 3, which included Kankakee, Will and three other counties. When things happened within our District, we would generally try to draw upon our own officers prior to going outside of our District.

In August of 1995 a 12-year-old boy (Christopher Meyer) went missing in Aroma Park, Illinois. This sleepy little river town lies on the banks of the Kankakee River (in Kankakee County). Our family had moved to Aroma Park in 1988 (when I was 18). Though our mailing address was Aroma Park, our residence was actually in a subdivision about 10 miles from town. We moved in during the early summer and I left for college that fall. I never really had a chance to "learn" Aroma Park like I did Peotone. Occasionally, I would run into town if we needed something, but never really did the "teenager exploration" of it. Although Aroma Park had the small-town atmosphere, it was also a short drive from Kankakee. That put it on the edge of something happening all the time. I spent a fair amount of time in and around Kankakee. To put it nicely, it was a place where I would always try to be aware of my surroundings.

Immediately upon Christopher going missing, foul play was suspected. Some of his belongings were found and he had been spotted with a guy who turned out to be a convicted murderer. Not privy to the details of the investigation, I will jump ahead and just say that we were told that Christopher may have ended up in Kankakee River State Park. The State Park system in Illinois is run by the Illinois DNR and enforcement in the parks is generally our responsibility. It was determined that a search of the park needed to be made. Sgt. Mathis assigned me to lead a search party in the hunting areas south of the Kankakee River. Those "hunting areas" had numbered parking lots and included lots numbered one through 10. Those parking lots were gravel and allowed access to the surrounding hunting area. The surrounding hunting areas are primarily timbered with some farm fields mixed in. There were also snowmobile and horse trails that travel throughout those areas. When I received my assignment, I knew that I wanted to key in on two areas—parking lots number two and seven. Those lots are desolate. Both are at the end of a long gravel road. All the other parking lots are relatively close to the highway (Route 113).

Before we started searching, I told everybody in my party that I wanted them to do a very thorough search of each area. I advised them that I would rather be slow and thorough than fast and miss something. The last thing that I wanted to have happen was to search an area—only to have Christopher found there later. I wanted to give his family closure while not having the guilt of knowing we had missed him. While keeping that in mind, I had also heard that the police were under the gun to try to find more evidence. If I am remembering correct, I believe there was some concern that the suspect may have to be released for lack of evidence in the coming days.

The search took place on a hot August day. Trying to be methodical, we started in parking lot number one and would carefully work toward lot number 10. Working our way through the lots, it continued to get hotter and more humid as the day progressed. I believe it was shortly after noon when they called the search off (due to the heat). At that point, we had only made it to parking lot number four. I was pretty confident we had not missed anything up to there. We did find and recover a couple of items of interest, but I never heard if they were important. Calling it for the day, I was told that we would be coming back to complete our search.

The very next day, I was told that Christopher had been found buried next to parking lot number seven. From what I was told, a psychic had guided a couple of Deputies to the area. Definitely not a big believer of psychics, I questioned if it was true. I didn't know the Deputies and never actually heard how they found Christopher. I have always had some guilt in not finding Christopher. I kind of felt like I had failed the family by not going to lots number two and seven first. I knew that both of them were the key lots to check and I did not make it there—not that I could have changed anything. The suspect in Christopher's murder was eventually charged and convicted. He was sentenced to death in Illinois.

In 2004, there were two openings in Rock Island County. After long discussions with Laura, we decided to make the move. Shortly after moving, I decided to do a patrol on the Mississippi River dike. Parking at Blanchards Landing, I hopped on an ATV and traveled down the dike into Mercer County. The dike is made from sand and stays along the river. It's hard to walk on because your feet are always digging into the sand. It doesn't really follow any roads and can get pretty remote at times. In one of the remote areas, I stopped the ATV and was taking a leak when I heard some gun shots. Following the shots, I located three guys walking along a timber edge with handguns. Closing the gap between us, when I identified myself to the subjects, one of them (Johnny) threw his gun into the brush. Reaching the guys, I ended up arresting

Johnny for being a felon in possession of a firearm. In Illinois, this is a custodial arrest and requires an officer to take physical custody of the subject—and yes, transport them to jail. That's kind of hard to do on an ATV. To make matters worse, we were well over a mile from a hard road. With Johnny handcuffed, I asked him if he wanted to walk a mile on the levy or ride on the front rack of the ATV. Johnny decided to take a ride on the rack. I called Mercer County Sheriff's Police and requested that they send a squad to help me transport Johnny. They agreed to have a squad meet me at the nearest road. I drove slow up to the next road and hid the ATV in the brush.

A short time later, Deputy Bill Glancey arrived to help me out. Over the years, I have met a lot of officers, but very few with Bill's integrity. I always felt like I could confide in Bill if there was something bad happening. During my time in this area, Bill progressed through the ranks and eventually followed in his dad's (Larry Glancey) footsteps by becoming the Sheriff of Mercer County. During our ride to the jail and back, Bill and I talked about a bunch of stuff, which included some of my predecessor CPOs. Bill said that some of them may have helped him with a murder case. Bill proceeded to tell me that the case involved a psychic.

Although I'm a skeptic, this had all the elements of a good conversation. A murder, CPOs and a psychic. Jokingly, I asked Bill how the psychic had worked out for them. Bill remained rather serious and told me that the lady was "spot-on". Surprised, I had to dig a little further. I asked Bill what happened. Bill told me that the psychic was a lady from central Illinois named Greta Alexander. I had never heard of Greta before, but my interest was definitely focused on what Bill had to say.

Bill proceeded to tell me that the first time Mercer County Sheriff's Department enlisted Greta's help was when they were investigating what was believed to be a satanic sacrifice. Yes, that's what I said. You must remember, I grew up as the traditional "all-American kid". Cars, girls, hunting, fishing and working were all real. The rest of "it" was just in the movies. With that in mind, shortly before I left Peotone, where I had essentially lived my entire life, I found out that the KKK was active in our community. Of course, we all knew about the Mafia to our north. Within weeks of moving to Illinois City, I heard that there was a local militia group. They were said to be well-armed and organized. And, of course, the police academy filled me in on biker "clubs" and street gangs. After knowing what to look for with the gangs, I started to see signs of them everywhere. Thanks to Bill, I now I had to be on the lookout for satanic worshipers. Are you kidding me!

Bill went on to tell me that his father had first talked with Greta while he was still attending Jr. High. As Bill was trying to keep his grades up, Larry had become an investigator for the Mercer County Sheriff's Department (MCSD). Bill said that the first "Greta case" didn't just affect his dad, but his whole family. As the investigation progressed, Bill was required to keep a loaded gun in his bedroom.

As the story goes, Larry was called to a house reference a complaint. The empty house had been listed for sale. While on the market, the owner's returned to check on it—only to find that someone had gotten inside. The house was a mess; there was blood all over the house. Everything in the house with a reflective finish had been written on in blood. One of the bedrooms had a huge pool of blood on top of the bed. So much blood that it looked like someone or something had been killed there. In the garage, Larry found six "rings" on the floor. The rings, outlined in blood, looked like there had been goblets or glasses sitting on the floor. As the blood spilled over the sides, the base of the goblets left their mark on the concrete.

Having saved an abducted girl once, Larry believed that he was once again seeing cult activity. Everything was pointing to a sacrifice on the bloody bed and a ceremony on the garage floor.

This was further corroborated with the fact that the full moon would shine directly through the bedroom window and onto the bed.

Confirming that it was human blood in the house, the investigation took a whole new look. The only problem was that there was neither a body nor a missing person to tie the blood to.

With little to go on, Larry heard about Greta. Making an appointment to meet with her, Greta asked that they bring something from the desecrated house and a map of Mercer County. Taking one of the bloody mirrors and a map, three Officers (including Larry) headed down to meet with Greta.

When they arrived, Larry and the other Officers were welcomed into Greta's home. Stepping inside, one of the first things that Greta told Larry was that he wasn't a "believer". An honest man, Larry agreed. Pointing at one of the other Officers, Greta asked him if he had three holes in his underwear. Embarrassed, the officer agreed that he did. Greta proceeded to tell the Officer that he was born in a house in Mercer County, not a hospital. The Officer again agreed with Greta's observations. Opening the map, Greta pointed to the spot where the Officer had been born. After the Officer confirmed that Greta was correct, she reaffirmed that Larry still didn't believe in her abilities. Although Larry confirmed her supposition, I find it hard to believe that he wasn't a little "on edge".

Asking for the mirror, Greta confirmed that a "man" had been sacrificed. Not just a human, but a man. Greta told the Officers that they were correct in believing that it was related to a satanic cult. She said that very few cults actually commit human sacrifices. She said that they generally stick to animal sacrifices. Greta told the officers that they needed to be aware that once a cult transitions into human sacrifice, they never go back to animals. Asking Greta why they wouldn't have any missing person reports, she told the Officers that the cults are very cautious. She said that they pick homeless people or the outcasts. The people that "nobody will miss".

Greta went on to warn the Officers that the cult's members can hold very powerful positions. She said that sometimes they suddenly quit their jobs without reason. Greta told the officers that although the cults won't generally "screw" with police officers, they might do stuff to their families. Greta advised the officers to watch people posing as salesmen or others who come to their houses for obscure reasons. Before Larry and the other officers left, they were told that the sacrificed man was in a cold, dark, damp place.

As told by Bill, his dad was a very driven officer who wanted to solve every crime in front of him. This case was no different. By the time I had an opportunity to write this book, Larry had passed away. As Bill recalled his dad's story, you could detect the frustration that Larry seemed to pass on to Bill. Larry had developed suspects, but ran into roadblocks on every front. Somehow the evidence was mishandled at the lab and the integrity of it was lost. Although the state's attorney at the time was a "pitbull", and was initially supportive of the investigation, he eventually told Larry to abandon it. Greta wanted to be put in a plane and told Larry that she could direct him to the missing man. It never happened. Larry was even warned by one of the suspects to "back off".

During the latter stages of the investigation, Larry received a call from an Iowa Police Officer. The Officer told Larry that he had heard about the cult investigation. He said that he would be retiring early and was willing to help Larry solve the case. Hearing about Greta, the Iowa Officer got angry and told Larry not to trust her. He said that Greta was a "White Witch". Even today, I find that response odd. I could see an Officer saying that he doesn't believe in the credibility of anything "supernatural". But why would an Officer try to revoke "supernatural" credibility with the use of a "supernatural" term—unless they believed in "supernatural" ability to begin with? That's just freaky!

Two days later, Larry received a call from Greta. She told him that she knew she had been called a "White Witch". He agreed. Greta asked Larry if he remembered what she had said about people in authoritative positions and people suddenly quitting their job. Needless to say, Larry remembered. The Iowa Officer was never given an opportunity to help in the investigation and the case was never solved. Bill said that his dad thought about this case for the rest of his life.

Obviously, my curiosity was peaked at this point. I wanted to know everything about Greta that I could. Bill explained to me that Greta would see in the "past, present and future". The problem was that you had to decipher what she was "seeing in". She would also see through the eyes of the victim. Bill said that it was like a puzzle. You had to put the pieces together and figure out what was meant by what Greta had told you.

By the time that MCSD needed Greta again, Bill was a Deputy. He had received a complaint about a missing Alexis man (Farmer). Farmer was said to be a religious 44-year-old who had a standard routine. Every day there were certain things that Farmer would get done—and returning home was one of them. On this day, Farmer and his truck had come up missing. Bill said that he had a gut feeling that something was seriously wrong. There was already a suspicion that Farmer's son (Jesse) may have been involved.

After a few days of Farmer not returning, MCSD called Greta and asked for her assistance. After answering a few questions, Greta confirmed that Farmer was dead. She said that they would be investigating a homicide and that Farmer had been shot in the back three times. She went on to describe Farmer's house both inside and out. Bill said that it was precise to a "T". Without prompting, Greta told them that two Deputies had already searched Farmer's house. After confirming that she was correct, Greta told them that they had missed something important in the "cluttered room". When she described it, Bill said that he knew exactly which room she was talking about. Greta went on to tell them that if they didn't solve the case within a couple of weeks, a blonde person would be next. Greta told them that she could see the blonde person being chased through a corn field. Bill said that he immediately had a fear for Farmer's blonde stepdaughter. Greta finished by telling them that she was seeing Colorado. As it turned out later, Jesse would try to use a trip to Colorado as his alibi.

For some reason, Greta could "see" more or "see more clearly" if she had personal items from the people involved. They made plans to go see Greta in person. Greta asked them to bring Farmer's ex-wife (Jesse's stepmother) and a picture of Jesse.

When they met with Greta, she looked back and forth several times between Jesse's picture and his stepmother. Looking directly at Bill and the other officers, Greta told them that Jesse was "evil". She then asked if they remembered the blonde running through the corn field (that she told them about). When they said yes, Greta turned her attention to the stepmother and told her that if she didn't cooperate and help solve the crime, she would be next.

Going back to Farmer's point of view, Greta said that she saw a dirt lane off a main road. Near the intersection, Greta said that she could see a small "quanset hut". Greta said that there was a roll of wire. Not a small one, but a large one like the power companies use. Greta told them that she felt like she was being sucked under. She said that there was a large eagle or bird. Greta told the Deputies that there were three people involved. Greta said that two of them had hoods and that she could see a fire. Greta told the Deputies that if they had not completed the investigation in two weeks, they should call her again.

Leaving the meeting, Bill said that they got a call from the Sheriff's Department. They had found Farmer's truck. It was parked below the big eagle sign at the Eagle Grocery Store in Moline. Check that one off the list!

When they got back, they tried to put the other pieces together. They were thinking that being sucked under could be in the pond on the neighbor's property. The Sheriff's Department arranged for a dive team to search the pond, but didn't find anything in the water. While Bill was on scene, one of the neighbors came down. Bill asked them when they last saw Farmer. He was told that they had seen Farmer the day that he disappeared. The neighbor said that they drove by Farmer while he was burning down an old shed (the fire?). After passing Farmer, the neighbor crested the next hill. Just on the other side, Jesse's truck was parked on the shoulder of the road facing the wrong way.

With the new information, MCSD got permission to harvest the bean field next to the burnt shed. With the field cleared, they searched it with a metal detector and found three rifle casings.

As the two-week period closed in, they called Greta once again. Speaking from Farmer's point of view, Greta told them that he was down the previously mentioned dirt lane. She said that you need to cross the new drain tube where the water is trickling. She said that they needed to pull into the farm lane on the right side. Greta said that they should stay on the farm lane through three jogs to the right. She said that "I" am right there, where the hoot owls are. The Deputies asked Greta if Farmer could see his house from where he was. Greta said that if he stood up and turned around, he could see it if there wasn't a big hill in the way.

Sharing the information with one of Farmer's hunting partners, they went out and found Farmer. Bill said that almost everything Greta told them was correct. He said that they turned off Route 67 onto a dirt road. Bill said that they drove down the dirt road until they crossed a brand-new culvert. Yes, you could hear the water trickling. Bill said that they immediately turned onto the farm lane to the right. He said that after following it through three jogs to the right, there was a tarp covered with clumps of weeds.

Bill said that when they pulled the tarp off Farmer, a hoot owl started "hooting". He said that it was about 2 p.m. when that happened. Bill said that the owl almost continuously hooted for five or six hours. He said that the owl didn't stop until they left the scene. In case you don't know it, owls very seldom hoot during daylight hours—let alone continuously hoot! Bill told me that Farmer's body was even lying as Greta had described.

I think that leaves us with the large spool of wire and being sucked under. As it turns out, the power company was working on the lines the day that Farmer's body was reportedly taken to where he was hidden. Yes, there was a large spool out there that day. Pope Creek (next to where Farmer had been buried) flooded at one point during the search. When it did, Farmer would have been covered with water. The rifle used to kill Farmer was eventually found in the cluttered room and the autopsy confirmed that Farmer had been shot in the back three times. I don't care how you "shake it", that's a lot of information confirmed!

In the following years, I ran into the old game wardens that helped secure the road during Farmer's recovery. They were able to confirm the hoot owl. Jesse was charged with murder and concealing a murder. Although he was acquitted of the murder charge, he was convicted of concealing it and spent a couple of years in an institution.

At that point, if Bill had 10 more stories to tell me, I would have listened to them all. Bill hinted about one more case that they could never prove and said that he had heard about another involving someone who had drowned. Bill said that the drowning involved an area fire department, but wasn't sure which one. I asked Bill if Greta was still alive. He advised that she was not. Bill said that Greta had indicated that she wouldn't be around much longer prior to her death.

With no solid leads on where to look for the next Greta story, life went back to normal after Bill dropped me off. Although it was dark when I finally reached my squad, I could see where somebody had run a key down the side of it. It wasn't just a little scratch, but down to the bare metal. I always suspected that it had been was one of Johnny's friends, but could never prove it. Now I had two more field reports to write. One for Johnny and the other for my squad.

Fast forward to the spring of 2017 and I needed to contact the fire chief of Colona, Illinois (John Swan). I had likely met Chief Swan previously, but never had an opportunity to sit down and talk with him. Chief Swan is a very dedicated fireman. I believe that he has served his community for over 40 years. Of course, as you sit and talk about the experiences and changes that occur in a 40-year career, you cover a lot of ground. While talking with Chief Swan, he mentioned that he had even worked with a psychic. I am sure that I immediately leaned forward in my chair. I told Chief Swan that I had talked with Bill Glancey about the psychic he worked with. Chief Swan told me that it was the same psychic—Greta. I told Chief Swan that I needed to hear what happened.

Chief Swan told me that he and Ty Massey (auxiliary Colona Police Officer) were responding to Rock River. He said that they had a report of a vehicle being swept into the flooded waters. Chief Swan was leading as he and Ty walked out onto a bridge to look for the vehicle. Making it a short distance out onto the bridge, Chief Swan suddenly heard an "aaaahh" yelled behind him. Turning back toward Ty, Chief Swan saw that he had fallen into the water next to one of the bridge supports. Chief Swan told me that he tried to get to Ty, but could not get there before Ty was swept downstream. Chief Swan said that Ty quickly disappeared below the surface of the river. Immediately, Chief Swan notified their departments and a search for Ty was launched.

You always hope to provide relief to the family of missing people, but flooded rivers rarely are willing to give up their secrets. The search had carried on for more than a week when Chief Swan was contacted by Greta. Like me, Chief Swan said that he was a skeptic—at best. There were several calls then that went back and forth between Chief Swan and Greta. Greta reportedly told Chief Swan at one point that she (Ty) had gone under water. Greta said that she could see rocks and sand as she went downstream. Greta said that she eventually ended up stuck in a log jam. Greta told Chief Swan that she could see something sparkling above the surface of the water. Chief Swan said that anybody could have told him what Greta did up to that point. Chief Swan advised that he remained skeptical of Greta and her visions.

One morning, Chief Swan said that he and one of the other firemen went down to the Colona boat launch. Chief Swan said that as he was walking down toward the bank, the other fireman received a call from Greta. Chief Swan said that Greta requested to talk with him. Taking the call, Greta told Chief Swan that he was standing on the bank of the river (he was). She then told Chief Swan that he could see two boats out on the river (he could). Third, Greta told Chief Swan that she saw something large and green behind him. Chief Swan said that he did not need to turn around. Chief Swan knew that Greta was talking about the big green fire truck parked in the lot (behind him). Chief Swan said that Greta now had his attention. Chief Swan told me that Greta again reiterated that she was stuck in a log jam and could see something shining or sparkling above the water. Later that day, Chief Swan said that he went to his house and wrapped several empty bottles in tape. Each bottle had a different colored tape on it. Chief Swan took the different bottles and launched them on the Rock River. A short time later, Chief Swan received a call from Greta. Greta told

Chief Swan that she was still stuck in a log jam. This time, Greta told Chief Swan that there was bottle with blue tape in the log jam too. Chief Swan said that he told one of his firemen to take their boat and go pull Ty out of the log jam where the bottle with the blue tape was. Launching their boat, the firemen went and pulled Ty from that log jam.

Chief Swan said that his curiosity later overtook him, and he had to see what the shiny object was. Chief Swan told me that he boated down to the log jam and looked around. He said that when he looked up, a sparkling light was reflecting from a power line insulator above him. Chief Swan said that the angle was such that a person in the log jam would have seen it sparkling.

After a little small talk about Greta, Chief Swan said that Greta had also helped one of his friends in the search for a little boy. Chief Swan told me that the little boy had gone missing from a little town called Aroma Park. My heart sank. I asked Chief Swan if the little boy had been buried at Kankakee River State Park. Chief Swan confirmed that it was Greta that had helped in the search for Christopher Meyer. Chief Swan said that the Aroma Park Fire Chief was a skeptic—just like him. From what I understand, the Aroma Park Fire Chief was at a gathering when he received a call from Greta. He was told that he needed to go to Kankakee River State Park. The Aroma Park Chief was given directions on how to find Christopher under a sheet of plywood by the area seven parking lot. That was just where they found him.

When I started this career, I was a psychic skeptic. Now, I feel there is no doubt that Greta had a gift. I only wish that I had an opportunity to talk with her myself. Was she given a gift from God? Was she able to talk directly with the soul of the missing person or was it something totally different? How can you literally see through someone else's eyes whether they are dead or alive? I have no answers, only questions. Hopefully, you have found this 22-year journey as interesting as I did!

THE BLUE THING

When I was hired in 1994, I felt like I was becoming part of the most honorable profession that there is. Loving the outdoors and wanting to be a police officer, I figured that "game wardening" was the perfect fit for me. I would be a police officer who got to take a little different approach. Although I would be able to help people and arrest "bad guys", my concentration would be on the Conservation Code. Within the first few months of my hiring, I came to the realization that my reality was not necessarily "Police Reality". I have never regretted my decision, but think that this is worth talking about.

As a game warden, 98% of police officers will accept you as one of their own. The other 2% will shun you or try to make fun of your position. Usually, the "two percenters", are the guys who hunt and occasionally step over the line. I believe that deep down, their intention is to diminish the position of a game warden and, therefore, the game laws. If they can do that with their peers, the game warden is the bad guy if they get caught poaching. Although many officers will have the "warden's back" while off the clock, very few are capable of choosing the warden's side if it ends up "green -vs- blue".

Having now spent over 25 years in conservation law enforcement, I have had plenty of time to think about **"Police Reality"**. In doing so, I decided that I wanted to define it in a way that everybody would understand how it works. I would say that there are four "things" - **"the Blue Thing, the Right Thing, the Wrong Thing and the Right for Me Thing"**. Although they are all self-explanatory, I feel obligated to further explain them - and their relationship in law enforcement.

The Blue Thing transcends all regular law enforcement in some way. It is strongest within a single agency, but connects all agencies that work together in a common area. You must remember that city, county and state agencies have to work together to be effective. Federal agencies are in the mix, but don't work with common patrol officers on a regular basis. Most of the time, the Feds would be working with either supervisors or special divisions within a smaller agency. Because of the reliance agencies and officers have on each other, they generally form a bond between them. All of that said, I have also seen pissing matches turn agencies and officers against each other.

I've worked the Chicago metro area, small towns and in places where back-up units don't exist. There's generally a big difference in "location attitude". In the big city, I've seen officers hold their badge up, shout out their affiliation and expect you to walk away (while they break the law). I've seen the sense of blue entitlement that allows the creation of people like a guy named Drew. I have also seen small city officers have similar attitudes within their jurisdictions, just not quite as brazen. As you continue further into rural areas, the frequency of this attitude becomes less common. These are not hard-in-stone characterizations of any of these officers or agencies, but rather generalizations that I have witnessed primarily amongst an agency's "two per centers".

The **Blue Thing** works on both sides of the spectrum. Simply put, it is the expectation of "professional courtesy". Some officers think they should receive it no matter what. Those same officers will likely give it no matter what. Some officers give professional courtesy to varying degrees and expect the same. Usually, the variables include where the other officer works and what the violation is. Finally, some officers just treat everybody the same—no matter who they are or where they work. Those officers would generally not ask for professional courtesy and will just "own" their mistakes. Because of their integrity, they will very rarely be caught breaking the law. If they are caught, they won't generally complain when they are held accountable.

The **Right Thing** and the **Wrong Thing** are pretty straight forward. Hopefully, people are brought up with the "Right Thing" instilled in their hearts. Even if they were not brought up in the best of homes, at some point in a person's life they realize the difference. At that point, they must make a conscious decision on where they will stand. Maybe I should say that they must make hundreds of those decisions every day. From holding a door for someone or saying "thank you" to picking fights with them— or worse.

The **Right for Me Thing** is pretty much as it sounds. It is the kindred brother of the Blue Thing. I have seen officers (and people in every other profession) do things with concern for what they will receive in return. Heck, that's how politics works. What these officers do has a purpose other than serving the needs of the public. By giving "professional courtesy", they "serve the needs" of an individual person or group (whether inside or outside of the Blue ranks). The officer in some way at some time may receive something in return. What they receive may not even have real monetary value. It could just be standing in the community. If you take care of someone with "power", you may have the ear of that person. If so, you indirectly have been given more power yourself. Of course, power itself will likely someday lead to some sort of compensation. You do not see any high-level politicians living on the bottom rungs of the social ladder. I think every person would attest to the fact that they have seen some "not so smart" politicians that have power and wealth.

I believe that in a perfect world, three of the "Things" are the same—the Blue Thing, the Right Thing and the Right for Me Thing. Just as you will never eliminate corruption in politics, you cannot separate the Blue Thing from the Right for Me Thing. The key is trying to keep the right people in the most powerful positions. Those people would be the ones who don't abuse the Blue Thing or get consumed with the Right for Me Thing. They set the standard for their agencies and what their subordinates will do. They are the officers driven by the Right Thing.

Although it sounds easy to keep "good people" in high-level positions, the officers who tactically use the Blue Thing with the Right for Me Thing create personal power. That power can lead them to into those high-level positions. Once they are there, who are they going to surround themselves with? You got it.

I probably spend too much time thinking about it, but officers should always be aware of people's (officer or not) true intentions. Those consumed with the Right for Me Thing should not be in the law enforcement community. Laws were created to make things fair for everybody. Not to be used for personal gain.

Welcome to Baited Island

Although I was hired in 1994, it takes about 10 months to complete training and hit the field. After working the summer on my own in 1995, I was itching to get into the hunting season. I think that any officer who calls themself a "game warden" looks forward to hunting season more than any of the others. Being proactive early that fall, Laura and I made a dove bait case together. Bait cases and over-limits are sort of the pinnacles of wildlife cases. Yes, there are many other great cases to be made, but you always hope to have a baited site for opening day.

For two weeks prior to duck season, Laura and I had been scouting hard. All the scouting had not turned up any baited sites. Laura had received a complaint from a chemical facility in the north end of Will County. The complainant said that the subjects hunting in the bordering duck blind had shot and recovered ducks on their property (the previous year). With chemical tanks all around, they did not want anyone coming onto their property. Laura decided to contact the local police department to reference the blind. Going to the P.D., Laura met with a guy I will just call "Chief". Laura discussed the blind with Chief and was told that they were not aware of the complaint. Of course, Chief offered to help should Laura need it.

It was the evening before opening day, and I was skunked. I decided I was just going to pick a random duck blind and sit on it the next morning. As the sun was setting that evening, I received a phone message. Back then, we did not have cell phones. The TCs (telecommunicators) would call us on the radio and give us people's phone numbers to call back. I had a calling card with a PIN number. I had to type the PIN number into a pay phone to make a call. You got pretty good at knowing where the pay phones were located.

Calling the person back, I was told that they wanted to remain anonymous. The person told me that there was a baited duck blind on the Des Plaines River. I was told that the blind was on the first island south of the Route 7 bridge. The caller told me that the bait would be on the upstream tip of the next island downstream. I was about to go off the air, but was not going to pass on this opportunity. I told Laura that I was going to go up and check on it. She said that she would go with me. By the time we arrived back in the Lockport area, it was dark. Hiding the old Dodge Ramcharger, we put on our hip boots and headed to the water. The Des Plaines River in this area is generally shallow. There are very few areas that are over three feet deep at normal water levels. The floor of the river is mostly gravel and rock. We slowly worked our way down stream to the first island. Honestly, I had been skeptical, but there was a duck blind on the downstream side. After we checked the blind out, we walked about 90 yards downstream to the next island. Sure enough, there was corn scattered all over the rocks on the upstream side of the island. We took bait samples and pictures of the area. Set up for the next morning, we headed back to the truck. As we were heading back, I asked Laura if she wanted to work the duck blind with me. She told me that she had committed to working the chemical plant blind.

Having not made a duck bait case yet, I called CPO Mark Simon. Mark agreed to meet me in the morning and help me with the investigation. Mark lived and worked in Will County before I got there. At that point, Mark had transferred to Grundy County (bordering county to the west). Mark was a traditional "game warden". It seemed that he liked to work hunters and fishermen more than anything else. If you had a question about local poachers, Mark was the guy to go to. Several years later, Mark became my Sergeant. Mark was a good Sergeant. He was never on my back. When it comes to that, less is definitely more.

Mark and I got out to the river just before sunrise and took up positions on the west bank. From where we were, we could watch the duck blind and the bait spot. I have to say, that as a rookie, I was kind of skeptical about making the case. I had seen a lot of pictures of bait cases and people talked about making them, but we were on the verge of getting one. It would put me 2/3 of the way to a "warden's trifecta". A "warden's trifecta" being dove, duck and deer bait cases all in one year.

Looking at the blind with my binos, there were three guys out there at sunrise. I couldn't believe things were working out as I had planned. I hate to admit it now, but I didn't watch the blind and hunters every time they shot. I think I was afraid to be seen and blow the case. By the end of the season, I had plenty of opportunities to sit on duck blinds and was confident enough to take more chances. I got to the point that I would rather be seen than not see something. The hunters started shooting at about 6:40 a.m. and finished a couple of hours later. When they began to take their decoy spread in, we started walking across the river toward them. As we reached the hunters, we identified ourselves to them. I realized we had two teenagers (B and M) and an adult male (LT). LT identified himself as a police officer. All three of the hunters admitted to killing their limit of ducks (15 in total). All three of them also said they did not know anything about the bait. Mark recovered a 16th duck that had dropped next to him. He said that the hunters never tried to recover it. With their group one duck over their limit, I secured more pictures of the bait and took some more samples. Because of the police connection, we decided not to issue citations on the spot. We ended up referring the case to the U.S. Fish and Wildlife Service for prosecution. LT was charged and found guilty of hunting waterfowl over bait. He ended up paying a $500 fine. USFWS asked that I charge the teenagers in State court. I ended up going to their houses and issuing them citations for $75 each.

When we left, Mark and I had a good story to tell. It would have been a better story if we did not have to say that we referred prosecution because of "who" we had caught. Excited to tell my story, I met up with Laura so we could share the stories from our first duck opener. Laura's morning had not gone so well. Laura sat on the blind by the chemical facility. She said that the hunters did everything exactly right that morning. They had all their required licenses, legal guns and ammunition and did not go onto the chemical company's property. Likely the reason everything was perfect was because one of the hunters was Chief's son. Yes, the same Chief that Laura had checked in with earlier in the week. Two checks on opening day of duck season and both were tainted.

Karma

The following year, Laura and I did not have a baited duck blind to work for opening day. After scouting the upper portion of the Des Plaines River (in Will County), we decided to spend opening morning sitting on a duck blind near Romeoville. Once again, the blind was on an island. This blind faced to the west, so we snuck into a position on another island northeast of it. Lying in the weeds about 40 yards away, we had a perfect view of the blind. By about 6:42 a.m., three hunters had reported to the blind. Except for the dew and bugs, I always loved these mornings. Nestled into our locations, we got our pads of paper out and started taking notes. Watching the hunters with our binos, they hunted for about two-and-a-half hours. Over the course of that time, we watched one of the hunters take over the limit and all three of the hunters shoot a duck on the water. Back then it was not considered sporting to shoot ducks on the water. For some reason, they decided to change the law a few years later. Maybe it got too hard for some guys to hit a flying duck? As the hunters retrieved their ducks, they carried them back and threw them into a common pile on top of the blind. As you duck hunters know, the piles are supposed to be separated so we know who killed what. This ended up being the perfect case for that law. Although the hunters had killed 15 ducks (their limit as a group), the one hunter killed six of them. By doing so, he killed one "for" another hunter. That's the nice thing about watching a blind from before the start of shooting hours. If you put yourself in a position close enough to the blind, you can actually see who shoots what for the entire hunt.

As the hunters picked up their stuff and got ready to go, we approached them from across the river. Identifying ourselves, we got the hunter's licenses and identified a couple more violations. As is typical, the hunter who had taken "over the limit" claimed that one of the other hunters killed his duck. We sorted out the over-limit and discussed why they had each shot a duck on the water. The last guy to shoot one on the water said that he was, "just ready to leave". That guy ended up being none other than "Chief". Yes, the same Chief that Laura had met the previous year. Sometimes karma is beautiful! Between all the hunters, we issued four citations, some written warnings and seized all the ducks.

Some years later, on an election year, I was called up to the Region Office by Captain Howard Brewer. Howard was a really good Captain. He had common sense and knew how "the system" worked. In the years that Fred was riding my back, Howard helped to diffuse some of my "browbeatings". Howard was always able to get us extra equipment at the end of the fiscal year. If there was money left in the Region budget, Howard made sure to spend it. I remember him saying that he couldn't articulate needing more money (for the Region) if he had money left over this year. Yes, that's how government works. I had a different Captain years later who seemed proud of the fact that he stayed under budget every year. Under him, we were missing some of the basic equipment that we had received under Howard. There's no two ways about it, good equipment helps you do your job better.

As for the call I received from Howard, he told me to be at the Region office first thing the next morning. The Region office was two hours away and on the other side of Chicago. He didn't indicate what was wrong, just that I had to be there. Normally, you are in trouble when you get that call. All night long, I had to wonder what the hell I had done. At least it wasn't hard to get up early the next morning. Arriving at the office, I met with Howard and one of the other sergeants. Howard told me that he had received a call from "Chief". Yes, the same one again. Apparently, Chief was concerned that I would possibly target him on an election year. At that point, I believe I hadn't even checked Chief in a couple of years. Howard told me that I didn't have to steer clear of Chief, but he wanted me to be aware of the political wheels that were turning. I didn't check Chief that year; in fact, I don't think I ever checked him again. It wasn't that I steered clear of Chief, but that I had already worked the area that he was hunting. I had hundreds of other places in Will County that I had not worked. If people are not checked, they grow complacent and tend to bend the laws in their favor. I always wanted to check people and locations that had not been checked before. I don't remember my route ever leading back to Chief's blind.

M was a different story. Laura and I caught up with him and his Grandpa as they hunted doves over bait in 2001. A couple of months after M's second arrest, I got a call at about 1 a.m. The guy on the line told me that he was calling about the free German Shepherd puppies. Groggy, I asked him what he was talking about. The guy told me that he was calling about the ad in the paper. I told him that he had the wrong number and hung up. The next day, I got another call at about 1 a.m. Again, the guy wanted to get a free German Shepherd puppy. Waking myself up, I asked him if he was calling about an ad in the paper. He advised that he was. I asked him what paper it was in. He said that it was in one of those free papers you get at the gas station. I explained that I didn't have any puppies and that someone must have placed the ad in there with my number. The next day, I got one of the papers and found that "I" was giving away free German Shepherd puppies. Everybody was to call after 12 a.m. because I worked second shift. Calling the newspaper, I talked with one of the supervisors. They said that they didn't verify people's information if they were offering stuff for free. For the next two weeks, we didn't answer the telephone after we went to bed. We never did figure out who put the ad in the paper, but thought that it was likely someone who we had arrested that fall. It was actually a pretty good joke on us!

Hunting the Preserve

Moving to the south end of Will County, you run into Des Plaines Conservation Area (DPCA). I spent a lot of time working the site and getting to know the people working at it. As the name states,

DPCA is primarily a hunting and fishing area. They also had a camping area and a busy boat launch. I have many stories from DPCA and you will likely get to read several of them. One of the employees at the site was Danny Gaddis. Danny could not have been a nicer guy. No matter when you saw him, he would joke around and smile. Danny always seemed to know some tidbits about illegal activity, but seldom shared them. I don't think he wanted to be caught up in the middle of any cases. That was always fine with me; I just liked getting the information when he would share it!

By 1997, I was getting into a lot of different things. I felt like I knew what was going on in Will County and was pretty comfortable with my patrol area. In the early fall that year, I was talking with Danny. He asked if I had ever checked Shrub Prairie Nature Preserve (south of Wilmington). Shrub Prairie? I didn't even know it existed. Danny told me where it was and said that I should probably check it some time. I asked him if someone was hunting in it. Danny said that he didn't know. He told me that it was a remote site and would likely be a good place for people to sneak into.

Opening morning of firearm deer season, I worked in other parts of the county. That evening, Laura and I didn't have anything in particular to work, so I suggested checking the Shrub Prairie Nature Preserve. The 146-acre nature preserve was a mixture of prairie and timber surrounded by private property. We decided to just drive out to the edge of the timber. I wouldn't normally do that, but the nature preserve was surrounded by open farm fields. I knew that if we walked in, the poachers would see us coming from a mile away. By the time we got to them, they would be gone. I figured that if we quickly drove across the farm field, they wouldn't be able to react fast enough to get out of there.

When we reached the edge of the timber, I drove along it until I found a well beaten path that went down into the nature preserve. Parking the squad, we got out and immediately walked down the path. When we got about 70 yards in, I saw a guy (I will call Sarge) in full camouflage. Sarge was hunched over with a shotgun in his hands. He had a tree stand sitting on the ground right behind him. I asked Sarge if he knew that he was hunting in a nature preserve. He admitted that he did. I seized Sarge's gun, hunting bag and tree stand. Laura found another unoccupied tree stand in the timber and a couple of guys hunting on the edge of the nature preserve. Those guys likely moved to the edges after they heard or saw us, but we couldn't prove it. The thing I always loved about catching someone hunting in a nature preserve during firearm deer season was that you were guaranteed a "two for one". They were hunting in a restricted area and would never be wearing blaze orange. The kicker for the blaze orange violation was that it showed intent to break both laws.

Sarge ended up pleading guilty to one violation and paying a $75 fine. He got all his equipment back. Some state's attorneys will not prosecute police officers for what they consider to be minor violations. In that regard, I can't complain about the plea deal. The other thing you must keep in mind is that some police officers get in trouble with their administration. I do not know if Sarge got in trouble with his administration, but I do know that I never caught him breaking any conservation laws again.

Floor-it Dave!

Jumping over to Grundy County, I was involved in an airplane detail on an early December day that same year. For this detail, CPO Simon had picked the stationing locations for the ground units. They then flew an airplane over the county, looking for guys poaching out of their vehicles (or other possible violations). When the guys in the airplane located something of interest, they would lead the closest ground unit over to the "target" by radio direction. The ground units on this day were two officer units. I was assigned to patrol with CPO Dave Hyatt. Dave was in my academy class. When we graduated, Dave was assigned to the District north of us. For this detail, we needed more bodies, so Dave came down to help. Dave was always funny, so I looked forward to working with him that day.

Of course, I must tell the academy story about me and Dave. I was the biggest guy in our Conservation Academy class and Dave was the smallest. Although he was small, to be funny, Dave would talk a big game. Returning to the dorm room after a long-wet day on the range, all of us were soaked and covered in mud. Dave didn't spare any time stripping down to his briefs. Strutting around like a rooster, Dave started talking smack. He told me that he could take me in a wrestling match. As I laughed at him, Dave kept egging me on. Finally, I agreed to wrestle with him. He came at me like a little miniature Sumo wrestler. No, Dave wasn't fat, but that was his wrestling stance. Bear-hugging my waist, I can remember giggling until I felt his hands trying to grab onto the rear of my underwear. I thought, you little son of a bitch, not today! His underwear was easy to grab onto - since it was the only thing he was wearing! I'm not sure if Dave's underwear was weakened by being wet, had been washed too many times or was his "break-aways", but as they reached his shoulder blades, they ripped right off him. I think Wild Bill (one of our other classmates) yelled, "Naked midget wrestling." Everybody laughed and the match was over as quickly as it had begun. As Dave reminded me later, Wild Bill was the one who instigated the whole thing. Either way, we all had a good laugh that night!

Back to the airplane detail. Dave and I were to be stationed south of Morris along a road near the sand pit. As we began to get set up, Dave told me that he had gotten a stuffed pheasant at a garage sale. Pulling it out of the back seat, it was pretty ratty. We stuck the pheasant on the north side of the road and pulled up a hilly driveway on the opposite side. Dave positioned us so we could see the pheasant with our binoculars. It actually looked real the way that we had it set up. We were in a pretty good spot;

we could get an airplane complaint or catch someone shooting at our pheasant. As we were sitting there, I thought I saw the pheasant move. Getting my binoculars up, I couldn't see it anymore. We hadn't seen a car and didn't hear a shot. Driving down to the entrance of the driveway, a red-tailed hawk was standing over the stuffed pheasant. The pheasant had been knocked over and was decapitated. The hawk had the pheasant's head in its talon. Shortly after recovering the pheasant, we were told that the airplane detail was over, and we could patrol freely.

More familiar with the area than Dave, I suggested going up along the north bank of the Illinois River. Working our way northeast, we issued a guy a couple of tickets for an untagged deer. Then we found a dirt road that went back toward the river. It's always good to drive down a desolate road. You never know what you will find at the other end. The road eventually took us into a field back by the river. From the edge of the field, we could see some guys goose hunting out in the middle of it. After watching them briefly, we drove out to the hunters. We really weren't looking for waterfowl hunters, but ended up getting violations on them.

After issuing the guys some paperwork, we started to drive back toward the field entrance. We hadn't made it very far before we saw a little maroon SUV driving in the neighboring field (east of us). The SUV was traveling very slowly in our direction. It looked like they were hunting from the vehicle. With the two fields separated by a hedge row, we stopped and watched as the driver (DC) inched along. You could tell that DC likely had either not seen us or didn't realize who we were. Dave and I agreed that we needed to go check DC.

Dave started off at a slow pace as we cut across the field. I kind of got on him about speeding up. I didn't want DC to realize who we were and be able to hide anything. I think Dave was worried about hitting something in the hedge row. As Dave sped up, DC must have realized something wasn't right. He came to an abrupt stop. As we reached the hedge row, DC did an abrupt U-turn and hammered on the gas. After tapping the brakes, Dave shot through the hedge row and hit the "rollers". Within a hundred yards or so, we were on DC's tail, but he was not stopping for us. As he sped through the field, DC reached across to the front passenger seat and began shucking shells out of his uncased shotgun. As Dave pulled up along the left side of DC, I rolled the window down and started yelling at DC to stop. The chase continued for about 40 yards through the field before DC finally came to a stop. As soon as DC hit the brakes, Dave did too. Because Dave had to be reactionary, we stopped just ahead of DC. I immediately jumped out of the vehicle and was greeted by DC with his badge being brandished in short order. He initially acted like he didn't know what was going on, but eventually admitted that he had made a mistake. As I was talking with DC, Dave saw another truck driving on the opposite side of the same field.

Leaving me with DC, Dave took off after the other truck. I watched as Dave chased the other truck down. In pretty short order, Dave was returning and had the truck following behind him. Hard to believe, but the guy in the truck (I will call him Sparky) was driving with a loaded gun inside. It's never easy deciding what to write in these situations. You want to be fair to everyone—Blue or not. It makes it harder when you have a mix of the two. I hopped in with Dave and we started discussing what we should do. As we talked, a third vehicle came pulling up behind us. We watched as the guy (I will call Ray) parked right behind Dave's Ramcharger. I hopped out and walked back to Ray's window. Ray identified himself as the landowner. Sure enough, there was a loaded and uncased shotgun sitting in the front seat. All I could think is, "Are you kidding me!" Securing the third weapon, I returned to the squad with Dave. We finished our discussion. DC was issued a citation for hunting with the use or aid of a motor vehicle. As a police officer, he could legally have a loaded gun in his vehicle (even though there was not an exemption in the conservation code for police). Sparky and Ray got loaded and uncased weapons charges. Sparky pled guilty and was fined $100. Ray pled guilty and was fined $75. The charge against DC was dismissed. The prosecuting attorney told me, "You cannot attempt to take something that is not there." If an attorney wants to, they can justify not prosecuting almost anybody. When I was young, it frustrated me to see what I considered to be the wheels of injustice turning. As I got older, I began to realize that I should not be frustrated about things that I cannot control. In my old age, I would tell the attorneys that I had a clear conscience. I had done what was right and the ball was in their court. These cases should not be about who is "Blue" or not, but about doing what is right. DC was the only one that had proven knowledge and intent to break the law by his "reaction" to our presence. He tried to "run" from us in the field. Blue or not, it didn't seem like a fair outcome. Not for me, but for Sparky, Ray and anybody else that was prosecuted for the same offense.

POACHER

Turning back the clock a bit, earlier that same year, Laura and I were out scouting for dove hunting areas. I always tried to scout during the day, on weekdays, in the last 10 days of August. To start with, that put me in the 10-day restricted baiting window. It also put me out scouting when people were generally at work (time of day and week). I didn't have to worry so much about poachers "catching me" looking for them. It would suck to "lose" a baited field because someone saw me in the area. When it happened, the hunters just never showed up to hunt. I would spend a lot of time working a field with no results.

The most effective way that I found to scout for dove hunting areas was simply by using a grid pattern. It generally took me two years to complete each grid. I would pick a rural part of the county and drive on either the north and south or east and west roads. Whatever I picked; I would do the opposite direction the following year. When I did it, I would start at the edge of my scouting area and drive as far as I could (while staying in my target area). I would then cut over one mile and go back the opposite direction until I reached the plane of my starting spot. I would continue this method of zig-zagging back and forth until I covered the target area.

While driving down gravel or paved roads, I was always looking for mowed and dirt "roads" traveling off the road that I was on. I say "roads" because many of them are really just mowed paths. That time of year, all the farmers are mowing their field edges, so you must focus on what you are really looking for. That would be any path that has been driven down for any purpose other than just mowing it. Most people have to drive in to prepare their hunting fields. The easiest thing to look for was just tire tracks in the loose gravel on the edge of the road. Sometimes you would follow the tracks back and not find anything. Other times you would find something good.

On this particular day, we were scouting between Beecher and the Indiana state line. As we were driving down Yates Avenue, we located a dirt road that traveled back in between a couple of fields. The dirt road had been heavily traveled. Driving to the west on the dirt road, it ended at a cut rectangular clover field that had been partially disced. The field was likely 10 to 20 acres in size. In each corner of the field, there was a pile of six to eight hay bales. The hay bales didn't appear to have come from that field. There was really no reason for the bales to be there. It was six days before dove season opened and we didn't see any bait. We also didn't see any doves. If they were going to hunt that field, they would have to bait it to bring the doves in. We figured that we would check the field one more time before opening day.

At 10:00 p.m. on the night before dove season opener, Laura and I drove back to Yates Avenue. Pulling down the dirt road, I parked back from the edge of the field. Exiting the squad, we walked toward the field. As soon as I got past the first set of hay bales, I started finding sunflower and safflower seeds all over the ground. There wasn't a sunflower or safflower plant anywhere near the field. The field was baited! Gathering up a sample of the bait, we hurried up and got out of there. The seeds would not be evidence unless we caught someone hunting the field. At that point, we didn't want to spend any more time there than necessary.

We didn't get much sleep that night. At 4:00 a.m. the next day, Laura and I found a spot to park my squad about a mile northwest of the baited field. At first, we were able to walk down the road, but then we had to cut across a standing bean field. To say there was heavy dew that night was an understatement. We may as well have walked through a creek. We were completely soaked from the waist down by the time we reached the edge of the baited field. Looking across the field, there was a standing corn field along the south end. We decided that the corn field would likely give us the best field of view while providing cover from being seen. By about 4:30 a.m., we were laying in between the corn rows. Surprisingly, the dirt wasn't muddy. Almost all the dew had stuck to the plants. Occasionally, it would drip on us. After a while of being wet from the waist down, I started to get cold and uncomfortable. I figured I just had to bear it for a little bit longer since legal shooting hours started at 6:25 a.m. I figured we would make our arrests and be on our way.

Over the next two hours, I must have checked the clock 20 times. Two hours seemed like four hours. As 6:25 a.m. approached, we figured that we would already have hunters staging in the field, but nobody had come. Shortly into legal shooting hours, we were listening to people shooting in the distance. With nobody in our field, we had to wonder if the hunters were running late or if someone saw us out there the night before. It was even possible that someone had found our "hidden" squad.

At 7:07 a.m., a Suburban came pulling into the field. Immediately my blood pressure went up. Not only did we have hunters coming, but a Suburban full of them! Looking at the license plate, it read "POACHER". Okay, it wasn't actually "poacher", but the word on the plate insinuated that it would be a scoundrel inside. Only the driver (Freddy) got out of the vehicle. Waiting for the other doors to open, they never did. Freddy walked to the rear of the Suburban and got a bucket out. He proceeded to dump bird seed into the bucket. Freddy started walking around the southeast corner of the field throwing seed all over the place. Returning to the truck, he filled the bucket again and scattered that one too. Freddy then drove around the field and stopped two more times. Each time he stopped, Freddy would get out and scatter five-gallon buckets of bird seed. I think by the time he was done, Freddy had scattered seven five-gallon buckets of seed throughout the field. The whole time Freddy was scattering seed in the field there was a flock of pigeons flying around him and landing in the field.

At about 7:33 a.m., Freddy left the field. Though we had not caught anyone hunting, there was some relief in the fact that Freddy obviously did not know we were there. We also figured that there was a good likelihood he would be coming back.

Eight, Nine and ten o'clock came and went without any sign of a hunter. I think that at about 10:00 a.m. Laura called the ISP telecommunicators and asked them to airlift us some food. Laughing, we knew that wasn't going to happen. At least it had warmed up and we weren't cold anymore. At about 10:50 a.m., a guy on a tractor rumbled into the field and quickly left. It seemed like he was just checking to see if anyone was out there.

Finally, at 1:37 p.m. POACHER and another Suburban came pulling back into the field. All I could think was, "Motherload!"

Both of the Suburbans were full of hunters. Six hunters exited each of the vehicles. After gathering their guns, the hunters broke into three-person groups. Those groups worked their way to the hay bale stacks in each corner of the field. After arranging the bales into blinds, Freddy put some decoys out.

Laura watched the hunters on the east side of the field, and I took the ones on the west side. With all the pigeons mixed in with the doves, we had to make sure that each hunter shot at a dove. We didn't want to let the hunters kill any more doves than necessary, but we needed to see each hunter actually try to kill one. If we didn't, they could claim that they were just shooting at pigeons (which would be legal). It took almost an hour and a half to confirm that each hunter had shot at a dove.

At about 3:17 p.m., Laura and I broke cover. Walking out into the field, Laura went to her side and I went to mine. We identified ourselves to the hunters and confirmed that they knew they were hunting over bait. Freddy identified himself as a police officer. What a horrible position to put us in. Not only was he hunting over bait with non-police officers, but he was the one that had been baiting the field. We ended up seizing all the dead doves, more bait samples and took a bunch of pictures. We issued a couple of citations for state violations (unplugged shotgun and a juvenile hunting over bait) and referred the rest of the cases to the U.S. Fish and Wildlife Service for Federal prosecution. The remaining hunters all plead guilty and were fined a total of $3,200.

Throughout my career, I had many enforcement situations where I did the "Right Thing" when it was definitely not the "Right for Me Thing". If I had done the "Blue Thing" instead of what was "Right", my life would have been much easier. I paid a penance for those decisions. I had an officer try to rally other officers into writing me citations. His reported goal was to get my driver's license suspended or revoked—so I could not work. I had officers in their squads wave at me with one finger and full agencies refuse to wave at all. I had jailers try to make my job hard to do. I had them refuse to take prisoners by refusing my paperwork. The same paperwork that had been accepted 100 times before. The only thing that had changed was the Jailer. One of the worst things that I dealt with was a useless assistant state's attorney who took me out into the hall and admonished me for five minutes in front of a crowd. After he was done getting his satisfaction, he informed me that he was going to drop the charges against "Blue" anyway. All of this and likely hundreds of other things in retaliation for literally doing what I truly felt was the "Right Thing".

Did I ever give "Blue breaks"? Yes, occasionally I did. If I believed that an officer did not intentionally break the law, I would generally give them a break. Did they ever run back and say that they got a break? Not that I recall. Normally, I would hear that I was an asshole for even completing a check of them. For all of it, I have no regrets and all my integrity.

Although I have spent quite a few pages talking Blue, there are many cases that I have not touched on. They would all be similar in one way—I had caught an officer who appeared to have intentionally broken the law. The worst cases and officers that I dealt with, I am not memorializing by even mentioning their cases. Those officers don't get to say that their story made it into a book. For me, the biggest shame was that the "two percenters" made it hard to know who I could trust. I wish they had just tried to do the "Right Thing".

ACCIDENTS

Like a lot of kids, when I was young, I loved water. I loved to swim, boat and fish. If I had an opportunity to mess around in a creek or pond, I almost always did. As I got bigger, my Grandma Sophie and Grandpa Joe would take my older brother (Jimmy) and I up to their cabin in Wisconsin. Grandma Sophie was an outdoors woman. She was an expert mushroom picker, could butcher every animal alive and loved to fish. I would definitely credit my love of perch fishing to grandma. When Jimmy went fishing with Grandpa Joe, grandma would take me perch fishing. When we returned, grandma would tell us to go and play while she cleaned the fish. She wouldn't let grandpa do it! Fillets in hand, grandma would cook the perch up with a big batch of homemade French fries. When we finished playing and ate our fish, grandma always had fresh baked strawberry pie waiting for us. Those were the days!

When I was thinking about becoming a game warden, I didn't think much about handling accidents. I thought about catching poachers and helping people. It didn't take long for that to change. Although I handled many different types of accidents, the only ones that I really came to hate involved water. The paperwork didn't bother me; it was the senseless injuries and loss of life. No matter what I did, I couldn't "fix" the accident after it had happened. I couldn't change what the families would have to deal with for eternity. In the latter part of my career, I grew to despise rivers. Quite simply, the damn things are dangerous! Although I don't hate water, I have a fear of it that I never had as a kid. Maybe it's a good thing, but it sure doesn't feel that way!

Most of the water-related accidents that I've handled involved boats. Boating accidents will usually fall into one of two categories—either collisions or environmental. As the word insinuates, collisions involve running into something. Sometimes, equipment failure or operator inexperience causes the accident. More often than not, they are caused by alcohol, bad judgment or intentionally doing something stupid. The really sad collision cases involved victims who had no choice. They themselves hadn't done anything "wrong". It was the "other guy". On the other hand, environmental accidents may involve rough waters, dams or falling overboard. These accidents are less likely to involve bad intentions. Quite often, they are the epitome of true accidents.

Although preventing collisions is hard to do, everybody will be moving in the right direction if they don't drink too much, maintain their equipment and make good decisions. If everybody just wears their PFDs (life jackets), half of the serious environmental accidents will disappear. Since none of the aforementioned is going to happen, I feel that I should talk about a couple of different environmental accidents. These cases will highlight a couple of things that may be helpful to avoid getting into or getting out of a bad situation.

I know this isn't a revelation, but the inherent danger of a river is the moving water. If you fall into a lake and swim to the surface, you will likely come up relatively close to where you fell in. If you fall into a river, you might not. You may think that you're just going to come up and swim back to your boat, but it's not that simple. If you're a real good swimmer or are on a slow stretch of river, you can tip the scales in your direction. The reality of a river is that many of them travel faster than you can swim. You may have a couple of fast bursts in you, but swimming is a resistance exercise that will tire you out very quickly, especially if you don't do it on a regular basis. Even though you can swim, how often do you actually do it? How long can you swim at your fastest pace? If the boat isn't anchored, it will drift with you, but it won't necessarily drift at the same pace. Even if you can get to the boat, can you get back into it? Depending on the situation and your abilities, you should always consider swimming downstream (at an angle) to the nearest bank. The river is like a never-ending treadmill. If you give it everything you have and go nowhere, that's exactly where you will end up.

One of the most dangerous obstacles on a river is a dam. Over the years, I worked several fatal accidents involving them. One such accident occurred in July of 2013 at the Steel Dam. At approximately 4:53 p.m., I received a report of the accident. I was told that one boater (Mark) was deceased and the other (Artie) was still stuck in the boil below the dam.

Responding to the Backwater Gamblers boat ramp, I hopped into a boat with another officer. Motoring down to just above the dam, we worked in conjunction with another rescue boat to get a rope out to Artie. Artie had been holding onto a floating tree and a PWC (personal watercraft). He was struggling to keep his head above water. As the other rescue boat floated the rope over the dam (and down to Artie), we drove the opposite end over to the north bank. Hopping out with the rope, I carried it over to the other first responders. When Artie grabbed on, they pulled him free of the dam and over to the bank. Artie had clung onto the log for over an hour. When he was finally pulled out, he was exhausted. Artie was taken to the hospital to be evaluated.

Heading to the hospital, I was able to meet with Artie. I explained to him that I was tasked with investigating the accident.

I asked him to tell me what had happened. Artie said that he and Mark were out boating on their PWCs. He said that they both had PFDs on. He told me that as they operated down the flooded river, there was very little traffic. The water was so high that the drop at the Steel Dam was only about 12 inches. At normal water levels, the drop would have been five to seven feet. Artie said that as he and Mark traveled downstream, they didn't even see the dam until they had crossed it. From upstream, it probably looked like it was flat. Once Mark and Artie were on the downstream side, they discussed whether they should try to go back up over the dam. Like most guys, Mark and Artie likely considered it to be a challenge. Artie decided that he would try to cross the dam at the same spot as where they had come down. Artie said that as he approached the dam, he was going just fast enough to keep the PWC moving forward. As Artie nosed into the roll of the dam, he said that the bow of his PWC got lifted and he was turned sideways. Tipping toward the dam, Artie said that he fell off the PWC. Artie told me that he tried, but couldn't climb back onto his PWC.

As Artie struggled in the water, he said that Mark pulled up and tried to help him. Artie grabbed onto the rear of Mark's PWC. When Mark hit the throttle, the engine bogged and Artie lost his grip. Within minutes, Mark was stuck in the boil with Artie. Artie said that the wash from the dam was slowly pushing them to the north (lateral to the dam). He said that at first, they were both holding onto a log. Artie said that Mark switched to one of the partially submerged PWCs. He said that shortly after Mark did that, he lost sight of him. Mark was found later floating downstream in his PFD.

Being further into my career, I had started to think more about why one person survived an accident when another did not. In doing so, I started to ask the survivors what they had done to survive. At the end of getting a statement from Artie, I asked him his thoughts. Having made it for over an hour in the boil of a low head dam, I was hoping that Artie would have some words of wisdom. He said that he just kept fighting. He didn't have an answer for why he had made it when Mark had not. I often thought that there had to be something more. For years now, I've wondered if time would change Artie's answer. I'm sure that he has thought about it a lot more than I have.

Having worked on several of these accidents, Artie's thoughts were consistent with the other survivors. Most of them just felt blessed to have made it out of the dam. The water was never going to stop coming and would never stop pushing them under.

Maybe there isn't a "secret" to surviving a low head dam. Some people get ejected from them as fast as they get into them. Like Artie, others get stuck in the boil until they are either rescued or killed. I've never gotten an explanation for why one person gets ejected when another does not. Maybe they just hit an area where the return wash is disrupted. I would say that anybody who finds themselves caught in a boil should be mentally prepared for a long stay. Don't hunker down and pass on an opportunity to escape, but don't be thinking, "I don't know how long I can make it." Have the mental resolve that you are going to make it—no matter how long it takes. When you get pushed under, get back to the surface. Usually, there are other things churning in the boil with you. If you're holding onto a boat, you're going to get hit every time it flips. If it's stuck in the boil, it will flip—and often. If it catches you just right, you may get knocked unconscious. If you find a straight round log to hold onto, you still have to worry about it flipping long ways. If it doesn't have branches, it might not uncontrollably roll like the ones that do. I've seen several people come out of dams that have been beaten up by whatever they were holding onto.

The best advice is don't end up in there to begin with. I know it sounds obvious, but put some thought into where you go boating. If there's a low head dam downstream, stay at least a mile up from it. If you have a regular boat, have an anchor. If the motor stops, put the anchor out before you try to fix it. Remember, in the river, the anchor only goes out from the bow. If you throw it in from the transom, when it catches, you might start taking water over the stern. If that happens, cut the rope immediately. If you try to pull it in, you will likely just pull the stern of the boat deeper into the water. Depending on how big your boat is, within a few seconds it could sink. Never put an anchor in from both ends. If it's not your lucky day, the bow anchor will come loose, and the boat will spin around (stern up stream). Of course, the stern anchor will hold. When it pulls tight, you will be in the same position as if you had just thrown it in from the stern.

Never Give Up

In late February of 2009, I received a call that a boat accident had occurred about three miles upstream of the Steel Dam. It was one of those late winter days when you could tell that spring was coming. The temps had hit the upper 40s at one point. Even though the air had warmed up, the river temperature was lacking behind. The water temperature was hovering in the mid-30s. On top of that, a storm front had come in. A mix of rain and sleet had started coming down.

By the time I arrived on scene, two (Snap and Crackle) of the three boat occupants had made it out of the water. The third (Pop) was still missing. Meeting with EMS on scene, I was told that the there was a witness to the accident. The witness saw the three subjects capsize in a canoe out in the middle of the river. When the canoe capsized, Snap swam to shore and got a "jon boat". Launching it, he returned to Crackle and helped him get to shore safely. Snap couldn't make it out to save Pop. Pop had disappeared under the surface of the water. Looking at the jon boat, there was some clothing and a PFD (life jacket) sitting inside. I asked EMS personnel if the canoe had been recovered. I was told that it had been. Sgt. Randy Heisch (Rock Island County Sheriff's Police) and a local patron went out and got it. They said that the only thing left in the canoe was a box of beer and two PFDs. Asking where Snap and Crackle were, I was told that Snap had been released and Crackle had been transported to the hospital.

Returning to my squad, I called Randy to hear exactly what he had found. Besides being a good officer, Randy was a really good human being. I knew that if Randy told me something, I could trust what he had said. I never saw a situation where Randy used his position to get something for himself. Literally, the only thing that I saw Randy do wrong over the years was make me late. Since I always enjoyed talking with Randy, I found that if we started talking, I had a hard time ending the conversation. More than once, I was talking with Randy when I should have been getting something else done! Okay, I suppose it was as much my fault as it was his.

Randy told me that when they got to the canoe, it was partially submerged, but right side up. He said that there was a PFD and a box of beer inside. A second PFD was floating in the water next to it. Randy told me that after they got the canoe to shore, the storm had started to lightning. He said that they had not made it back out onto the river yet. After EMS searched for Pop, we had to suspend our water operations for safety. The weather continued to get worse. I took pictures of the scene, the canoe and the jon boat. When I got done, I headed to the hospital.

Arriving, I located Snap standing outside of the emergency room. I identified myself to him and confirmed his identity. I asked Snap if he would go in and tell me what had happened. He agreed. When we sat down, Snap told me that he lives there on the Rock River. He said that he, Crackle and Pop were talking and decided to go out fishing in the canoe. Snap told me that Pop was in the front seat, Crackle was in a lawn chair in the middle and he was in the back. Snap told me that they were taking turns paddling as they headed for the bridge. When they got out toward the middle of the river, the canoe capsized and all three of them were ejected from the boat. Snap said that they tried to turn the canoe back over, but couldn't get it done. Snap told me that he and Crackle decided to swim for shore. Snap made it to shore first, ran into the garage and grabbed a jon boat. Dragging it down to the river, Snap said that he could still see Crackle swimming for the bank. Launching the boat, Snap told me that he rowed out to Crackle. He said that when he got to Crackle, he had him hold onto the transom as he pulled him back to shore. Snap said that he last saw Pop holding onto the canoe in the middle of the river. Snap said that he couldn't make it out to Pop before he disappeared.

I asked Snap why the canoe had tipped over to begin with. He started to get upset as he told me that either Crackle or Pop must have leaned too far to one side. I asked Snap how many PFDs he had in the canoe. He told me that he thought he had two. After we talked about the other equipment, I asked Snap how much alcohol he had to drink. Snap said that he had four or five beers before the accident. Snap ended up writing a statement for me.

When he was done, I walked back and met with Crackle. Crackle was still under medical observation. We introduced ourselves and I asked Crackle what had happened. Crackle confirmed Snap's recollection of the accident. Crackle went on to tell me that when the canoe capsized, he could not get his shoes or coat off. Crackle told me that as he and Snap swam for the bank, he knew that he would not be able to stay above the surface of the water. Crackle told me that he took a deep breath and went under water. Crackle indicated that he thought it might be the last breath he would ever take. Crackle said that when he got to the bottom, he pushed himself back to the surface at an angle toward the bank. After trying to swim again, Crackle took another deep breath and went back under water. Crackle told me that the water didn't seem as deep this time. Pushing off the bottom again, Crackle said that he was starting to become exhausted. When he got to the surface,

Crackle said that he could barely swim at all. Repeating the cycle a couple more times, Crackle admitted that he didn't know if he would survive. He really couldn't swim anymore when he got to the surface. Crackle told me that the last time he came up, he was at the rear of Snap's boat. He said that he grabbed onto the boat as Snap grabbed onto him. Crackle couldn't remember much after that. I got a statement from Crackle and left the hospital.

The weather continued to deteriorate for the next few days. The Rock River in the area of the accident went from about 12 feet deep to around 17 feet deep. Although we searched for a couple of weeks, we never did find Pop.

There are several things to talk about with this accident. First, never add an elevated seating position to a narrow watercraft. Have PFDs and wear them in a canoe or kayak. Think twice about canoeing in bad weather or in cold water. Although the capacity was not exceeded, with three people, it becomes more likely that two of them will lean to the same side causing an excessive weight shift. Last but not least, adding alcohol to the situation increases the likelihood that the other risks involved will be exploited.

Just as important as what led to the canoe capsizing, is what happened after it did. While two PFDs were in the canoe, nobody put one on (even after it flipped). I have heard many people say that you should always stay with the boat. I would agree that under many circumstances, it is the best option. However, many older boats didn't have built-in flotation. If those boats take on enough water, they will just sink and disappear (unless they have air trapped inside). If you buy one of those older boats, add permanent flotation to it. If it doesn't sink, you will have something to grab on to.

The most important point is similar to the dam accident. Crackle knew that he wasn't going to be able to swim all the way to the bank. He took the deepest breath he could, went down, and pushed off the bottom. He kept doing it until he was rescued.

He indicated that he didn't think he could have kept doing it all the way to the bank. On the other hand, I think that he would have made it. I don't think that Crackle would have given up, especially when he knew that what he was doing was working. His mindset was right. Try to stay calm and figure out how to survive. No matter what situation you find yourself in!

Anchors Away

Although I could write many chapters about accidents, I have covered most of the main points that I wanted to make. The last "almost accident" that I wanted to talk about is one of my own. In June of 2013, I received a report of an illegal hoop net. Hoop nets are commercial fishing nets used on the Mississippi River. One of the requirements for their use is that they are to be checked every 72 hours. If they aren't checked as required, the fish will start to die inside of the net. Once the fish die, turtles will climb in to get a free meal. Since hoop nets are set completely under water, the turtles can't come up for air and die as well. Before long, everything is decomposing and filling up with gas. At that point, the net will float. Fish eating birds end up seeing the floating fish and come down to get their free meal. Sometimes, they get caught in the net and end up dying too. It's a big snowball that just keeps getting bigger.

On this occasion, the complainant stated that the hoop net was in Velie Chute. Velie Chute is a part of the Mississippi River that cuts through Andalusia Island. Launching a boat near Andalusia, I told the Illinois State Police (ISP) that I would be out on the river.

The river was high and there wasn't much traffic that day. I headed straight for the chute. About 100 yards in, I located the floating net on the west side. The dead stuff inside was stinking really bad! There were 11 fish and seven turtles in it. The turtles and some of the flathead catfish were pretty big. You could tell that some of the turtles had been dead for a long time. The plates on their shell had actually started to slide off. I took pictures of the floating net and figured that I would just pull it into my boat real quick. I tried to lift the net straight up out of the water and realized that it wasn't going to be that easy.

It was time for plan two. When I first tried to pull the net in, I was pulling against the anchor too. Hoop nets have giant anchors that keep them in place. I decided that if I pulled the anchor in first, I might be able to flip the net in. The anchor had gotten hooked on a log or root, so it took me a while to get it loose. Once I got it into the boat, I set it on the floor and wound the anchor rope up. I still couldn't lift the net straight up into the boat. It was too heavy and cumbersome. Turning the net so the hoops were lined up with the side of my boat, I pulled the top of the rungs over the side. I tried to pull the bottom of the rungs up and flip the net into the boat, but it kept slipping off the side of the boat. I knew that I was consciously trying to keep from getting the dead fish "slime" on me, but I was starting to get frustrated. I decided that I didn't care how slimy I got, I was tired of "failing"!

Lining the top of the net's rungs up once again, I got them into the boat. Grabbing the bottom of the rungs, I pulled as hard as I could. The net didn't just flip into the boat and land at my feet. It slowly continued moving in my direction until the fish started to slide into the boat. Then, they all came at once. I tried to step back and let everything come in, but my foot got caught on the anchor. I couldn't step back, but my body was already going in that direction. As I fell out of the other side of the boat, I can remember grabbing for anything that I get a hold of. Needless to say, there wasn't anything to grab onto.

When I was fully under water, I opened my eyes and could only see green. I never touched the bottom, but came up right next to the boat. Reaching up, I grabbed onto the side of the boat. I tried to pull myself up, but couldn't get my chest over the side. With my entire uniform on, I was carrying at least an extra 30 pounds. I worked my way to the rear of the boat and stepped on the lower unit. Pulling on the transom, I was able to climb up into the boat.

I had my radio on my belt and my cell phone in its holder. The holder was clipped onto my shoulder strap. Worse yet, I had my personal cell phone in my thigh pocket. I couldn't call anybody and couldn't get any calls. Thinking about it, I figured that it didn't really matter. I didn't "have" to call in. If ISP had tried to call me, they would just think that I couldn't hear them over the sound of the boat motor.

Sitting down for a few minutes, I took off some of my soaked clothes and equipment. Striping off my duty belt and bulletproof vest, I relieved myself of the 30-pound anchor. I thought about how lucky I was to have on my PFD. Not just any PFD, but the one that I had purchased. Although the DNR had issued us both regular and inflatable PFDs, I had purchased my own work PFD several years earlier. The regular PFD issued by the DNR was outdated and the inflatable one was a manual unit. In order to fill the inflatable PFD with air, I had to pull the handle on the bottom of the vest. The handle punctured a CO_2 cartridge, which filled the vest up with air. That is, unless the CO_2 cartridge failed. On my issued inflatable vest, the CO_2 cartridge had repeatedly come unscrewed. In an emergency, I didn't want to risk pulling the handle only to have it fail. I went and bought my personal PFD. Mine had extra flotation and some mesh areas to help keep me cool. I figured that I needed to counter the "extra 30 pounds" that I was always carrying.

Like most situations, as I sat there, I started to think about what I had done wrong. Obviously, I had set the anchor in the wrong place. When I pulled the net in, I hadn't done it "under control". I should have put my personal cell phone somewhere in the boat. With everything else going through my head, I kept thinking about my PFD. When I had fallen into the water, the only thing that I thought about was getting back to the surface. I wasn't frantically swimming because I knew that I had my PFD on. Almost as fast as I had fallen in, I started coming back toward the surface. Then I thought about the inflatable PFD. If I had worn it, would I have had the composure to pull the handle? Would I have frantically tried to swim for the surface (as I kept sinking) and never pulled the handle? Would the CO_2 cartridge have come unscrewed again? I don't know the answer to any of the questions. I do know that having the "regular PFD" made it so that I didn't make a fatal mistake that day.

When I finished daydreaming, I walked up to the bow of the boat and emptied the hoop net. I took pictures of the fish and turtles. One fish was still alive, and all of the turtles were dead (or so I thought). I released the fish right away. It took me about a half hour to get everything together and take pictures. Just as I was about to leave, I saw one of the turtles move its foot. At first, I thought I was just seeing things. Then it moved again. I messed around with the turtles for about five minutes and was able to release three of them on the island. I'm not sure if they actually lived. They were pretty lethargic.

Getting back to the boat launch, I figured that I needed to call ISP. I may have missed a call from them. When I got through to the TC (telecommunicator Lori Delos Reyes), she asked me if I was alright. I was surprised that Lori would ask me that. I told her that I was. Lori asked me to immediately call her on the telephone. I told her that I had fallen into the river and didn't have a working phone. Lori asked me to call her when I got to one. Loading up my boat, I made my way to a phone and called Lori. She told me that I must have keyed up my mic when I was falling over the side. Lori said that what she had heard on the radio wasn't good. She tried to call me and got no response. Trusting her gut, Lori started the cavalry in my direction. I believe it included Iowa DNR, ISP and the ISP airplane. I can't tell you how important good TCs are to the officers in the field. They never get the credit that they deserve.

They save lives and help with arrests by simply using a radio and a telephone. Lori was one of many great TCs that I had an opportunity to work with over the years.

I truly hope that you think about and share what I have written in this chapter. It won't save you in every situation, but may help in some of them. Although you think it will never happen to you, many others (including me) have thought the exact same thing. The mistakes made during boating season weigh on many people, not just the ones directly involved.

A WARDEN'S REALITY

Every person has life lessons constantly molding their perception of reality. I will not say that my life lessons have been any better or worse than anybody else's. I will say that to help you understand who I am, you need to know how I got to where I am. You should also have the opportunity to see both the good and bad things about being a CPO. In doing this chapter, I hope to help you better understand my reality. I also hope to settle my own soul. Most importantly, I hope that you look at these stories with a thought toward how you could have changed the results by altering the events that lead to them. Although it sounds good, it may not always be possible.

I've told this first story many times throughout my life. Although it's not a "game warden story", I have told it more times as a game warden than any other. As game wardens, we often get requests to speak to kids groups. If the group is of an age that it would be proper to tell this story, I tell it. I hope that those kids and their parents (if they are present) realize what could have happened and think about the decisions made before, during and after.

It was the early spring of my fifth-grade year. For my birthday, I had asked for fishing equipment. I got a new tackle box and a bunch of lures. I can remember my tackle box clearly. It was a Plano three tray. It was better than everybody else's tackle box in my whole family (with the exception of Dad's). Dad had a big white tackle box that had four or five trays. I couldn't wait to get out and use my new equipment. I am sure that I was repetitively asking Dad when we could go fishing.

That following weekend, Dad asked me what I wanted to do for my birthday. Of course, I said that I wanted to go fishing. My Dad owned Jim's Body Shop. He generally worked from 6 a.m. to 5 p.m. during the week. On weekends, he would start at 6 a.m., but would only work until about noon. Dad said that he had stuff to do at work that Sunday, but would drop me off on his way. I was super excited. Dad was going to drop me off at Peotone Sportsmen's Club. The Sportsmen's Club consisted of two little lakes on the north edge of Peotone. One lake was right next to Harlem Avenue. In this area, Harlem Avenue is just a gravel road. The second lake was separated from the first lake by a narrow strip of land. When I say that the first lake is right next to the Harlem Avenue, I mean that there was not even a ditch. You could pull off onto a wide shoulder and cast your line into the lake. There were no houses right next to the club. There were one or two houses about a quarter of a mile north of it.

In preparation for my trip, I rounded up all of our old fishing poles. Like most fishing families, we had a pile of poles that were less than perfect. Some had broken rods, some were out of line and some had reels that had outlived their parts. I also had my "tried and true" Zebco 808. My Grandma Sophie had given it to me for fishing in Wisconsin. I knew that if all of the other poles didn't work, my 808 would.

When Sunday morning came, I was up and ready to go. Dad took me out and dropped me off. I decided to fish right next to Harlem Avenue. I had so many poles that it would have been hard to carry all of them around the lake. I put some stink bait on my

808, cast it out and set it off to the side. Although it was sunny, it was not real warm. There was a light breeze that cut through my clothes. I occasionally took a break from fishing and would work on making a wind break. I worked on the extra poles for a while and was able to get a couple of them to work. The rest of the poles needed something more than I was capable of doing.

Done with the poles and having my wind break done, I started focusing on the fact that I was not catching any fish. I knew that I had not planned very well. I should have gotten some night-crawlers. I decided to look for bait in the ditch on the other side of the road. Any worm or bug would do. I walked across the road and started looking in the ditch. I couldn't find anything. I couldn't even find a bug moving around. As I started walking back across to my fishing spot, I saw an old van south of me. It had crossed the tracks from Route 50 and was coming my way at a pretty good clip. As the vehicle continued to speed up, I jogged across to my fishing spot. As the van approached me, I saw there was one guy in the driver's seat (I will call him Dick). As he passed me, Dick actually swerved off of the road toward me. He came about three feet from hitting me. I was scared at that point. Watching the back of the van, I can remember thinking, "Please don't stop, please don't stop, please don't stop." As the van approached the entrance road to the club, I saw the brake lights come on. Clear as day, I can remember the next thought in my head was, "Please don't turn around, please don't turn around, please don't turn around." Dick backed out and started to come back toward me. My stress level was through the roof as I again thought, "Please don't stop, please don't stop, please don't stop." Of course, Dick slowed to a stop right next to me.

A couple of weeks before this incident, we had a "Stranger Danger" demonstration at school. During the demonstration, the speaker talked about maintaining a reactionary gap between you and a stranger. They also told us that you should always carry change for a pay phone. Parking in the road, Dick got out of the van. He had overshot me by about 20 feet. When Dick exited the van, I still had my reactionary gap. Dick acted like he had not swerved at me. With a smile, he asked if I was catching any fish. I told Dick that I had not. I explained that I had not had a bite. He asked why I thought I had not gotten any bites. I told him that I didn't have any live bait. As Dick stepped toward me, I stepped back. Dick told me that he needed to go to Kankakee. He asked me if I knew where Kankakee was. I told him that I did. My Grandma June lived down there. Dick asked me for directions to Kankakee. I told Dick that he needed to drive south on Harlem Avenue back to Route 50. I advised him that he needed to go south on Route 50 through Peotone and the next town that he came to would be Kankakee. Dick corrected me. He asked me if the next town was not Manteno. I told Dick that he was right. I told him that he also needed to go through Manteno. Dick acted like I had enlightened him. Dick told me that he had a problem with the seat in his van. Dick said that his seat would slide forward and back while he was driving. Dick told me that he needed someone to hold the seat while he put the bolt back in. Dick asked me if I would hold the seat for him while he put the bolt in. Quietly, I said, "No". Dick raised his voice and said, "What?!" Louder, I said, "No." He yelled, "You little mother fucker!" I'm sure there was more, but I had turned and was running toward the club entrance road. Looking back to see if he was chasing me, I saw Dick kick my tackle box out into the middle of the lake. Then he grabbed the pile of "broken" fishing poles and threw them into his van. As I turned and ran east on the entrance road, I saw my tackle box sinking out in the lake. I do not remember seeing the van that time, but was thinking that Dick might be trying to follow me. I knew that the entrance road would lead me back to the railroad tracks. Dick would not be able to follow me up onto the tracks. I had spent a lot of time catching snakes along the tracks and might be able to elude Dick there.

When I reached the tracks, I looked back toward the lakes and could not see Dick. I looked south toward the railroad crossing and could not see Dick or his van. There were no vehicles on the gravel road that followed along the side of the railroad tracks. Looking across Route 50, I had forgotten that the North Peotone Motel was directly across the road. I could see the glass phone booth in the frontyard. I had some change in my pocket and just needed to make it to the phone booth. I really didn't want to cross Route 50 for fear that Dick may be on the road. I really just wanted to hide. Looking up and down Route 50, I could not see Dick anywhere. I decided to run for it. Running to the phone booth, I went in and closed the glass door. I hated that Dick could see me through the glass if he drove by.

There were two types of pay phones back then. One type, you had to dial first, wait for the amount, deposit it and the call would be completed. The other, you had to put your money in first and then dial the number. I put my change in and dialed Dad's number. It wouldn't go through. I tried it both ways several times, but could not get the phone to work. Having not seen Dick again, I knew that I needed to run to Dad's body shop. I figured if I got up by the tracks, I could run down the tracks and across town to the shop. I never thought about calling collect or running to my house (which was actually a little closer).

I ran back across Route 50, down the tracks and across town. The whole time I was nervous that I would see Dick's van. When I got to the shop, I was crying and told Dad what had happened. He took me to talk with a police officer. I told the officer what had happened. He wanted to know if I knew the license plate number. No, of course I didn't. Dad took me back out to the Club where we found the Zebco 808 on top of a bush. The only really good pole that I had, and Dick had not stolen it. There was nothing else left.

As a kid, I didn't want to tell this story, but was likely forced to tell it 10 times. In August of that year, my Uncle Wally Rokus (a

Kankakee City police officer) wanted me to come look at a van they had found at the Kankakee County Fairgrounds. He said that it matched the description I had given him. I was still afraid. I wanted to forget that it had ever happened. I refused to go down and look at the van. I can remember Wally trying to talk my mom (his sister) into taking me down there. She didn't. My Uncle Wally was the toughest guy I knew. Not only was he a police officer, but he was an all-around "tough guy". Every person that ever talked about Wally had a story about him kicking someone's ass. I don't know if anyone ever beat him up. With all of that said, I was still too afraid to go.

Looking back now, I thank God for the Stranger Danger program. I also wish that I had gone down and looked at the van for my uncle. I wonder how many little kids Dick lured into his van, and what happened to them. In writing this story, I also realized a personal connection (due to circumstance) to Christopher Meyer's tragedy. I wonder if I subconsciously thought about it at the time? Would Stranger Danger have helped him?

In what is obviously different ways, I suppose that Dick and Uncle Wally pushed me toward being a police officer. Dick because I never wanted to be that vulnerable again. Uncle Wally because I always wanted to be as tough as him. I went on to lift a lot of weights, study Hapakido and become a defensive tactics instructor. I am likely still not as tough as Wally was. I can also say that I have disliked vans for the majority of my life!

Coach Eb

Moving ahead to high school, my favorite coach was Terry Eberle. On more than one occasion, Coach Eb called me "Smiley". Apparently, while I was in high school, I would smile at the drop of a hat. He was not my favorite coach because of how he coached, but because of his positive influence on my life. Coach Eb liked to joke around, but would also have serious "life" talks with me. Like most kids, I didn't always feel like everything was going perfect.

Coach Eb was an outside voice that helped me to believe in the path that I had chosen. He encouraged me to stay on that path. He told me that if I did, everything would work out in the end. He was right, and it did. That is not to take anything away from my parents or the rest of my family. They made me who I am. Coach Eb was simply the "outside voice" reinforcing that my parents and family had done a good job.

Over the years, I became good friends with Coach Eb's son, Jason. While we were in college, Jason and I got summer jobs at the local bucket factory. If we weren't working, Jason and I would hang out together. One afternoon, as Jason and I were getting ready to go out, we were sitting in Jason's living room talking with Coach Eb. Coach Eb suddenly had a massive heart attack. All that I could do to help Mrs. Eberle (a nurse) and Jason was to assist in getting Coach Eb onto the floor. Mrs. Eberle performed CPR until the ambulance arrived. Coach Eb passed away that day. I always wished that I could've done something more. Prior to that, I had not given much thought about being in that situation. Even if I had been mentally prepared for what happened, I do not know that I could have helped Coach Eb. I could definitely have helped Mrs. Eberle—if she would have let me. I will not forget Coach Eb and will forever be grateful to the Eberle family. They gave me much more than friendship. Of course, I went on to learn CPR, first aid, and have been trained in being a first responder. I've never just gone through the steps to get a certificate; I try to learn what I can. I also find myself constantly thinking about what I need to do if something goes "bad".

Although the first two stories in this chapter were from before I was an officer, they were important events in my life. They were important in molding what was "reality" to me. They likely moved me toward where I ended up. As I recognized my own personal deficiencies, I tried to address them. I tried to ready myself for what police work was about to throw at me. I thought that I had done well in my preparation. In "reality", I was prepared, but not for everything. The next stories represent some of my darker days while being a game warden. I could not have changed the results, but maybe somebody closer to the situation could have. In "reality", some things you just have no control over.

Joshua and Ashley

By 2002, Laura and I were the parents of three-year-old Garrett. We took him everywhere and did almost everything as a family. On this particular December day, I happened to be working near Des Plaines Conservation Area. I received a call that a couple of fishermen had found a human body on the Des Plaines River. I was told that it was located in a cove near Big Basin Marina. One of the fishermen was identified as a guy I will call "Alex". Alex was a tournament bass fisherman. I had received numerous complaints about Alex over the years and was hesitant to believe the validity of what he was reporting. I still responded as quickly as I could.

Arriving at Big Basin, I drove through the neighboring corporate area and over to the bank of the cove. Parking my squad, I could see Alex out in his boat. Alex quickly advised that the body was next to the bank. He pointed toward the bank directly in front of me. Approaching the edge of the bank, I can remember seeing a bunch of white puffy stuff floating around in the water. It looked like a bunch of giant cottonwood seed balls. It was December and there definitely shouldn't have been any floating around. Reaching the edge of the upper riverbank, I looked down. The bank dropped about three feet to the surface of the water. I could see a little kid (later identified as three-year-old Joshua Gleeson) floating next to the bank. Joshua had brown hair and was only moving with the surface of the water. He had a t-shirt on that had floated up around his neck and head. I really didn't want to believe what I was looking at. Joshua was literally the same size as my own son.

The local media outlets were known to monitor ISP frequencies. When I went back to my squad, I "generically" called the incident in to the Illinois State Police. I did not want the media breathing down my back before I had officers there to help secure the scene. ISP was sending back-up units and crime scene investigators. It seemed like it took hours for another officer to get there. In actuality, it was likely about 10 minutes. Having to run all of the traffic over the radio, I started to worry about a news helicopter or airplane flying over. I felt like I needed to cover Joshua up. The only thing that I had with me to cover Joshua was one of those plastic silver heat blankets. Even though it would not be normal protocol, I broke it out. It just seemed like the right thing to do. I covered him up and waited. Back then I did not read a daily newspaper or watch the local news every day. As the cavalry started to arrive, I was told that there were two missing children from Dwight, Illinois (Joshua and his five-year-old sister Ashley).

When the crime scene investigators arrived, we removed the heat blanket and they started processing the scene. About the same time, CPO Matt Lentz arrived and was helping as well. Matt was a relatively new officer. He had moved into an open position on the north end of Will County. Laura had been one of Matt's FTOs, so I had gotten to know him pretty well. Although Matt was a very nice person, we didn't get to work together very often. On this particular day, it was nice to have two game wardens. When it came time to pull Joshua out of the water, Matt and I put our hip waders on and were supplied a "water body bag". I had not seen one prior to that day. It is the same size and shape as a regular body bag. It just happens to be made out of mesh (so the water can drain out). Matt went to the north side of Joshua (by his head) and I went to the south side (by his feet). Because Joshua was right up against the bank, we put the bag in the water on the opposite side of him. With the bag open, we tried to pull it under Joshua. The bag got stuck on a branch or something under water. Pulling it a couple more times, we had the same issue. The last time we went to pull it, I told Matt to pull it hard. When we did, Joshua's little body rocked in the water. It rocked him enough that it caused his shirt to pull down from his face. What a beautiful little boy. I had an incredible sadness and anger that overcame me. We got Joshua secured in the bag and lifted him up onto the bank. He was turned over to the investigators and I was ready to leave. I had a long ride home that night. Since becoming a parent, I had not experienced anything like that.

The following day, Ashley's body was recovered from below the I-55 bridge. I was not there when she was recovered. Although I would like to have seen the case through, maybe it was best. As it turned out, Joshua and Ashley's father admitted that he had shot both of his children in the head. I did not see any evidence of the injuries on Joshua. After killing his children, their father apparently wrapped them up and threw them into the river from the I-55 bridge. There was a sleeping bag recovered during the search of the water. I think all of the "white puffy stuff" was actually the fill from the sleeping bag. The father ended up pleading guilty to the murders of his children and his girlfriend. He was sentenced to life in prison in Michigan. They believed that all of the murders had been committed up there.

To this day, I can see Joshua's little face in my memory. I also continue to get the same anger and sadness that I felt that day. Having thought of this case a thousand times, where did we go wrong as a society? The only thing that Joshua and Ashley did, was trust their father... Although I know that Joshua and Ashley will forever be missed, they will never be forgotten.

Carter
Several years later, I was notified of a boat accident that had occurred on the Rock River. On this occasion, the accident occurred at around 4:30 in the afternoon. I did not receive notification of the accident until over an hour later. A large time gap between the occurrence of a boat accident and the reporting of it

is not uncommon. Sometimes, the accident involves a single sub-ject who is later reported missing. Other times, people intention-ally do not report the accident. Those people are usually drunk or decide to get their "story straight" before they report it. The last and most common issue that I experienced was a combination of technical and knowledge-based complications. Although they are different, they are also combined. Most boat accidents are reported to 911 from a cellular telephone. The call will generally go to the nearest cell phone tower and be routed to the county in which that tower is located. Sometimes, that tower is on the other side of a state or county line. When the telecommunicator realizes that the accident occurred in another jurisdiction, they will try to forward the call to the proper agency. It may be forwarded sev-eral times. When the call gets to its final telecommunicator, you have to hope that they realize that the DNR should be the primary investigating agency. If they do not, the case may not be referred to the DNR until the responding agency has already started an investigation. This is especially true in urban areas. In those areas, game wardens are not as "involved" in community affairs (as they are in the rural areas). Most urban police officers know that we exist, but many do not understand what we really do. In rural areas, it can be quite different. We will commonly work in tandem with the County Sheriff's Police. Some agencies will even request our assistance for calls that are not conservation-related. Sometimes, we just happen to be the closest back-up unit to their location.

Although the forwarding of a 911 call should not take very long, I have seen a single call be forwarded as many as three times. That particular call went from Rock Island County to Rock Island City to Davenport (Iowa) and finally to Scott County (Iowa). Keep in mind that the caller is going to hear "911, what is your emer-gency?" four times. On that occasion, after they heard it the fourth time, an investigating agency responded to the call. The case was referred to us hours later. Although we are frustrated in those cases, the complainants are likely livid. This would be especially true if they have family or friends needing medical attention (even though medical may already be en route).

Getting back to Carter, I responded to a house along the Rock River near Geneseo, Illinois. The delay in this particular case was just figuring out who had jurisdiction over the incident. The scene was secure when I arrived, but there were still witnesses available to tell me what had happened. Great Grandma and Great Grandpa lived in a house along the Rock River. Grandpa (47), Grandma and 2½ year old Carter Tjarks had come to visit. Grandpa was going to hang out with Carter, while Grandma and the great grandparents went to the store. After Grandpa and Carter went for a ride in the golf cart, they decided to go for a boat ride. Like all kids, Carter loved the water. Walking down onto the dock, they had to decide if they were going in the pontoon boat or in a Sears V-bottom. As they pondered which boat, Carter kept playing in the water and Grandpa kept telling him to get out of it. After checking out the pontoon boat, Grandpa decided that they would take the Sears out. Unhooking the Sears, Grandpa climbed into the stern and was preparing to go. Although unhooked, the Sears would remain in place until Grandpa was ready to go. This is because the Sears was pushed up under the dock and rode higher in the water than the bottom of the dock. There was constant pressure pushing the top of the Sears boat up against the bottom of the dock.

As Grandpa worked on getting everything ready to go, Carter continued to play in the water. He was also climbing in and out of the Sears boat and walked over by the pontoon boat. One of the last things Grandpa remembered was picking Carter up and putting him back into the Sears boat with him.

Grandpa was a diabetic and had been so since he was eight years old. Occasionally, Grandpa would have a hypoglycemic event that he called an "episode". During his episodes, Grandpa would go into a trance-like state. He would appear to be alert, but was actually in a semi-awake comatose state. When Grandpa was a kid, he could tell when he was about to have an episode. Grandpa said that as he got older, he could not tell when one was coming on. Grandpa's doctor told him that this was not an uncommon occurrence with age. Yes, as they were getting ready to go, Grandpa went into an episode.

Sometime later, Grandma and the great grandparents returned home from the store. After unloading the car, Great Grandpa walked down to check on Carter and Grandpa. When he arrived on the dock, Grandpa was unresponsive, and Carter was nowhere to be found. Running back to the house, Great Grandpa told everybody what had happened. They called 911 and started a search for Carter. Great Grandpa enlisted the help of some local fishermen who found Carter floating down stream. Carter was without a life jacket, but did have bright blue shorts and sandals on. The fishermen said they were able to see Carter's clothes just below the surface of the water. Pulling Carter from the water, one of the fishermen performed CPR as the other drove him back to the dock. At the dock, emergency personnel took over CPR. Carter was transported to the hospital but could not be revived.

When I got on scene, I walked (and talked) through the entire incident with Grandpa, Great Grandpa and the fishermen. During the walk-through, Carter's life jacket was located at the golf cart. It was still in storage condition (straps wrapped around it). Grandpa said that Carter had taken it off prior to getting on the boats. Completing the interviews and investigation, it was determined that the incident did not constitute a "boat accident".

Interviewing family members in cases like these can be difficult to say the very least. Grandpa was notified of Carter's death minutes before I had to interview him. At that moment, I would rather have been doing almost anything else. I actually felt guilty for doing a job that I had to do.

Over the years, I have capitalized on the only positive that comes from a case like this - knowledge. I've told this story to diabetics, people with other medical conditions and their families. I have also used this story to highlight that some "mistakes" can never be reversed.

For my part, I can say that whenever I have responded to missing children reports, I am very aware of nearby accessible water sources. Not only do I want them cleared, but I want them posted until the child is recovered (so they don't end up in there).

For Carter's family, I can only wish that I had been on the river checking fishermen that day. I know that they would want all of you to understand the risks and variables which caused this tragedy to occur. Although PFD awareness is commonly discussed, the awareness of medical conditions (and their effects on others) is not a common talking point.

The Sad Reality

While I was still working in Will County, a hunter told me about hunting alligators in Florida. This was long before it was popularized on TV. I took a fancy to the idea. This particular hunter had actually hunted them with a bow and arrow. The arrow had a string attached and they would pull the alligator in after it had been shot. Once the alligator was boat-side, the hunter would hit it with a bangstick to put it down. I was never in a position to go on one of those hunts, so it was nice when the TV shows came out. I was able to watch somebody else do it!

One morning while I was patrolling south of the Quad Cities, I was asked if I would be able to help capture an alligator. You can bet that I was available for that - and I wouldn't even have to go to Florida! After I committed to assisting, I was given the rest of the details. A young man had moved to Mercer County from another state. Once here, he found a job, rented a trailer (out in the country) and acquired two dogs, a snake and an alligator. The young man apparently ran into some tough times and ended up taking his own life. He did so by shooting himself in the head (while he was in bed). My excitement was dashed, but I still had a job to do.

Arriving at the trailer, I met with Mercer County Sheriff's Police and two Illinois State Police Investigators. One of the Investigators was Tad Nelson. I had met Tad several times. You won't find a nicer person. Tad was serious when he needed to be, but would joke around when it was appropriate. Walking toward the trailer, the smell was overwhelming. Apparently, there had been over a week between the suicide and the discovery of it. The dogs and the alligator had been stuck in the trailer the entire time. Animal control had already secured the dogs. The alligator was still in one of the bedrooms. I was told that the alligator was between four and five feet long. Without anyone feeding the alligator and dogs for a week, it was believed that they had consumed part of their owner. The animals and their feces were going to be tested to see which ones had done it.

Getting a catch pole from animal control, Tad and I had a brief planning session. I was going to stick the catch pole loop around the alligator's snout and pull it tight. Once tight, I figured that I would be able to grab the alligator's body and Tad could tape it's mouth shut. Easy enough - right?

After our brief planning session, Tad and I went into the trailer. I don't know that I have ever smelled something so bad. Besides the decomposition odor, there were animal feces all of over the trailer. Stepping into the bedroom with the alligator, I could see it lying under the long dresser. It was in a "perfect" position. The tail was sticking out on my side and the mouth was sticking out on the other.

I snuck along the side of the dresser until I could see over the far side. Lowering the catch pole noose down, I was able to slip it around the alligator's snout. I pulled it as hard as I could. Cinching the noose around the alligator's snout, it started "fast" walking backward. As it tugged on the catch pole, the noose started to slip. I immediately told Tad that it was slipping. Pulling free, the alligator continued moving toward Tad.

About the time I let Tad know that the alligator was free, I heard the bedroom door slam. Looking over, I saw that Tad was no longer in the room. By the closet, I saw a square board with "Wally" written on it. I put the board between me and the alligator. Without carpet on the floor, the alligator had a hard time gaining traction. As I backed the alligator into a corner by the door, it kept hissing and snapping at me. Once I had it pushed tightly into the corner, I stepped on the alligator's head. Setting the board aside, I reached down and picked the alligator up by its snout. I told Tad that I had caught the alligator. He opened the door and taped it's mouth shut. Carrying the alligator outside, we secured it in the animal control van.

All of the animals and their feces were eventually tested for human remains. From what I was told, the dogs were the culprit. It definitely wasn't like hunting in a swamp, but it is the only alligator that I have ever caught.

Every officer will deal with suicidal situations in their career. None of them are good. Most of the time, you are either too early or too late. If you are too early, you may never even know that the situation existed. If you're too late, you will likely never know what has driven the person to where they are. I have been on both sides of the "coin", but have been too late more often than not. In those cases, I helped to secured the scene (as if a murder had occurred). You would hate to lose evidence - if there was "foul play" involved.

In the situations where I was on time, I was able to help get the person to a care facility. Hopefully, as I talked with them, I struck the right "chord". I always wanted them to see the value in their life and remind them that they have something to look forward to. It doesn't have to be something big, just something.

When that day comes, they already need to have the next future event picked out. I know that doesn't fix the root of the problem, but it is a very important driver for people. In my Grandma June's last year, she often said that she would not make it to Christmas. She passed away on 12-25-1999. In my heart, I know that she had reached her goal!

Every police officer has stories which they will never forget. These are some of the cases that have weighed heavy on my heart and molded my "reality". When I was a young officer, responding to these types of cases was interesting and exciting. As I have gotten older, the realization of how precious life is has made it just part of the job. As many officers will tell you, "We do not get paid for what we do every day, but rather what we might have to do every day."

AWR - MACI

In June of 2018, I had been working on this book for about six months. Although progress was steady, it was not fast. My pace was hindered by both speed and time. I am not a fast typist and I could only spare a couple of hours a few days a week. I had already completed my chapter "A Warden's Reality". As a supervisor, at this point in my career, my job duties had switched to primarily being administrative. Deep down, I believed that I had made it past the worst cases of my career. I knew bad things could happen at any time, but was having a case of wishful thinking.

On the evening of 06-18-2018, I was working on paperwork at the District Office. The District Office is in Rock Island and was within walking distance of both the Rock and Mississippi Rivers. I was trying to get caught up on my administrative Sergeant's duties. Being a Monday night, I didn't anticipate being interrupted. At about 6:30 p.m., I received a call from the Illinois State Police (ISP). I was told that a boat had gone through a dam. There were no further details. They didn't tell me where I needed to go or if there were any occupants on the boat. This was far from my first dam call and I knew that I would need to respond to see what was going on.

Expecting the worst, I collected my gear and called ISP on the telephone. I asked for clarification on the location and situation. I was told that the accident had occurred at the Steel Dam in Milan, Illinois. ISP told me that there were three occupants in a canoe that had gone over the dam. I was told that all of the occupants had been ejected into the water. ISP confirmed that rescue personnel were responding to the north side of the dam (by the quarry).

That information took my "response pace" from fast to leave everything on the desk and go! The Steel Dam is a low head dam. I would guess that most large low head dams have killed someone. The Steel Dam is no exception to the rule. In fact, it is one of the worst dams that I have ever seen. We had two guys on personal watercraft get stuck in the Steel Dam a few years earlier. They were wearing life jackets, but only one of them made it out alive.

Just a few miles from my office, I arrived at the north side of the Steel Dam in less than 10 minutes. The north side of the dam connects to the south bank of Vandruff Island. It is a remote access location that is vehicle accessible. There is an elevated wall on the bank where the Steel Dam meets the bank of the island. Downstream from the elevated wall, there is a cemented rip-rap bank. On this day, the drop from the upper pool of the river (above the dam) to the lower pool (below the dam) was approximately two feet. There was a swift current both above and below the dam. On the downstream side, there was a heavy backwash and boil.

Parking in the grass, there were several rescue vehicles and numerous rescue personnel on scene. I could see a Backwater Gamblers ski boat above the dam. The Backwater Gamblers are a local water ski team that performs "ski shows" upstream from the dam. They practice throughout the week and have weekly shows. People will go out to watch both the practices and the shows. On this night, they were trying to assist in the rescue of the people caught below the dam.

Exiting my squad, I grabbed my throw bag and PFD. Putting on my PFD, I walked to the elevated wall. I could see a child (later identified as Maci Chavez) and an adult female (Mom) struggling in the backwash below the dam. Maci and Mom were approximately 200 feet south of the elevated wall. Between us (approximately 70 feet south of me) was a large tree that had become hung up on the top of the dam. It bridged from the top of the dam to approximately 20 feet out into the river below the dam. The log then disappeared below the surface of the water. The log formed a bridge with an open triangle gap underneath it. Both Maci and Mom appeared to have PFDs on. I was told that Maci did not appear to be in good physical condition. The backwash kept drawing Maci and Mom back into the water cascading over the dam. When they got close to it, they would be driven down into the boil. Their life jackets would bring them back to the surface just to go through it again.

Meeting with Blackhawk Fire Department personnel, I was told that they were going to lower an inflatable rescue boat over the dam. I asked if we had a rescue boat coming up from downstream. That is the only way that I have ever seen someone successfully pulled out of a low head dam. I am not saying that someone could not be pulled from the upstream side, but the force of the water coming over the dam is incredible. I was told that Rock Island Fire Department (RIFD) had a boat coming up from downstream. Looking at what was going on, I knew that we needed the RIFD boat there immediately. I called ISP on the radio and asked them to contact RIFD. I wanted to see how long it would be before RIFD would be on the scene. If we had a boat on the downstream side, I was pretty sure that we could get the rescue done. I went back to watching Maci and Mom. I felt helpless as they kept getting pounded by the water. Even though only a couple of minutes had passed, my frustration was growing quickly. I had not heard from ISP, so I called them on the telephone. Asking them again how far RIFD was out, I was told that they would not be able to get their boat up to the dam. Even with the high water, there are some shallow rocky areas downstream from the dam. RIFD's boat is big and drafts a lot of water. The one thing that I had truly believed would work was not going to be there in a few seconds (as I was hoping).

Not willing to give up on our downstream boat, I called Jim Daviess. Jim is the owner of a local boat dealership (Ted's Boatarama). Ted's Boatarama has a private boat launch on the Rock River. They're located about five miles downstream from the dam. Although it was after hours, I was hoping that Jim or one of his guys would still be around. Jim answered his cell phone and I quickly explained the situation to him. Jim told me that he was getting a boat and would be launching as soon as he could. It was great having Jim as a contact—he always answered in a pinch!

With a long rope, the Blackhawk Fire Department tied their inflatable rescue boat off to the stern of the Backwater Gamblers ski boat. Directed by Blackhawk FD personnel on shore, the Backwater Gamblers boat lowered the rescue boat over the dam to Maci and Mom. Floating tight to the dam, the rescue boat kept getting caught in the cascading water. It would push one side of the boat down while flipping the other side up. Then the upstream side would flip back up and it would all start over again. With the rescue boat between us, you couldn't see Maci and Mom long enough to be able to tell if it was helping or hurting the situation. I was afraid that it was just something else that was pounding on them below the dam. Within a few minutes, it was clear that Mom was not going to be capable of getting into the rescue boat. Blackhawk Fire Department personnel decided to pull the boat out. They were going to send it back with firefighters on board.

The firefighters would be able to help Maci and Mom get into the boat.

As the Backwater Gamblers boat started back upstream, the lead side of the rescue boat initially dug down into the water below the dam. It was obviously not easy for the Backwater Gamblers' ski boat to pull it out. As they pulled it further into the cascading water, the rescue boat suddenly popped up and cleared the top of the dam. Maci and Mom were drawn back into the dam and got hit with a wave of water. When Maci went under this time, my heart sank with her - something just wasn't right! Mom came back up, but Maci did not. I stood there looking for Maci, hoping that she would suddenly appear, but it never happened.

The rescue boat was brought back to the bank of the river just above the dam. Blackhawk Firemen (Shane Littlejohn and Scott Bowers) had suited up in rescue float suits. Littlejohn and Bowers got onto the rescue boat and were pulled out into the river. When the rescue boat was lowered over the dam, Littlejohn and Bowers got out of the boat and pulled Mom over to it. They secured Mom to a floating harness that was connected to the south end of the rescue boat. The firemen gave a signal to pull them out. Relayed to the Backwater Gamblers boat, they started to move upstream. The rescue boat was again met by the force of the dam. Digging in, it had not moved very far when the rope broke. All three subjects and the rescue boat were now caught in the backwash and boil.

Clear that the stranded subjects would need to be pulled out from the downstream side, an effort was started to get a rope to the stranded subjects. Because of the log bridging up onto the dam, efforts to get a rope connected from the downstream side were nearly impossible. We needed to have three points of contact on the rope to get the job done. The Backwater Gamblers boat (with one end of the rope) needed to go to the south side of the tree. The guys on the downstream end of the rope needed to be able to keep the rope tight while we tried to lift the center of the rope (with another rope tied off to it) from our elevated position (on the dam).

Theoretically, once it was all tight, we would be able to guide the center of the rope over the tree. The span of rope ended up being too long and heavy. On top of that, our communication was not good enough. If we all had a chance to talk about what we needed to do before we started, I think that it may have worked. As we got one thing into the right location, another section of the rope would go slack or get caught in the water. The bridging log had thwarted our efforts.

Even though our effort to get the rope to them didn't work, it did let Littlejohn and Bowers see what we were trying to do. They began to work their way toward the elevated wall. I had been looking at my throw bag and knew that it only had 50 feet of line in it. When Littlejohn, Bowers and Mom had made it to the "log bridge" (approximately 70 feet out), they hit a little bit of a slack spot in the current. They were not safe, just not getting beat up as bad. Looking around, I found the end of a "heavy rope" hanging on the handrail. I attached the end of it to the end of my throw bag rope. I tried to throw my throw bag to the stranded subjects. It fell approximately 15 feet short. Pulling the bag back in, it was wet and substantially heavier. On the second throw attempt, I got closer but ran out of line. I had not put enough rope outside of the handrail. It got caught on the rail and stopped the bag in the air. I believe it was the third throw when I had diagnosed all of my shortcomings. The fireman next to me held the extra rope outside of the handrail while I got the rest of the throw rope ready to go again. I can remember thinking, "You're fucking going this time" as I turned and wound up to make a hard throw. I kind of felt like I was throwing the shot put or discus again. I'm sure that I grunted as I whipped the rope as hard as I could. Not only did I make it to them, but I shot the rope over the log bridge and about 10 feet past them.

The rope was out there. We just needed to get it into the hands of Littlejohn and Bowers. Draped over the log, the rope was suspended out of the water on our side of the log bridge. I let slack into the rope and tried to work it over to Littlejohn and Bowers. They worked their way around to our side of the rescue boat and were able to grab onto my rope. The rope in my throw bag was not real strong. I really wanted them to pull the heavy rope (the one that I had tied off to) over to them before we started to pull them out. That said, that they were ready to get out of the backwash and were signaling for us to start pulling. We handed the end of my rope down to the rescue personnel on the lower bank and they started pulling. I ran down and we were able to get the subjects and boat out of the wash. It was hard pulling. The Steel Dam did not want to give the people or the boat up. As we were trying to get them out, my throw bag rope broke! Thank God the end of the heavy rope had made it out to them. The remainder of the heavy rope was handed down from the top of the elevated wall and we began to pull it again.

Looking at our angle, we were pulling everybody from the nearest point of the bank. By doing so, we were actually pulling them into the elevated wall as we tried to pull them out. I told the pullers that we needed to get a better angle. We needed to clear the end of the elevated wall. Looking downstream, there was a set of rocks that jutted out into the river (about 10 feet downstream). I moved down onto the jutted rocks and we started pulling at the new angle. As the rope got real tight, I saw that the other end of the rope was still tied to the stern of the Backwater Gamblers' boat. I started yelling at the boat to cut it loose. When they did, we pulled Mom, Littlejohn and Bowers free from the dam.

Once we got them to the bank, I helped Mom get untangled from a log and the rescue boat. Mom was exhausted. As I helped her get to a seated position, I saw there were two life jackets attached to her. One was tied around her waist with the other tied to the first one. The straps were twisted, which made them tight to Mom's body. There was no way to untie the life jackets quickly. I figured that I would have to cut them off of her. The rocks were real slick where I was standing. I can remember thinking that I didn't want to slip with my knife - and accidentally stab Mom! I cut the life jackets free without incident and tossed them up onto the bank. I was later able to identify one of the life jackets as the one that Maci had been wearing. Mom was having trouble engaging in conversation. She was wet, very cold and would sob about the loss of Maci (as she tried to talk). I confirmed with Mom that there had been four people on board the canoe when they launched (Mom, Maci and two boys). Mom was eventually secured to a board and pulled up the riverbank.

I heard a boat below the dam and saw a Moline Fire Department boat approaching from downstream. Walking down, I made contact with the Moline firefighters. They told me that they had recovered the two boys from downstream. I was told that the boys were in good shape (uninjured). I could see the two young males sitting in the bottom of the boat. Moline FD said that one of them was wearing a life jacket when he was found, and the other didn't have one on. Mom later told us that he had lost it while he was in the backwash (below the dam).

Once the boys were out of the wash, they swam to where they could stand on the bottom. One of the boys had made it all of the way to the bank and was actually walking back toward the dam when he was located.

Prior to leaving the dam, I took pictures of the it and the rescue equipment. I talked with the other rescue personnel and did some unorganized debriefing. There was a unified frustration common amongst all the people involved. We had saved Mom, but had not been good enough to save Maci.

After Mom was transported to the hospital, I knew that I still needed to help complete the investigation. As a general rule of thumb, the Illinois Conservation Police are taxed with conducting boat accident investigations. When I was out of sight of the rescue crews, I had to pull over to the side of the road. I knew that if I had to talk with anybody, I was going to cry. Collecting myself, I did the best that I could to relay the information to Laura. I figured that I would just have to complete the investigation (as I have had to do so many times). It was a cut-and-dried case and there was no sense of another officer having to deal with the mental burden of a case like this. I was overruled. Since it was a fatal, I was going to need one of our Boat Accident Team Investigators (BAT) to complete the primary report. Luckily, CPO Audrey Jones (a BAT Investigator) was in the area investigating another case. I called Audrey and asked her to respond to the hospital (to attempt to get a statement from Mom). I let Audrey know that I would be trying to locate the canoe and recover it for evidence.

Contacting Moline FD, I was told that the canoe had been tied off at the downstream end of the island. Responding to the address, I contacted the owner of the residence. I knew him pretty well. He used to work at the Rock Island County State's Attorney's office. I told him that I had heard the canoe (from the accident) was located at his house. He agreed and invited me into his backyard (along the river). As we walked toward the back yard, I was told that he had flipped the canoe over to empty the water out of it. I acknowledged that I understood. Reaching the canoe, we flipped it right side up. The bars on the inside of the canoe were bent. The homeowner assisted me in carrying the 17-foot canoe back to my squad. I had to flip my tailgate down, rest the canoe on the roof and tie it in place. Once it was secured, I transported it to the District One Evidence Facility. When I got it into a lighted area, I took pictures of the canoe and secured it in the facility.

About the same time that I completed my work at the evidence facility, Audrey was completing her interview of Mom. We met at the District Office for a few minutes and discussed the case. Audrey told me that she had just completed the hardest interview that she had ever done. I thanked Audrey for the help, and we discussed the upcoming week. Now we needed to find Maci.

Heading home for the night, I thought that Audrey and I were ready for the following day. It was a restless night. I kept thinking about what had happened and needing to find Maci the next day. I got a call at 1:00 a.m. I answered the phone and a news reporter started asking me about the search for Maci. I was groggy and was likely a little "short" with the reporter. I felt like I had just gotten back to sleep when the phone rang again. It was 5:00 a.m. and another reporter wanted some information. At that point, I figured that I may as well just stay up and get the coffee started.

In less than an hour, my plans for the day were thrown into a tailspin. I got a call from Audrey. She was watching the news and saw that Maci had been found. I was relieved but very surprised. As far as I knew, nobody had been searching for Maci since 11:00 p.m. The news wasn't saying if Maci was found dead or alive. I wondered if we had not totally missed her making it to shore. Did I need to call the search off? Wanting to confirm what was being said, I started calling the agencies involved in the rescue. Some of them had heard that Maci was found, but none of them had been the one to find her. About that time, we started getting inquiries from Maci's family. They wanted to know where Maci was. I figured that I would go to the coordinator for all bodies recovered in Rock Island County—the coroner's office. Reaching the Coroner, he checked with his personnel and was able to confirm that a body had not been recovered (in Rock Island County). Calling the news agency that was putting the information out, I reached the reporter who had "broke" the story. He said that he had gotten the information from a police sergeant. He did not know who the sergeant was, but was able to tell me what police department he worked for. I called their department and confirmed that they had NOT found Maci. They could not find a sergeant who had spoken with the reporter. What a pain! Now that's a story that a reporter should NOT have run until they confirm their information!

Talking about the case with Laura, we decided to divide up the job duties. Laura was going to handle the media and keep the family informed. With what had gone on earlier that morning, it was not going to be an easy task. I had Audrey come back to Rock Island County and we were going to search for Maci. Although Audrey lives two hours away, it made sense for her to come back. She is both a BAT member and a sonar operator. Audrey brought her sonar boat and we conducted searches for Maci. We checked the surface of the river from the mouth to the Steel Dam and ran sonar in a "zig-zag" pattern for almost a mile downstream of the accident.

After Audrey and I had completed our initial search of the Rock River, Laura called me. She said that Christian Aid Ministries Search and Rescue (CAMSAR) had offered to assist in our search. I had never worked with them before, but had heard that they were a reputable search team. Laura told me that they had a "fancy" sonar unit and were willing to come and try it. I have been involved in body recoveries that only lasted a couple of hours and others that have gone on for weeks. I had one on the Rock River where we never recovered the missing person. Whether you are using sonar or hooks, if you hit it hard early, you might get lucky. If not, you will be waiting until the person floats. Depending on body composition, what they have ingested, water temperature and depth, it could be a couple of days or a couple of weeks. It has been said that in extreme water depth, a person may never float. We don't have that in the Quad Cities, so it's just a matter of time. We were really hoping to get "closure" for the family on the first day.

Making contact with the Illinois CAMSAR Coordinator (Ralph Kropf), I was again told that they have an advanced sonar system. Ralph offered to come and search the area. I agreed. About the time that I got off of the phone with Ralph, a strong thunderstorm came in. We had to delay our efforts for a few hours, but had a break coming in the storm.

While we were waiting, the CAMSAR crew got their equipment ready. CAMSAR uses a "command trailer" in conjunction with their sonar boat. Inside their trailer, they have a computer system and TV monitors to review the sonar data. As they are running sonar in their boat, they will save the data on an SD card. When the card fills up, they run them up to their command trailer, download what they have and fill up another card. It's a lot easier to see what's on the bottom of the river with a 40" TV monitor than it is with a 10" sonar monitor. To save time relaying SD cards, I obtained permission from Allied Stone (the quarry) to set up the command trailer next to the dam. When the storm finally broke, Audrey went with the CAMSAR crew to assist in the sonar search and I conducted another surface search on the Rock River.

At approximately 7:45 p.m., I received a call from Ralph. I was told that they had identified a "target" that they believed was worth diving on. I was told that it was in the right location and about the right size.

At approximately 7:51 p.m., I called the Big River Rescue and Recovery dive team (Mark Poulos). Mark was able to contact his team members immediately and agreed to dive on the target. Having worked with Mark several times before, I knew that we were getting the best that the Quad Cities had to offer.

At approximately 8:30 p.m., Mark and his dive team arrived at the quarry. After readying their equipment, Audrey got onto the CAMSAR boat with them and they were taken out to a position upstream from the dive target. They tried to anchor about 10 times, but the anchors wouldn't hold. Not only was the current swift, but the bottom is mostly gravel (with some boulders mixed in).

Coming back to shore, the divers told us that they needed to locate some better anchors. Getting permission from Backwater Gamblers, we went over to their facility and borrowed two heavy anchors from them. When CAMSAR added those to the two they were already using, they were able to get the boat to hold.

It was probably 10:30 p.m. when the divers were finally ready to get into the water. The dam's swift current, debris and air bubbles had made is so Audrey's sonar couldn't create good images of the river bottom. CAMSAR's sonar could see through some of the obstructions. Although the target had been the right shape and size, it didn't show any appendages (but you can't always see them). As Ralph had said, it was also near where we would have expected Maci to end up. With what we had, we were cautiously optimistic as the divers descended. Within 20 minutes, we got word that the target had been identified as a large rock.

When CAMSAR pulled the anchors, I saw their boat start heading downstream. I called Audrey and asked her what they were doing. She said that they were just doing a quick check for other targets. At that point, Audrey had been working for 17 hours straight. We had put so much effort into the search, that nobody wanted to give up. As a supervisor, I knew that Audrey still had to drive two hours to get home. I hated having to be the one to make the call, but it was the right thing to do. We suspended the search for the night. If something happened to Audrey on her way home, it may have been my fault. I didn't want to live with that guilt.

Making the decision to suspend the search, took the recovery into the next phase. With the big boulders, swift current and dam, it would have been hard (and dangerous) to use a drag bar. We would likely have lost hooks on every pass and even have gotten the drag bar caught. In a worst-case scenario, one of the recovery boats would have been sucked into the dam themselves. Instead, we would be conducting surface searches every day until Maci was found.

I was able to coordinate three boats to search the Rock and Mississippi Rivers every day for the next four days. At about 11:00 a.m. on the following Saturday, I received notification that somebody had found Maci. While someone was driving on a road along the Mississippi River, they saw Maci floating near the bank. Andalusia firefighters and the Rock Island County Sheriff's Department were the first agencies to respond. They asked if they should pull Maci out. Protocol dictates that we get pictures and a GPS location before we remove a body. I asked the fire personnel to wait—unless they could get the necessary information. When I arrived, Maci was still in the water. Getting the necessary information, I told the firemen that they could remove Maci. One of them said, "What, a game warden without waders?" I said, "No, I have two sets. I will go get her." Walking back to my squad, I got on my waders and walked out to recover Maci. Once I had pulled her close to shore, the firemen helped me complete the recovery.

Although it pales in comparison to what Maci's family has gone through, that was a tough week for me. Whether at the dam or thereafter, we all did the best that we could with what we had to work with. I found that with this case, it helped me to talk about it. In one of Laura's first talks with Mom, she was told that Maci was kind of a smart aleck—just like our own kids. I was told that while they were stuck in the backwash, Maci said, "Mom, why are they just standing there...don't they know that I'm too young to die?" When Mom was later quoted in the newspaper, the wording was a little different. I'm not sure exactly what was said, but we all knew that Maci was too young to die. We will all forever wish that we could have done more.

THE LITTLE THINGS

Alot of little things happen in every profession. "game warden-ing" is no different. Although little things will not individually make up a chapter, hopefully a mix of them will. These stories contain some of the "little things" that I found funny on a daily basis.

Many times, it's not the person that we remember, but what they said or did. On this particular summer evening, I was working In Kankakee River State Park. It was about 9:00 p.m. when I decided to go check the remote areas of the park. Going to the south side of the river, I headed toward parking lot number seven. Lot seven has a driveway that's about half a mile long with a parking lot at the end. Whenever I went to lot seven after dark, I would always turn off my headlights while I was traveling down the driveway. If there was anybody in or near the parking lot, I didn't want them to know that I was coming. People would commonly "park" in their cars (in the lot) or park and walk down to the river.

When I got to the parking lot, I could see the outline of a vehicle on the far side. Turning my parking lamps on, they lit the car up well enough for me to see that it was empty. Parking my squad, I got out and looked in the vehicle's windows. The stuff sitting inside told me that I was looking for several subjects fishing down by the river. I took my flashlight and binoculars as I headed for the riverbank.

Separating the bank of the Kankakee River from Lot seven was about 50 yards of heavy timber. I got onto one of the trails and started working my way toward the river. I still didn't want anybody to know that I was there, so I walked slowly without using my flashlight. When I got about 20 yards into the timber, I could see the glow of a fire near the riverbank. As I got closer, I could hear people talking by the fire. From the heavily timbered upper bank, there was a drop of a couple of feet to the lower bank of the river. The lower bank consisted of rock and gravel and was only exposed during normal water levels.

As I continued working my way toward the subjects (Hickory, Dickory and Doc), I was trying very hard not to break a branch or use my flashlight. It took me several minutes to get within 10 yards of them. I could see four fishing poles anchored up and down the bank. A small fire was burning in the rocks. Hickory, Dickory and Doc were talking real loud and laughing as they sat by the fire. I needed to wait and find out who was "actually fishing". For five minutes, nobody went and tended to the fishing poles. They just continued to sit there and laugh. I suppose my curiosity overtook me, so I decided to get close enough to hear what they were saying. Working my way from tree to tree, it took me a few minutes to close the gap between us. I was now standing on the upper bank right behind Hickory, Dickory and Doc. On one of my last steps, something crunched under my foot. Hickory looked back to see what it was. I held still while he retrieved a flashlight. Hickory shined it through the timber, but didn't come to investigate the sound.

After a short break in the conversation, Dickory asked, "If you had to 'do' a guy, who would it be?" They all erupted in laughter. In fact, it was hard for me to keep from laughing. Within a few seconds, Doc said that he would pick "Gary Coleman". Hickory and Dickory started hysterically laughing again. After they both ripped on Doc for a while, Hickory said that he would at least pick somebody good-looking—like Rob Lowe. Suddenly, Doc apparently realized what Dickory had actually said. He yelled, "Wait, wait, I thought you meant that if I had to let a guy do me!" After they all started laughing again, Doc said that since Gary Coleman was short, his dick would be too! He said it wouldn't hurt so bad.

They all laughed for a while and finally decided to check their fishing poles. Hickory Dickory and Doc all went to different poles. After they reeled them in, they each cast the poles back out. I waited until everybody sat back down and got comfortable. Turning on my flashlight, I stepped down onto the lower bank and identified myself to the subjects. I advised them that I needed to check their fishing licenses. Dickory told me that he was the only one fishing. He said that all the poles were his. Hickory and Doc agreed that they weren't fishing. I advised the subjects that I had been there for a while and had seen all of them fishing. One of the guys asked me how long I had been there. I told him that I was there since before Gary Coleman. They all laughed. I issued the illegal fishermen citations. I kind of hoped that they would contest their tickets so I could tell the judge my story. Hickory and Doc ended up pleading guilty and paying $75 each.

Fountain of Youth

You might need to be as old as me to fully appreciate Hickory, Dickory and Doc. The next story is multi-generational. Both young and old "potheads" alike can have a comical point of view. Some of them get so addicted to weed that it starts to run their life. They always want to argue whether or not weed is bad for you. I would say that if you get addicted to it and spend money on it (when you should be paying for something else), it's bad for you. They also want to argue whether or not it's a gateway drug. Pretty easy, how many cocaine, meth and heroin users used pot first? I never did a formal survey, but most of the ones that I ever talked to had!

On this particular spring day, I was on bicycle patrol at Milliken Lake. I always liked bicycle patrols in the parks. It was faster than walking and I could get to remote areas. Stealth was the other benefit. People didn't recognize me until it was too late. If they were doing something illegal, I could get to them before they stopped doing it or hid what they had.

As I rode around the lake, I saw there was a small truck parked in the furthest lot from the entrance. Normally, those would be the people that I wanted to check first. It always seemed like the "bad guys" went to the far end. They wanted to see me before I could get to them. Kind of like facing the door in a restaurant.

Since there were very few people in the park on this day, I headed toward the small truck. When I was within a few hundred yards, I could see two people (Ralph and Alice) sitting at the picnic table by the truck. Ralph was sitting on one of the seats and Alice had a seat on the tabletop. As I closed the gap, I watched as both subjects started looking at me. When I was about 30 yards away, Ralph and Alice looked at each other and said something. Looking back at me, Ralph dropped a cigarette from his right hand.

Pulling up in front of Ralph and Alice, I asked them what they were doing. Like everybody else, they were doing nothing. Ralph was 73 years old and Alice was about 25. No, she wasn't his granddaughter. Looking on the ground between Ralph's feet, I could see a half smoked joint. I picked it up and told Ralph that I had seen him drop it. Ralph immediately started complaining about the cannabis laws. I asked Ralph if he had any more. He said that he didn't and emptied his pockets. I asked Ralph if he had any cannabis in his truck. He again said that he didn't. Walking over to the truck, I looked in the open driver's window. Stuffed into a strap on the sun visor were three more joints. I pulled them out and showed them to Ralph. He immediately started complaining about the game warden picking on the "old guy". I told Ralph that he was old enough to know better. He said, "How the hell do think I got this old!"

I seized the evidence and filed a possession of cannabis charge on Ralph. The charge was eventually dropped. The state's attorney's office decided to let Ralph have a senior discount! Ralph ended up being the oldest person that I have ever arrested for possession of cannabis. He's also the oldest guy that I ever met with a 25-year-old girlfriend! I guess there's something to be said about bridging the gap with a "common cause".

The First Amendment

Not two months later, I was working at Kankakee River State Park. It was a hot Saturday afternoon. If you go north of Route 102 along Rock Creek, the creek bed is down in a canyon. The canyon walls are all rock and get up to about 50 feet high. There are several rock ledges along the creek that look out over the canyon. People would go sit on the ledges. Some of the people would fish in the creek, some would swim, and some would just sit there and smoke pot. Of course, fishing is the only legal "past time" of the three.

Walking on an old road that parallels Rock Creek, there's a thin strip of timber between the road and the rock ledges. The timber was thick enough that I couldn't see the ledges through it. Each time I found a trail, I walked out to see if there was somebody sitting on the ledge. As the ledge came into view, I would stop and glass it with my binos. If there wasn't anybody on the ledge, I would walk out and glass the surrounding area. Whether somebody was in the creek or on another ledge, it was a 50/50 chance that they were doing something illegal.

On this particular day, when I walked out onto one of the ledges, I saw that there was a young man (Bud) sitting on the next ledge upstream. Looking at Bud with my binos, I could see his open tackle box. From the angle that I had, I couldn't see Bud's fishing pole.

I walked back out to the road and went down to Bud's trail. Sneaking down his trail, I stopped when I could see Bud. He was sitting on the ledge and looking down into the canyon. I watched Bud for a few minutes, as he had yelled back and forth with somebody down in the creek. Normally, I would wait for Bud to pick up his fishing pole, but there wasn't anybody else on the ledge. Bud would have a hard time claiming that it was somebody else's pole.

I decided to go ahead and check Bud. Sneaking within a few feet of him, I verbally identified myself. Bud was startled as he turned to look at me. I stepped toward Bud's tackle box, as I continued to look for his fishing pole. I didn't see it. Looking down, I focused on Bud's tackle box. There wasn't any tackle in it. It was full of pot and pot smoking paraphernalia. For a 15-year-old kid, Bud had amassed quite an array of pot smoking devices! Bud admitted that he wasn't fishing. He was just smoking pot. I bent over and closed Bud's tackle box. Picking it up, I told Bud that he needed to walk with me up to my squad. As he stood up, Bud argued that I couldn't arrest him for pot. When he reached his feet, Bud said, "You can't arrest me for weed, it's my religion... and I have the freedom of religion!" I laughed and told Bud to get moving.

Leave it to a 15-year-old to come up with that one. He was probably just waiting for an opportunity to tell somebody about his "religion". Bud got a free ride to the park office and had to call his mommy. She didn't seem to be amused about his choice in religions! With Bud being a juvenile, I referred him for prosecution. Maybe the state's attorney's office believed in his freedom of religion too. Bud wasn't prosecuted. I'm not an advocate of monetary fines for juveniles. The kids don't pay them anyway. If the parents are complacent in their duties, maybe a fine will open their eyes. I do believe in community service and impact panels.

It would be nice if juvenile offenders and their parents had to sit through an impact panel. After the lecture, the kids could spend a few Saturday nights doing some community service. The timeliness of the labor is just as important as the type and amount.

Coffee

I always hated coffee as a kid, but one game warden case changed that for me. Farmer Fred had heard some trucks driving up and down his road at about 3 a.m. Looking out his bedroom window, Fred saw a truck sitting in the road outside of his home. He said that a spotlight came on inside of the truck. As it searched the field, the light found a deer. Almost immediately, Fred said that he heard a loud gun shot. The light went off and the truck sped off down the road.

Getting into his own vehicle, Fred said that he headed in the direction of the poachers. Searching the area, Fred found a truck that looked like the poacher's truck. He got the license plate number and returned to his house. Getting on his tractor, Fred drove out into the field and recovered the deer. He didn't want the poachers to come back and get it. Although he wasn't sure that he had the poacher's license plate number, Fred figured that nobody else would be driving around at 3 a.m. The next morning, Fred gave us a call.

Responding to Fred's house, I got the story, the deer and the license plate number. After confirming that the deer had been killed with a rifle, I tracked down the license plate number. It returned to a local family. Since the poachers had not recovered the deer, Laura and I decided to stake out their house. Maybe they would try to poach another one.

The first night, we watched the house nearly all night long. After about midnight, there wasn't any more movement around the house. We stayed in position until about 5 a.m. Just before daybreak, we headed home.

On the second night, I was getting REALLY tired around midnight. I told Laura that I needed to go get something "strong" to drink. Driving to the closest gas station, Laura grabbed a Diet Coke, and I tried a coffee. It was probably more creamer than coffee, but it did the trick. At the end of the night, we still didn't have an arrest for the poached deer. Although I was pooped, I couldn't believe how well the coffee had helped me stay awake.

At the start of the third night, I got another coffee. After sitting on the house for a couple of hours, Laura and I decided that we were spinning our wheels. Although we didn't have much to go on, we decided to go interview our suspect (Tom).

Arriving at Tom's house, we met with him and identified ourselves. At first, Tom wouldn't admit to anything. After a little talking, Laura and I got him to crack. Tom admitted to sitting in the bed of his buddy's (Jerry) truck with a 7 mm rifle. Tom said that after he shot the deer, they went back to his house and swapped out their trucks. Trying to be sneaky, they parked Jerry's truck and hopped into Tom's. They wanted to drive back past the dead deer. Kind of like a movie murderer going back to the crime scene. During the drive-by, Fred found Tom and Jerry and got their license plate number. That's right, the house that we had been watching for two days wasn't actually related to the truck that was used to poach the deer. Both Tom and Jerry had trucks with CB antennas. That was what Fred had recognized! Their trucks weren't even the same color. Tom ended up receiving three citations and pled guilty to all of them. He was fined $600. That case led to a career of drinking coffee. The first few years, I had to load it up with creamer and sugar. Now I drink it with just a touch of cream.

When I moved to the Quad Cities, I found a local gas station (Fort Bragg) that had good coffee. Not only was their coffee good, but the owner (Steve Bragg) was really nice. He never treated me like "the game warden"; he just treated me like a friend. I shopped there when I was both on and off duty. I always liked buying stuff from people that I know.

One morning, I stopped in at Fort Bragg to get some gas and a coffee. After filling up at the gas pump, I walked in to fill up my coffee cup. Like most mornings, Steve and his buddy (Jim Palmer) were joking around and greeting customers from their table. When I walked in the door, they were laughing out loud. As they greeted me, I asked Steve and Jim if they were solving all the worldly problems. Steve laughed and told me that they were. He said that they had them all solved but the last two. I laughed and asked Steve if they were still working on "food and hookers". Steve and Jim laughed again and agreed that they were.

As Steve and Jim continued to talk, I walked back to the coffee pots and filled up my cup. When I was done, I knew that Steve wouldn't allow me to pay for my coffee. It was the same routine every time I stopped in. Like always, I had to try to pay. I felt like I was stealing it, if I didn't. When I got to the register, Steve gestured to the cashier and she refused to take my money. Thanking both, I made my way to the door.

Just as I was about to step out, Steve yelled at me. He declared to have solved the last two worldly problems. I laughed and said, "Oh yea?" Steve said, "One you eat and the other you don't!" We all laughed as I continued on my way. Steve passed away a few years later. Fort Bragg changed hands and was never the same.

Coffee has helped me make a lot of cases over the years. Sometimes I needed the shot of energy and other times I got a tip during the morning social stop. I have even caught poachers and dope smokers who were pumping gas. When people know where the game warden gets his coffee, they tend to find him there when they need him.

The Gate

The Joliet area has numerous old quarries around it. In order to build the roads and buildings south of Chicago, they needed an awful lot of sand, gravel and stone. When the quarries go defunct, they almost always fill in with water. The water is usually deep and clear. Some of the quarries have been turned into private diving and fishing areas, while others were eventually opened to the public. The ones that are recently closed usually are waiting for the owner to decide their fate. Whether they are private or public, there's almost always people swimming and fishing in them.

There was a semi-closed quarry located between Channahon and Joliet. Instead of actively digging in the quarry, the owners were using the Des Plaines River frontage for their business. I had responded to several complaints at the quarry over the years. Usually, it was people swimming or fishing without permission.

The east side of the quarry was bordered by a large piece of BP property. Following 911, BP wanted everybody prosecuted who had found their way onto their property. BP was concerned that somebody would accidentally or intentionally damage an oil pipe or a storage container. Because of BP's proximity to the quarry, I would park in the quarry and go on foot patrol in BP. Several times I was successful in catching poachers in BP.

On an early October morning, I decided that I would go see if anybody had snuck into BP or the quarry. Getting off I-55, I headed toward the quarry gate. The quarry gate was always open. I could drive right in and find a spot to park.

As I approached the gate, I saw that it was closed, and a vehicle was parked behind it. It wasn't just "any vehicle", it was a squad car. Immediately I started thinking about what must have happened. Was it going to be a drowning, a business accident or something criminal? Pulling up to the gate, I exited my squad. As the officer (Chief) at the gate got out of his squad, he walked toward me and said, "Thank god you're here!" I don't think I ever heard that from another police officer, so I wide-eyed asked him what happened. A little stressed, Chief proceeded to tell me that he had parked in the quarry last night and fell asleep. He said, "And they locked me in!"

I asked Chief if he was supposed to be off duty already. He said that he was and asked if I had a set of bolt cutters. I likely chuckled as I told him that I didn't have any. Chief said that he would be alright. He had already called the Channahon Fire Department. They were coming to get him out. As I pulled away, I passed a Channahon ambulance. I never did ask the quarry workers if they saw Chief sleeping in there. I also never saw the gate locked again.

What Sign?
In order to be a CPO, you can choose a few different paths. I chose the path of going to college and getting a bachelor's degree. For my last semester of college, I did an internship with the Illinois Conservation Police. There were different options for internships, so I chose the one that would give me the most job exposure. Wanting to stay close to home, I got assigned to work with CPO Eric Bumgarner in Kankakee County. Over the course of four months, I didn't have an opportunity to see everything that a CPO does, but got into a pretty good variety of casework.

Eric was always fun to work with. If we weren't in the middle of working on something, we were joking around about something else. Eric held me accountable when I screwed up, but would try to teach me when he had the opportunity. He always joked that he was the hose of knowledge.

A week before firearm deer season, Eric and I were patrolling on the east side of Kankakee County. It was mid-morning, and we were traveling down a back road. Out that way, almost all the roads are "back roads". We were paralleling the Kankakee River in hopes of finding a poacher. In that stretch of river, it's bordered on both sides by timber. It affords a lot of opportunities for both outdoorsmen and game wardens.

Working our way to an area where there was an open field between the road and the timber, we stopped to glass the wood line with our binoculars. About 200 yards away, we could see a vehicle that had pulled back into the timber. There was a guy (Indy) walking around by the car with a blaze orange hat and coat on. Indy appeared to be working on something near the rear of the vehicle.

Eric decided that we would sneak across the open field to Indy. Parking our squad, we got out and started across the field. We didn't low crawl, but tried to stay as low as we could while walking across. Although it was open, there was a little ridge and some timber between us and Indy. If we couldn't see Indy, he most likely couldn't see us. I tried to keep it so that I couldn't see Indy while still being able to see his car.

We made it across the field to the edge of the timber without being seen. Kneeling next to the little ridge, Eric and I watched as Indy moved a gun and some other stuff around at the rear of the vehicle. Looking closely, I could see a deer leg sticking up in the rear of the vehicle. I just knew that the guy must have poached a deer! It wasn't firearm deer season, and nobody would go archery hunting in blaze orange. Whispering back and forth, Eric decided that it was time to go check Indy. Following Eric over the ridge, he identified us to Indy. I was expecting Indy to be really nervous. We literally had him "red-handed". Indy stayed calm as Eric went through the check. As I got closer to the deer, I could see the tag on it. It wasn't like anything that I had used before. Relatively quickly, Eric completed the check, handed Indy his paperwork and told him to have a good day. I was thinking, "What the hell?"

Heading toward the squad, when we cleared the timber, I asked Eric what was going on. He said, "Let's get the hell out of here, we crossed over into Indiana!" Both of us laughed as we hurried back to the squad. It could happen to anybody who works in a border county. It was before GPS mapping was popular and there weren't signs posted on every road crossing the state line. Needless to say, Eric and I laughed about it for the rest of the day. That day, the hose taught me to pay closer attention to street signs and maps. We were likely doing a little too much talking and not enough looking.

Sons

The last story for this book will not be a warden story, but a family story. My entire family loves to fish. Garrett would never pass on an opportunity, but Nathan and Kaylee sometimes had "better things to do".

In the spring of 2009, Nathan and Kaylee were five years old and Garrett was 10. Somehow, we were always running late when it was time to go fishing. Inevitably, we would end up rushing around. Having to work that day, when I got home, I polled the possible participants to see who was interested in going. When I asked Garrett, he was all in. He was immediately up and finding his fishing equipment. Checking on Kaylee, she had other plans. Reaching Nathan's room, I asked him if he wanted to go and was countered with a question. He asked me if Garrett was going. When I told him that he was, Nathan said that he was going to stay home.

At first, when I left Nathan's room, I didn't give it much thought. As I was loading stuff into my truck, I thought about it more and started to get irritated. Not that Nathan (or Kaylee) didn't want to go, but that Nathan and Garrett must have gotten into an argument. Obviously, Nathan didn't want to go because his brother was going. As I passed Garrett in the garage, I questioned him about the argument with his brother. After Garrett denied having an argument, I told him that they just needed to get along. I explained that I didn't have time to schedule separate fishing trips for each kid.

When we finished getting everything loaded up, Garrett and I were off on our next adventure. As we headed down the road, Garrett told me that I had unjustly "gotten on" him about Nathan. He said that after we had talked in the garage, he went back in and asked Nathan why he wasn't going. Nathan said that he didn't want dad to be lonely. He said that if Garrett wasn't going, he would have gone—so that his dad didn't have to go fishing by himself.

Yea, I misread that one. Kids are amazing. Just when you think you know what's going on, they throw you a curve ball!

REFERENCES

Case Reports:

95-2-366 08-1-337-035B

97-2-337-003 08-1-337-060

97-2-337-005 2009-1-337-003B

97-2-338-032 2009-1-337-019C

97-2-337-045 2009-1-337-037U

97-2-337-052 2009-1-337-057

97-2-337-057 2010-1-337-033C

98-2-337-002 2011-1-337-007C

98-2-337-042 2012-1-337-039

98-2-337-045 2012-1-337-049

99-2-337-036 2013-1-337-018

99-2-337-044 2013-1-406-022B

00-2-337-032 2013-1-337-024

00-2-337-039O 2013-1-337-032

04-2-337-002 2013-1-337-046C

04-1-337-036 2014-1-337-032

04-1-337-043 2015-1-337-030C
05-1-337-015C 2018-1-469-013B
05-1-337-018
05-1-337-050
06-1-337-004J
06-1-337-017C
07-1-337-041

Newspapers:
Tierney, Tim and Bils, Jeffrey, "BOY'S BODY FOUND IN WILL COUNTY"
Chicago Tribune, August 16, 1995

Times Staff, "Boy drowns in boating accident"
Quad-City Times, August 17, 2008

Mellen, Karen, "Dad pleads guilty to killing his kids"
Chicago Tribune, August 19, 2003

Nessler, Marc, "Mom of drowning victim recalls tragedy at Milan's Steel Dam"
Quad-City Times, June 21, 2018

Sage, Lydia, "DEAD POLICE OFFICER TY MASSEY TO BE HONORED"
Dispatch-Argus, February 27, 1994

Mc Elligott, Walter L., "Dillinger, Infamous Story, Man"
Peotone Vedette, May 15, 2000